DRAG AS MARKETPLACE

Contemporary Cultures,
Identities and Business

Edited by
Mikko Laamanen, Mario Campana,
Maria Rita Micheli, Rohan Venkatraman
and Katherine Duffy

BRISTOL
UNIVERSITY
PRESS

First published in Great Britain in 2025 by

Bristol University Press
University of Bristol
1–9 Old Park Hill
Bristol
BS2 8BB
UK
t: +44 (0)117 374 6645
e: bup-info@bristol.ac.uk

Details of international sales and distribution partners are available at bristoluniversitypress.co.uk

© Bristol University Press 2025

British Library Cataloguing in Publication Data
A catalogue record for this book is available from the British Library

ISBN 978-1-5292-3744-3 hardcover
ISBN 978-1-5292-3746-7 ePub
ISBN 978-1-5292-3747-4 ePdf

The right of Mikko Laamanen, Mario Campana, Maria Rita Micheli, Rohan Venkatraman and Katherine Duffy to be identified as editors of this work has been asserted by them in accordance with the Copyright, Designs and Patents Act 1988.

Cover design: Nicky Borowiec
Front cover image: Stocksy/Igor Madjinca
Bristol University Press uses environmentally responsible print partners.
Printed and bound in Great Britain by CPI Group (UK) Ltd, Croydon, CR0 4YY

FSC
www.fsc.org
MIX
Paper | Supporting
responsible forestry
FSC® C013604

With admiration to all who
'glitter and be gay'

and the people who cannot
show who they are

with the hope we can all shine one day

Contents

List of Figures and Tables

Figures

Tables

Notes on Contributors

Alina Both is a third-year PhD student at Aarhus University (Denmark). Her thesis work at the Department of Management deals with omnichannel customer experiences and brand narratives in retail settings. With a BA in English and Intercultural Business Communication and an MSc in Service Management, her research often takes an interdisciplinary angle, drawing on narrative theory. Her methodological competencies centre around qualitative investigations which enable insights into consumers' unique stories and subjective experiences.

Jan-Hendrik Bucher is a PhD student at the Institute for Marketing and Customer Insight (IMC-HSG) at the University of St. Gallen (Switzerland). In his qualitative research at the intersection of marketing, sociology and psychology, he explores novel market and consumption phenomena. Jan-Hendrik graduated with a master's degree in Brand Management and Marketing Communication from the University of Southern Denmark.

Mario Campana is Associate Professor of Marketing at the University of Bath School of Management (UK). He obtained his PhD from Bayes Business School and has previously worked at Goldsmiths and the University of Bristol Business School. Mario's research interests centre on consumer research and CCT. His research programme focuses on three consumer research domains: materiality, diversity and inclusion, specifically within LGBTQIA+ and alternative economies. His recent work has been published in journals including *Journal of Management Studies* and *Journal of Public Policy & Marketing*.

Katherine Duffy is Senior Lecturer at Adam Smith Business School, University of Glasgow (UK). Kat's research interest lies broadly within consumer culture and primarily explores two research domains: sustainability and clothing circularity, and the digitalization of consumption. Her approach is qualitative and interpretivist. Her research is published in a range of international journals including *Journal of Management Studies*, *Journal of Business Research*, *Consumption Markets and Culture*, *Journal of Retailing and Consumer Services*, *Journal of Marketing Management* and *Gender Work and Organisation*.

Paul Haynes is a member of the Department of Marketing at the School of Business and Management at Royal Holloway, University of London (UK). His core research interests include analysing the impact of consumer culture and networks on innovation and marketing practice. He holds a PhD from Lancaster University with a thesis on Deleuze and the role of non-linear dynamics in innovation.

Khyati Jagani is Associate Professor of Marketing at FLAME University (India). She has also worked at the School of Business, Florida State University as a Visiting Doctoral Scholar. She holds an MBA in Marketing from IFHE, Hyderabad and a BBA in Marketing from Saurashtra University. Her present research is in the area of MMORPG NFT games, influencer marketing, compulsive consumption, metaverse and advertising. She has co-authored several research articles in journals such as *Electronic Commerce Research*, *International Journal of Pharmaceutical and Healthcare Marketing* and *Health Marketing Quarterly*. Her domain knowledge lies in the field of qualitative research and mixed methods.

Mikko Laamanen is Research Professor of Sociology of Consumption at Consumption Research Norway (SIFO), Oslo Metropolitan University (Norway). His research draws from the sociologies of consumption, organization and social movements to focus on the everyday politics of technology, inclusion and social change. His current project focus is on inclusive digital platforms, subcultural consumption communities and sustainable arts. His research has been published in *Current Sociology*, *Information Communication & Society*, *International Journal of Consumer Studies*, *Journal of the Academy of Marketing Science*, *Journal of Marketing Management* and *Social Movement Studies*.

Pauline Maclaran is Professor of Marketing and Consumer Research in the School of Business and Management at Royal Holloway, University of London (UK). Her research interests focus on cultural aspects of contemporary consumption, and she adopts a critical perspective to analyse the ideological assumptions that underpin many marketing activities, particularly in relation to gender issues. She has published her research in many international journals and has recently co-authored *Gendered Marketing* (Edward Elgar, 2022) and *Contemporary Issues in Marketing and Consumer Research* (3rd edition, Taylor & Francis, 2023), and co-edited *The Routledge Companion to Marketing and Feminism* (2022).

Mark McCormack is Professor of Sociology at Aston University (UK), having previously worked at Durham University, Brunel University and the University of Roehampton. His research examines social trends related to gender and sexuality, including transgressive leisure such as illicit drug use and pornography consumption, and queer cultures. He has published on drag performers' perspectives on the mainstreaming of British drag, and the impact of COVID-19 on queer nightlife in London.

Maria Rita Micheli is Associate Professor of Strategy at IESEG School of Management (France). She obtained her PhD at Rotterdam School of Management, Erasmus University. She has been a research fellow at Kellogg School of Management. Her research revolves around knowledge transfer and innovation, with particular emphasis on how organizations and individuals leverage knowledge to enhance innovation and introduce new paradigms. Her recent research has been published in *Organization Science, Journal of Management Studies, Journal of Public Policy & Marketing* and *Creativity and Innovation Management*.

Bình Nghiêm-Phú is Associate Professor at the School of Economics and Management and Graduate School of Social Sciences at the University of Hyōgo (Japan). Most of his research aims to understand consumers' perceptions and evaluations of the characteristics and images of products, services, organizations and places. He adopts approaches of applied psychology theories to the implementation of marketing, logistics, management and education activities.

Raian Razal is a PhD graduate at Aarhus University (Denmark). His research interests lie at the intersections between branding and social movements and LGBTQ+ cultures. His theoretical views are sympathetic towards queer theory and having a decolonizing critical eye on social justice issues. He leans heavily on qualitative methods – discourse analysis, phenomenological interviews and netnographic methods – as part of his immersion in consumer culture theory.

Pia Seimetz is a PhD student at the Institute for Mobility (IMO-HSG) at the University of St. Gallen (Switzerland). She completed her bachelor's and master's degrees at the University of St. Gallen. This was followed by employment in the luxury goods sector, in consulting, as well as in startups, all of which had a strong marketing focus. In her research, she is interested in the intersection of marketing and diversity/inclusion topics.

Luigi Squillante has a degree in Applied Social Science from the University of Rome, Sapienza (Italy) and holds a joint PhD in Computational Linguistics from the University of Hildesheim (Germany) and in Philology, Linguistics and Literature at Sapienza, where he has also been Adjunct Professor of Digital Humanities. His current research interests focus on queer studies and the impact of neoliberalism in contemporary culture.

Rohan Venkatraman is Lecturer in Marketing at Deakin University (Australia) who primarily examines how consumer identities challenge and are challenged by marketplaces. His primary stream of research examines the interplay between bodies, emotions and practices that constitute consumer performances of identity. He is also interested in how marketplaces structure inclusion and exclusion of consumers through power hierarchies such as stigma, as well as aesthetic and taste hierarchies.

Shayne Zaslow holds a PhD in Sociology from the University of Virginia (USA). His scholarly interests include gender, sexuality, art and popular culture. He has previously published works on drag performance as well as co-authored pieces in LGBTQ+ public health. He resides in Brooklyn, New York, and currently works as a research scientist in public education.

Acknowledgements

This book has been a fabulous journey for all of us, as editors and authors. We would like to thank colleagues and friends at Consumption Research Norway at Oslo Metropolitan University, University of Bath School of Management, IESEG School of Management, Birmingham Business School and University of Glasgow for their support.

A very special thanks to Paul, our editor at Bristol University Press, and his team for all the encouragement, feedback and support throughout this journey. Our gratitude goes out to the reviewers whose comments and suggestions guided the development of the book.

Most importantly, we are grateful to the authors whose 'werk' made this project become true!

1

Introduction: What are Marketplace Cultures of Drag?

Mikko Laamanen, Maria Rita Micheli, Mario Campana,
Rohan Venkatraman and Katherine Duffy

Drag is a highly stylized art combining extravagant costumes, exaggerated make-up and entertaining personae in musical and theatrical performances. Drag as an artistic practice challenges gender stereotypes and the epistemic regimes of gender (Butler, 1990), establishing a non-fixed gender reality. While scarcely represented in the field of consumer research, the appeal of drag has increased in recent years due to its visibility in the cultural and media mainstream. Traditionally performed in LGBTQ+ venues, drag has recently 'gone to the market': the contemporary drag marketplace represents a multimillion-dollar industry that reaches far beyond traditional queer venues and audiences. With its increased popularity, drag has evolved into an international consumer pastime, with drag performers-cum-celebrities featuring on national tours, in concerts and at large-scale events, appearing regularly in television shows, movies and advertising, developing their own brands, products and collaborations. This newly acquired visibility allows for contemporary drag to highlight its boundary-spanning nature across art, politics, lifestyle and entertainment. Drag is indeed, as this book shows, a profession – a product bought and sold – but also a political act.

A *drag queen* may be described as a professional male performer appearing as a female character (Newton, 1979); she is 'the realisation of the "veiled woman" … such is the androgynous power of the drag queen that what lies behind the veil may represent reassurance as much as alarm' (Baker, 1995: 128, 130). Drag as female impersonation is anchored in the contested myth that the term *drag* would date back to Elizabethan theatre and stand for DRess As Girl, an acronym for a role where the male actor would portray a female character (Baroni, 2006). Women impersonating hyper-masculine characters on stage are *drag kings*. For a long time, if impersonating a female character, women were called *faux queens* or *bio queens* (Nicholson, 2017). These distinctions are increasingly antiquated and it is widely accepted (as well as practised) that persons of *any* gender (women, men, non-binary) may be drag queens and drag kings.

During its long history, drag has been a staple of both high and popular culture traversing opera, theatre, cinema, popular music and 'the club'. A drag performance, regardless of genre or context, includes entertaining by, often, lip-syncing, singing, comedy and audience engagement. Doing drag can be differentiated from transvestitism as a situational and exaggerated performance, whereas transvestitism is engaged with for (sexual) pleasure gained from cross-dressing, passing for and being treated as a member of the opposite sex (Geczy and Karaminas, 2013). Beyond a performance of gender (Butler, 1990), drag is a performance of a profession that, as a commodity, fuels the entertainment industry in pubs and clubs, movies and, more recently, reality TV shows (Gamson, 2013). The performance of drag is mainly associated with being *on stage*, with the social, political and economic setting of that stage defining how drag is perceived, oppressed or appreciated and mobilized. Various older and newer media allow for extending the concept of stage and staging drag beyond the more traditional venues and out across the globe. Drag is a form of entertainment that often incorporates subversive political acts, a 'means to comment on culture from the outside of the mainstream' (Brennan and Gudelunas, 2023: 8). Drag includes standing up for political convictions in a frock, carrying on the tradition of drag performers on the front lines of gay liberation.

In the increasing commercialization of queer subcultural products, drag is mainstreaming and becoming a lucrative market (Kates, 1999, 2002, 2004; Chasin, 2000). Until very recently, consumer research has overlooked drag as a cultural or commercial phenomenon (for exceptions, see; Frankel and Ha, 2020; Campana and Duffy, 2021; Canavan, 2021; Campana et al, 2022; McCormack and Wignall, 2022; Venkatraman et al, 2024). Studies examining drag as a consumption object (such as a product or brand) and/or as a system of consumption (market) remain scant. Consequently, this book establishes the study of drag as a marker of a marketplace; one that warrants closer attention to the phenomenon and its dynamics. The interdisciplinary chapters in this book address this key omission in our current knowledge of the intersection of drag and markets, analysing themes such as the marketization of drag, drag's impact on the LGTBQ+ community, and the social and political implications of drag identity and performances – overall, the nature of the drag marketplace. The individual chapters present the multiplicity of drag phenomena (that is, not just drag as part of or pertaining to *RuPaul's Drag Race* and/or reality TV), while the global perspective of the book further considers non-Western contexts.

This introduction outlines the different perspectives of the subsequent sections of the book, highlighting the shifts in meanings attached to drag: deviance, cult, mainstreaming and dissident politics. While these perspectives complement and contradict one another, they illustrate how drag captures the attentions of audiences throughout its history, testifying to the iconicity of drag and the makings of a marketplace culture.

Drag in (sub)cultures and markets

In its long history, doing drag has carried both stigma and pride in deviance. To understand drag, we need to engage with its history (or, better, *herstory*). Over time, contours between gender and gender-appropriate conduct and vesture have alternated between more liberal and more restricted (and back again). The appropriateness of dressing up in a frock is context specific. For instance, it is fully accepted for members of religious groups to wear a cassock or a gown (the religious habit) with no connection to cross-dressing (Garber, 1992). Outside religious institutions, men would 'frock up' on the theatre stage as this was historically an all-male environment. Shakespearean theatre, castrati in opera (later developed into 'trouser roles' – young men portrayed by female singers), the onnagata in Kabuki and the dame in pantomime all refer to men playing the roles of women on stage (Senelick, 2000). While women were not allowed to play theatre, drag would tellingly appear in the theatrical scene where it would be acceptable as a mere enactment of a role (and thus, not a form of sexually deviant behaviour; Boyer, 2016).

Over time, the social and political response to drag has waxed and waned. Roger Baker (1995) claims that the decline in the popularity of drag in the UK was related to the gimmick of post-war servicemen in dresses wearing off. Over time, acceptance has also been affected by the status and background of performers. For instance, Newton (1979) recounts the societal position of drag performers in the US after the Second World War, often considered part of a deviant profession at the margins of society. In her famous study on drag queen cultures, Newton's informants saw themselves as 'specialised' 'professionals' in the left field of showbusiness yet still 'in the ball park' (Newton, 1979: 6). She goes on to highlight the status differences between stage and street performers, or performers whose drag persona stays on the stage compared with those whose drag transcends their everyday lives. For either group, drag meant precarity and susceptibility to stigma and existing in the margins of society.

Parodying both the patriarchy of the society and the hyper-masculine nature of the gay male community (for example Geczy and Karaminas, 2013), drag queens and kings are not only shunned on a societal level but also among gay subcultures. Seen as effeminate, drag queens have a difficult and marginalized standing on many levels. To some extent, this marginalized position of drag in the economy, society and the gay community made it necessary to 'pass' (Newton, 1979; Rupp and Taylor, 2003; Berkowitz and Belgrave, 2010) – the concept of passing refers to being able to avoid the (gender/race/class) critical gaze in public. Here, drag communities were a means of collective resistance. For example, the ball circle depicted in Jennie Livingston's 1990 documentary film *Paris is Burning* allowed both individual and collective escape from the harsh realities faced by the oppressed gay and black communities. Dorian Corey, one of the drag performers featured in the documentary, defines passing as being undetectable: 'when they can walk out of that ballroom into the sunlight and onto the subway and get home and still have all their clothes and no blood running off their bodies' (quoted in Hilderbrand, 2013: 59). The documentary opened an underground subculture of drag balls to a mass audience: it examined and catalogued various facets and struggles of the ball community as well as introducing a cultural vocabulary of drag (that has since mainstreamed), such as reading, spilling the T, throwing shade and forming houses.

Throughout this coexistence of stigmatization and acceptance, drag has expressed prideful deviance within a countercultural or subcultural cult, with the performance of drag becoming a distinctive element in embracing the minority status of being gay or queer. The complex evolution of drag over time and in different contexts has led to expressions such as genderfuck (confusing the relationship between gender and the assigned sex; Heller, 2020), which were at the core of the performances of charismatic individuals and collectives, such as The Cockettes and glam-rockers like David Bowie. Gender confusion has always come with moral outrage. For instance, we may trace the origins of genderfuck to the famous castrati of the Italian opera as a proto-form and early cult of drag. When castrati performed in London, newspapers claimed that 'the mere voice of the castrato could turn women into hermaphrodites and men into effeminate sodomites' (Englund, 2020: 62). Playing on this, the queer and drag domain heralded an era of gender-bending and confusion (Meyerowitz, 2002) with mainstream, but particularly subcultural (Haenfler, 2022), audiences.

John Waters' films featuring his muse Divine (a drag queen also affiliated and performing at the time with The Cockettes) gained cult status and following from the early 1970s. The trashy, tabooless and lewd Waters–Divine collaborations *Multiple Maniacs*, *Pink Flamingos* and *Female Trouble* gained infamy for their shock value. These movies featured the voluptuous Divine as 'the filthiest person alive', performing an execution of her rivals, being raped by a giant lobster (a scene later emulated by Róisín Murphy in her music video 'Movie Star') and shooting up liquid eyeliner. The most notorious act to seal Divine's fame, and the cult of her drag, was the coprophagia performed at the end of *Pink Flamingos*. Similarly, the 1975 film version of the West End rock musical *The Rocky Horror Picture Show* (RHPS), became a staple of midnight screenings. In the movie, two seemingly innocent, normal young people, Brad and Janet, are stranded in a storm at the castle of Dr Frank-N-Furter, a transvestite scientist from outer space. The plot follows a trail of decadence including creation of life, gay marriage, sexual experimentation, incest and cannibalism that finds its culmination in the floor show. The characters perform a three-part drag number, 'Rose Tint My World', in which they all embrace their individual transformations away from the patriarchal norms of the US towards their 'demise' from which they could never return. RHPS screenings soon generated a specific audience participation with rules and rituals (Senelick, 2000).

Divine (aka Harris Glenn Milstead) was about to attempt crossing over to the mainstream in a trouser role as Uncle Otto in the television show *Married With Children* when he suddenly passed away in 1988 (Jay, 1994). Other drag performers achieved mainstream success in the same period. Daniel Patrick Caroll and Barry Humphries, for instance, brought their classical drag characters Danny La Rue and Dame Edna Everage to mainstream audiences, achieving great popularity. A wave of drag mainstreaming came with films taking on drag as a central motif. The years from 1994 to 1996 saw the releases of *The Adventures of Priscilla, Queen of the Desert; To Wong Foo, Thanks for Everything! Julie Newmar;* and *The Birdcage.* While these films portrayed drag in a generally positive and empowering light, some commentators (such as Kirk, 2004 and Rehling, 2009) claim that, beneath such benevolent vail, loom old-fashion notions of gender and racial supremacy frocked up anew. In a similar vein, *Some Like it Hot* is 'a film very much about heterosexual men in disguise to preserve their lives who find themselves in heterosexual heaven' (Baker, 1995: 231). The men are shameful of the charade (almost) all the way through:

I tell you, Joe, they're on to us. And they're gonna line us up against the wall [gestures with an imaginary machine gun shooting them down]. And then the cops are gonna find two dead dames and they're gonna take us to the ladies' morgue and when they undress us, I tell you, Joe, I'm gonna die of shame. (Jerry/Daphne, *Some Like it Hot*)

The 'dragged up' comedies of more recent years maintain a similar subtext. While the drag character Albert is central to *The Birdcage*, as are Dorothy to *Tootsie* and Euphegenia to *Mrs Doubtfire*, none of these movies is about drag but about gendered roles at home, in family life and at the workplace. More importantly, in all cases, the lesson to learn is about male superiority in these settings, particularly after the men have encountered their femininity through (a bit of) cross-dressing.

The driver of drag's contemporary popularity in the mainstream is *RuPaul's Drag Race* (RPDR). The show started in 2009 and subsequentially reshaped the idea of drag for mainstream audiences, setting a new standard relative to the cultural products just mentioned. RuPaul, the self-proclaimed Supermodel of the World, introduced a new reality show combining elements of *America's Next Top Model*, *Project Runway* and *America's Got Talent*, aimed at finding the next US drag superstar. The show has become an empire. Indeed, RPDR has matured into its 16th US season along with separate all-star seasons and several international versions as well as *[international version] vs the World* seasons. Further spin-offs include *Drag U* and the podcast series *What's the T* as well as web series and podcasts created by queens from the show (such as *UNHhhh*). Fans engage further at conventions (DragCon in Los Angeles, New York and London), seeing RPDR queens on tour around the world and at *RuPaul's Drag Race LIVE!* in Las Vegas. On top of this, the franchise and RuPaul have brought out various products ranging from chocolate to games and music albums. If mainstream popularity is measured in numbers, the finale of Season 16 reached 708,000 viewers in the US, with a rating of 0.84 in the 18–34 age demographic (Sim, 2024); the show's X profile (@RuPaulsDragRace) has over 1.2 million followers; and the show has won several awards, including 27 Primetime Emmy Awards.

Beyond the performances, RPDR promotes a queer community narrative in a continuation of *Paris is Burning*. These take the form of the contestants' personal experiences of doing drag and, often, being gay/queer. In confessional segments, often taking place between the preparation for the main challenge and the runway show while the queens are transforming, the contestants share how they have been shunned by their families, struggle with their career choice or illness, or generally being queer in contemporary life. These powerful personal experiences are juxtaposed with RuPaul's motherly advice, her illustrious mantras (for instance, 'If you can't love yourself, how can you love somebody else? Can I get an amen up in here?' at the end of every episode) and illustrations of general gay history of overcoming stigma and legitimating the art of drag. This platform for gay history and queer identity veils both the commercial and entertainment logics of the show (Daems, 2014): the undercurrent of commercialized drag is not deep under the surface. Product placement is ubiquitous and, according to Gianatasio (2014), functions on two levels:

> viewers can get heavily invested in such series, rooting for their favourite players, and that can strengthen the bond with sponsors whose products and services play into the competitions ... [since] it's understood that contestants compete for cash or prizes, so the balance between content and commerce feels less strained than in scripted fare.

Indeed, the queens battle for thousands of dollars and several other prizes and, while doing so, develop their entrepreneurial flair. Illustrations of how RPDR has become a vehicle for commercial interests and how the queens should embody these are multiple. For example, in setting up the Hello Kitty challenge in Episode 11 of Season 7, RuPaul educates the contestants on how the savvy drag queen must brand her Charisma, Uniqueness, Nerve and Talent (her proverbial CUNT) for marketplace penetration. Neither the show nor its host hides this commercialization; they rather flaunt it. Before RPDR, RuPaul had a daytime TV talk show and a recording career later augmented by mainstream movies and television series. The 2017 LGTBQ+ issue of *Entertainment Weekly* introduced RuPaul as an 'underground superstar' who shot to international fame to become a 'phenomenon and cultural icon' (Snetiker, 2017). RPDR has, since its early days, had a major influence in creating and driving markets. RuPaul herself is a global business venture and a self-proclaimed marketing mogul, as she said in the 'Drag Fish Tank' episode of *RuPaul's Drag Race*: 'I'm a marketing genius! I marketed subversive drag to 100 million muthafuckas in the world. I'm a marketing motherfuckin' genius over here.'

In addition to the marketing for several companies (such as Boobsforqueens. com and Absolut Vodka), fashion and music are riding the high tide of drag popularity, with RPDR queens appearing on fashion runways and in clothing ads (Schneier, 2016) and the music used in the show's 'lip-sync for your life' section seeing substantial surges in sales and streaming (for example, Whitney Houston's 'So Emotional' Spotify activity spiked by 650 per cent and it streamed over 933 per cent more after being used in the Season 9 finale; Crowley, 2017). Nevertheless, these expanding product portfolios of programming, events and nicknacks might backfire on the 'brand' of RPDR. For instance, a fan commented on the launch of the Drag-Race-themed 'Mad Libs' game on YouTube:[1] 'I love him, but Ru is literally the Krusty the Clown of drag; there's no product he won't put his name on. Coming soon; RuPaul's ringworm cream, "ditch that itch, bitch!"'. The sentiment of this fan is shared by several others who prefer the earlier, less-mainstream versions of the show and of RuPaul.

So, RPDR confirms the claims made earlier of the difficulties and polarization that might emerge with the mainstreaming and commercialization of drag. In this respect, the backlashes observed for RPDR recall those experienced by *Paris is Burning*, the documentary that inspired the challenges among contestants featured in RPDR. The popular glory of *Paris is Burning* was shadowed by the perception that the documentary portrayed the community in a celebratory instead of realistic light, that is, as a marginalized and disempowered community. This appears in the way in which most of the ball participants seem disengaged from their own communities, resolute in copying to attain the lifestyles of the rich and white yuppies. hooks (1992: 155) illustrates this point by saying that 'consumer capitalism undermines the subversive power of the drag balls, subordinating ritual to spectacle, removing the will to display unique imaginative costumes and the purchased image'. Madonna went on to appropriate voguing from the very same community (the dance practice can be traced back to the 1960s from two possible New York origins: the back rooms at Stonewall Inn or the Riker's Island prison complex; Hilderbrand, 2013).

Despite its increasing commercial value, drag remains political in the public heteronormative gaze where 'to choose to appear as "female" when one is "male" is always constructed in the patriarchal mindset as a loss, as a choice worthy only of ridicule' (hooks, 1992: 146). By being in the margins of the heteronormative society, we can affirm that members of the drag community 'make us not only question what is real, and what "must" be, but they also show us how the norms that govern contemporary notions of reality can be questioned and how new modes of reality can become instituted' (Butler, 2004: 29). Drag remains a cornerstone of the gay identity (Garber, 1992) and it has, since the 1960s, existed as political resistance and a form of subversive enactment of 'eleganza'. Butler (2004) juxtaposes two views: the politics of drag either reduced to parody or resembling a model for political intervention and participation. While drag as parody has always taken issue with the politics of everyday life at home, drag has also been used in the mainstream to point out problematic issues in society with regard to minorities. Thus, camp and irony in drag can forge the queer community identity and sustain it during its struggles as well as poke a stab at the sensibilities and valuations of the bourgeois society (for example as John Waters has done with his films; Rhyne, 2004). Indeed, drag queens and kings have been on the frontlines of LGBTQ+ activism due to their high visibility, for instance during the Stonewall uprising and its subsequent commemoration in Pride parades. In such settings, as Newton (1979) would argue, kings and queens would join in, having little social standing or acceptance to lose through their activism. Then, at minimum, drag carries with it the potential of a radical agenda. Cross-dressing without the attempt of passing as a cis woman connected with the agenda of gay liberation and radical drag saw the combination of a frock and a beard flipping the bird to ideas of conformity and expectations of gender (Jacob and Cerny, 2004; Connell, 2005).

With respect to RPDR, the ninth season of the show made a strong political statement. The season went to air in a US under Trump, in March 2017, and was promoted with the slogan 'Drastic times call for dragtastic measures'. The 'pussification of America', a central macho-chauvinist issue of Trumpism, became a key advocacy point for drag (Kornhaber, 2017). Subsequent seasons have prominently featured the government voter registration website during the credit roll. Thus, while the RPDR community might be seen to be selling out by going mainstream, and certainly some performers are following the age-old principle of wearing a frock for pay cheques, some use the platform in the manner pointed to by the radical drag communities of the past. A more recent example from RPDR has seen recent winners Bob the Drag Queen and Sasha Velour both taking a stand for the position of the queer community and exploring how drag might be utilized as a mechanism to teach and mobilize the community (in the RPDR celebrity impersonation challenge 'The Snatch Game', Sasha Velour discussed how he had contemplated doing Judith Butler – 'but will you make it funny?').

As evident in the newly found mainstream success of drag, the subculture has become acceptable and the repressed have become heroes of the liberal West. There's a 'pull towards' the profession of mainstream drag (compare with Newton's categories of queens), and working as a drag performer may not carry the stigma it used to within the contemporary social zeitgeist (McCormack and Wignall, 2022). Given that the position of drag in consumer culture treatises has been fringy at best, the aim of this book is to open avenues of research into drag as a marketplace. Studies in consumer culture are increasingly identifying the body as a site of political, social and cultural resistance within countercultural forces (Ourahmoune, 2017). In studies of social protest, such understanding is part and parcel of theorizing: there is no protest without the body. Consequently, we can establish that drag challenges the established order not only with corporeal acts of playing with gender and sexuality but through signification acts that can lead to political mobilization and resistance via various media and global markets. This prospect may be reassuring to those among us who believe that the increasing mainstream popularity of drag will ultimately lead to its diluted politics.

About this book

Following this introduction, the book has three main parts, with seven chapters, that focus on different aspects of drag marketplace. The chapters cover the various forms of drag marketplace, both online and offline. Within online drag marketplaces, the contexts range from websites to social media platforms; in the offline domain, the chapters explore drag-themed markets, events and performances. In each chapter, the authors demonstrate how the specific marketplace supports the expansion of the reach and appreciation of drag culture. At the same time, they highlight tensions and evolutions emerging over time relative to the social and political aspects of drag. Different methodologies are leveraged in the chapters while exploring a variety of empirical contexts in different countries and social domains. The chapters are complemented by a conclusion by the editors and a final part, an epilogue of two chapters by Pauline Maclaran and Mark McCormack.

The authors of Part I, 'Politicizing Drag Identities', explore political and social issues of drag, highlighting the power of drag to challenge societal norms and address political and social concerns. Drag is explored in the realm of politics and identity, at the intersection with issues of gender, sexuality and self-expression. Chapter 2, by Luigi Squillante, offers an interpretive exploration of *RuPaul's Drag Race* to account for its success in elevating drag to be a worldwide cultural phenomenon and further integrating queer instances into pop culture. Employing a Foucauldian lens of discourse and utilizing a qualitative approach, Squillante considers several elements of the show and explains how they can be interpreted as examples of compliance to contemporary neoliberal norms in terms of both pedagogical and performative acts. The chapter also discusses how and why such dynamics can play an important role in facilitating the acceptance of new drag models within the mainstream culture. Squillante explores these dynamics across three identified themes within a neoliberal frame: individualism, self-confidence and condemnation of idleness. The chapter discusses how employing Foucauldian concepts for analyses of media and queer issues allows for interpretation of the neoliberal 'Ru-presentation' of drag both as a device pointing at disempowering the perception of the otherness of queer individuals and as a mechanism to facilitate celebration of drag for its 'marketable specialness' rather than its cultural subversiveness. *Drag Race* is illuminated as a 'privileged case' to demonstrate marketization and adherence to the values of neoliberal citizenship. In turn, the show can foster a discourse of integration in addition to that of exclusion of queer citizens as analysed in different contexts. Finally, Squillante highlights that the cultural integration driven by the show appears inextricably connected to queer homologation and 'normativization', thus becoming another example of the implicit power relationships, expressed by cultural phenomena, that pervade social dynamics.

Chapter 3, by Paul Haynes, conceptually examines the impact of the appropriation of womanhood as represented by drag performances. Drag is compared with 'blackface' to consider a possible negative impact of drag on women, particularly in providing a space for mobilizing portrayals of women and stereotypes that deny women agency or are morally offensive and misogynistic. Haynes employs Deleuze and Guattari's (1986) notion of 'minor literature' to compare blackface and drag. For Deleuze and Guattari, the term 'minoritarian' does not refer to someone from a minority; it means being different from the embodiment or approximation of the standard used to *define* a majority. By extension, Haynes states that the 'minor' appropriation of identity, found with drag but not blackface, creates its own identity standard, reversing the traditional narrative construction. Haynes also highlights that, as drag has evolved to be a more inclusive mode of performance and expression – as evidenced by the diversity of stories that underpin contemporary drag culture – it becomes clearer that attempts to capture an essence of drag and draw it into mainstream entertainment faces resistance from the very performers and performances it hopes to commandeer. The chapter suggests implications for rethinking the practice and the continued marketization of drag performances, which are considered through the insights of a 'minor gender' lens. Haynes argues that, in exploring the implications of drag and its continued evolution, it becomes clear that much more is at stake in the appropriation-inappropriation of clothing, posing and performing than mere amusement.

In Part II, 'Marketizing Drag', the authors explore the processes that are leading drag to be increasingly commodified and incorporated into the wider entertainment industry, with a focus on commercial success. While the opportunities emerging from marketization are identified and described, the potential tensions between commercial interests and political aspects of drag are also highlighted. In particular, the tension around authenticity vs marketability is discussed, using different perspectives and methodologies across a range of empirical contexts. In Chapter 4, Both, Razal and Venkatraman draw on theorizations of artisanship and artisanal brands to examine how brands leverage the creative power of drag performers as they seek to co-create meaning in the marketplace. The authors first explain how and why the notion of artisanship offers a lens through which brand-consumer interactions – especially around authenticity and trust – can be examined. They explain how drag performers can be considered as exemplars of artisans, drawing on auras of uniqueness and charisma – emerging from their multiple artistic practices – and how they represent key figures in the LGBTQ+ cultural imaginary. As such, drag performers can be viewed as direct and symbolic links between the queer community and the marketplace. Using an interpretive netnography of drag culture, and focusing on queen-brand interactions on social media, the authors theorize on the dynamics that underpin the market view of drag performers as craftspeople and artisans. They identify two framing mechanisms – 'skill and expertise' and 'charisma and vulnerability' – that shape how drag artists are viewed by audiences. They then identify two signalling mechanisms that brands seek to adopt as they use drag artists to represent them in the marketplace – 'artisanal transformation' and 'queering the brand'. These framing and signalling mechanisms work in parallel to cement the notion of the artisan drag performer within consumption ideologies and marketplaces.

In Chapter 5, Seimetz and Bucher delve into the topic of legitimacy and how it has changed over time within the subcultural drag scene in Berlin. Specifically, they explore the conflicts and collaborations that occur during the legitimization process between two subgroups within the drag community: the Tunten and the Drag Queens. Tunten is a radical form of drag performance that is highly charged with political messages. It is characterized by its deliberately untidy aesthetics and bold make-up and costumes, all of which are used to make political statements. In contrast to the glamorous Drag Queens, Tunten is seen as more subversive and without a focus on mainstream acceptance. Despite the unique and innovative performances, the radical nature of Tunten has led to it being marginalized within the broader LGBTQ+ community and the drag scene itself. Seimetz and Bucher identify three stages of the relationship between the Tunten and the Drag Queens. In the first, characterized by conflicts and rivalry, there were heated conflicts between Tunten and Drag Queens, resulting from their different approaches to politics and performance. Drag Queens were more accepted in the mainstream because they rejected the political aspect of Tunten. As a result, the broader LGBTQ+ community supported the mainstreaming of drag, which marginalized Tunten even further. In the second stage, collaboration between these two previously divided subgroups grew. This collaboration and mutual acceptance contributed to a more unified and diverse drag community in Berlin. Performers worked together towards common goals, leading to a legitimacy spillover from Drag Queens to Tunten. The third stage – of unity and diversity – describes the current atmosphere in the Berlin drag scene, which is characterized by collaboration and mutual acceptance: Drag Queens and Tunten respect and accept each other; collaborations are not exceptions, but the norm. Instead of insulting each other, Tunten and Drag Queens talk nicely about each other's performances; they watch each other's shows and go to parades together. Coherent with this close contact, Tunten and Drag Queens take elements of each other's style and integrate them into their own aesthetics. Overall, this chapter provides insight into how groups can acquire and transfer legitimacy in different social and cultural contexts. The chapter argues that legitimacy can spill over from one group to another through collaboration and acceptance, and notes that conflict resolution within members of the same subculture can enable illegitimate subgroups to gain legitimacy.

Chapter 6, by Binh Nghiêm-Phú, brings forward the connection between non-drag-fans and drag performers as celebrity endorsers. The chapter examines the context of Japanese non-fan consumers and their perceptions of drag celebrities, while also taking into consideration fans and anti-fans. The relationships between drag celebrities, fans and anti-fans often occur on social networking platforms. Nghiêm-Phú particularly explores non-fans' behavioural intentions towards beauty products that drag celebrities endorse. Nghiêm-Phú conducted 17 interviews with young Japanese non-fan consumers. These interviews show how the non-fans consider drag celebrities as having a positive and suitable image to serve as commercial endorsers of cosmetic products, but the influence of drag celebrities might be weaker than non-drag celebrities in the same product category. Similarly, across the fan groups, the non-fans considered that the images of fans and anti-fans were relatively vague, with the former being considered younger than the latter. While exploring the emerging topic of non-fan consumers and drag celebrities in Japan, the chapter extends the theorization between the different fandom categories. Nghiêm-Phú makes recommendations for strategies to manage drag celebrities' images and their relationships with fans and anti-fans in order to avoid negatively influencing non-fan consumers.

In Part III, 'Digitizing Drag', the authors analyse how digital technology and online platforms have transformed the world of drag performance, entertainment and related industries. The factors leading to the increase of digital platforms as a marketplace are analysed, and the strategies to engage consumers are described through different lenses and methodologies. In Chapter 7, Shayne Zaslow discusses the impact of the digital shift on drag performances, their aesthetics and community ties. Anchored on studies on the corporeality and liveness of an artistic performance and drawing on a five-year longitudinal engagement in a US drag community, Zaslow argues how the digital shift, as with many other marketplaces and practices, was amplified by the pandemic, which closed live performances and drag-community interactions. Rediscovering liveness comes through in the interviews that Zaslow conducted with 38 drag performers as well as ethnographic observations of attending (offline and digital) performances. Where digital performances were born out of a pandemic necessity, the performers and audience learned to navigate the different platforms and affordance to the performance. Digital drag has further expanded the marketplace itself in the communities it reaches, in the styles of drag it creates space for and in the performance opportunities it affords through 'cybernetic drag' as the fusion of technology and drag. This leads to the creation of an art-cyborg, described as a creative entity transcending boundaries between technology and materiality, as well as between reality and fantasy, and between body and machine. Overall, the chapter suggests a fundamental rethinking of drag, body and community, authenticity and engagement, leaving open questions for further exploration of these themes.

In Chapter 8, Khyati Jagani describes the process through which drag social media influencers (SMIs) generate followers' engagement, trigger persuasion, and promote drag shows. In the empirical setting of India, Jagani leverages netnography and in-depth interviews to identify a process consisting of five stages: attention and curiosity, desire and conviction, participation, event activation, and nurturing and prospecting. First, Jagani introduces the hierarchy of effects (HOE) model. This discusses the impact of advertising on consumers' decision-making processes, covering a series of stages for advertisers to follow to achieve purchase behaviour. The chapter extends this model by showing the steps through which consumers can be involved and provide feedback on the products (drag shows). In addition, the new model suggested in the chapter adds to the HOE by including the final stage of nurturing and prospecting (whereas the HOE model ends at the purchasing stage). In turn, Jagani claims that this additional step closes the promotion loop, explaining how repeated purchases over time (repeated attendance at drag shows) can be triggered.

The Conclusion draws together the key contributions of the book and suggests possible research avenues for the exploration of drag cultures in the marketplace, both offline and online. It also summarizes the main points, themes and arguments that have been presented and circles back to the Introduction, highlighting how the different chapters contribute to the understanding of drag marketplaces. Some questions are left open to the readers, encouraging them to think more deeply about the evolution of drag marketplaces, and suggesting alternative and complementary interpretations for future enquiry.

The book concludes with Part IV, a two-chapter Epilogue in which Maclaran and McCormack provide their readings of the impact of the drag marketplace on contemporary capitalism, marketing and consumption. Maclaran reflects the marketing of drag in and through the movie-cum-musical *Kinky Boots*, while McCormack picks up on personal experiences with drag to inform what consumption of drag may feel like. The conclusion of both is that this book will offer ways to inspire further research in drag, marketplaces and consumption. We, the editors and the authors of the different chapters, hope this will be the case, but, paraphrasing RuPaul's favourite one-liner, '*you'll* be the judge of that'.[2]

Notes

[1]   youtube.com/watch?v=Q6tzU0mYdaA&ab_channel=WOWPresents
[2]   See the first episode of Series 26 of *The Graham Norton Show*, youtube.com/watch?app=desktop&v=VitU2ZR_-lY&ab_channel=BBC

References

Baker, R. (1995) Drag: A History of Female Impersonation in the Performing Arts, New York: New York University Press.

Baroni, M. (2006) 'Drag', in D.A. Gerstner (ed) Routledge International Encyclopedia of Queer Culture, Abingdon: Routledge, p 191.

Berkowitz, D. and Belgrave, L.L. (2010) '"She Works Hard for the Money": Drag queens and the management of their contradictory status of celebrity and marginality', Journal of Contemporary Ethnography, 39(2): 159–186.

Boyer, K.A. (2016) 'Behind the Glitz & the Glam: Drag culture in the 1960s to modern day', The Odyssey, [online] 15 August, Available from: theodysseyonline.com/glitz-glam-drag-culture-1960s-modern-day [Accessed 10 March 2024].

Brennan, N. and Gudelunas, D. (2023) 'Post-RuPaul's Drag Race: Queer visibility, online discourse and political change in a global digital sphere', in N. Brennan and D. Gudelunas (eds) Drag in the Global Digital Public Sphere: Queer Visibility, Online Discourse and Political Change, Abingdon: Routledge, pp 3–12.

Butler, J. (1990) Gender Trouble: Feminism and the Subversion of Identity, New York: Routledge.

Butler, J. (2004) Undoing Gender, New York: Routledge.

Campana, M. and Duffy, K. (2021) 'RuPaul's Drag Race: Between cultural branding and consumer culture', in C. Crookston (ed) The Cultural Impact of RuPaul's Drag Race, Bristol: Intellect.

Campana, M., Duffy, K. and Micheli, M.R. (2022) '"We're all Born Naked and the Rest is Drag": Spectacularization of core stigma in RuPaul's Drag Race', Journal of Management Studies, 59(8): 1950–1986.

Canavan, B. (2021) 'Post-Postmodern Consumer Authenticity, Shantay You Stay or Sashay Away? A netnography of RuPaul's Drag Race fans', Marketing Theory, 21(2): 251–276.

Chasin, A. (2000) Selling Out: The Gay and Lesbian Movement Goes to Market, New York: Palgrave.

Connell, R.W. (2005) Masculinities (2nd edn), Berkeley: University of California Press.

Crowley, P. (2017) ' "RuPaul's Drag Race" Yields Impressive Streaming Boosts for Whitney Houston, Ariana Grande & Dolly Parton', Billboard, [online] 17 July, Available from: billboard.com/pro/rupauls-drag-race-yields-impressive-streaming-boosts-for-whitney-houston [Accessed 10 March 2024].

Daems, J. (ed) (2014) The Makeup of RuPaul's Drag Race: Essays on the Queen of Reality Shows, Jefferson, NC: McFarland & Company.

Deleuze, G. and Guattari, F. (1986) Kafka: Towards a Minor Literature, Minneapolis: University of Minnesota Press.

Englund, A. (2020) Deviant Opera: Sex, Power & Perversion on Stage, Oakland: University of California Press.

Frankel, S. and Ha, S. (2020) 'Something Seems Fishy: Mainstream consumer response to drag queen imagery', Fashion and Textiles, 7(1): 23.

Gamson, J. (2013) 'Reality Queens', Context, 12(2): 52–54.

Garber, M. (1992) Vested Interests: Cross-dressing and Cultural Anxiety, London: Routledge.

Geczy, A. and Karaminas, V. (2013) Queer Style, London: Bloomsbury.

Gianatasio, D. (2014) 'RuPaul Dresses Up Product Placement', Adweek, [online] 10 August, Available from: adweek.com/brand-marketing/rupaul-dresses-product-placement-159385 [Accessed 10 March 2024].

Haenfler, R. (2022) Subcultures: The Basics (2nd edn), Abingdon: Routledge.

Heller, M. (2020) Queering Drag: Redefining the Discourse of Gender-Bending, Bloomington: Indiana University Press.

Hilderbrand, L. (2013) Paris is Burning: A Queer Film Classic, Vancouver: Arsenal Pulp Press.

hooks, b. (1992) Black Looks: Race and Representation, Boston: South End Press.

Jacob, J. and Cerny, C. (2004) 'Radical Drag Appearances and Identity: The embodiment of male femininity and social critique', Clothing and Textiles Research Journal, 22(3): 122–134.

Jay, B. (1994) Not Simply Divine, New York: Fireside.

Kates, S.M. (1999) 'Making the Ad Perfectly Queer: Marketing "normality" to the gay men's community?', Journal of Advertising, 28(1): 25–37.

Kates, S.M. (2002) 'The Protean Quality of Subcultural Consumption: An ethnographic account of gay consumers', Journal of Consumer Research, 29(3): 383–399.

Kates, S.M. (2004) 'The Dynamics of Brand Legitimacy: An interpretive study in the gay men's community', Journal of Consumer Research, 31(2): 455–464.

Kirk, M. (2004) 'Kind of a Drag: Gender, race, and ambivalence in *The Birdcage* and *To Wong Foo, Thanks for Everything! Julie Newmar*', Journal of Homosexuality, 46(3–4): 169–180.

Kornhaber, S. (2017) 'Why Drag is the Ultimate Retort to Trump: RuPaul versus the White House' The Atlantic, [online] 15 May, Available from: theatlantic.com/magazine/archive/2017/06/rupaul-gets-political/524529/?utm_source=twb [Accessed 10 March 2024].

McCormack, M. and Wignall, L. (2022) 'Drag Performers' Perspectives on the Mainstreaming of British Drag: Towards a sociology of contemporary drag', Sociology, 56(1): 3–20.

Meyerowitz, J. (2002) How Sex Changed: A History of Transsexuality, Cambridge, MA: Harvard University Press.

Newton, E. (1979/1972) Mother Camp: Female Impersonators in America, Chicago: University of Chicago Press.

Nicholson, R. (2017) 'Workin' It! How female drag queens are causing a scene', The Guardian, [online] 10 July, Available from: theguardian.com/lifeandstyle/2017/jul/10/workin-it-how-female-drag-queens-are-causing-a-scene [Accessed 10 March 2024].

Ourahmoune, N. (2017) 'Embodied Transformations and Food Restrictions: The case of medicalized obesity', Journal of Business Research, 75: 192–201.

Rehling, N. (2009) Extra-Ordinary Men: White Heterosexual Masculinity and Contemporary Popular Cinema, Washington, DC: Lexington Books.

Rhyne, R. (2004) 'Racializing White Drag', Journal of Homosexuality, 46(3–4): 181–194.

Rupp, L.J. and Taylor, V. (2003) Drag Queens at the 801 Cabaret, Chicago: University of Chicago Press.

Schneier, M. (2016) 'Why the Fashion World is Obsessed with "RuPaul's Drag Race"', The New York Times, [online] 24 September, Available from: nytimes.com/2016/09/25/fashion/why-the-fashion-world-is-obsessed-with-rupauls-drag-race.html [Accessed 10 March 2024].

Senelick, L. (2000) The Changing Room: Sex, Drag and Theatre, London: Routledge.

Sim, B. (2024) '9 Milestones & Records that Prove "Drag Race" Season 16 was HERSTORIC' Out Magazine, [online] 23 April, Available from: out.com/gay-tv-shows/rupauls-drag-race-season-16-records-achievements-list#rebelltitem9 [Accessed 28 April 2024].

Snetiker, M. (2017) 'RuPaul: From drag to riches', Entertainment Weekly, 23 June.

Venkatraman, R., Ozanne, J.L. and Coslor, E. (2024) 'Stigma Resistance through Body-in-Practice: Embodying pride through creative mastery', Journal of Consumer Research, doi.org/10.1093/jcr/ucae015

PART I

Politicizing Drag Identities

2

The Neoliberal 'Ru-presentation' of Drag as a Key to Success and Acceptance

Luigi Squillante

It is slightly past 6 pm on 13 May 2019 and the Orpheum Theater in Los Angeles is packed with an excited crowd. The audience is paying tribute to a group of drag performers who, just a few minutes before, had been photographed at the entrance runway, Hollywood-diva style, and are now fiercely walking the catwalk on the theatre stage in their majestic outfits. Roars come from the crowd, as one by one the queens are introduced. The camera pans over the audience, as we see people clapping vigorously: there are young men screaming in exaltation, women with incredulous open mouths, and drag queens with exaggerated make-up waving at their idols and peers. Finally, a voiceover announces the entrance of the 'Queen of Queens'. The audience gives a standing ovation, as a drag queen dressed entirely in elegant green appears on stage.

We are watching the Grand Finale of Season 11 of the talent show *RuPaul's Drag Race*, and RuPaul – the host – has just entered the scene: she is ready to serve the audience a spectacular event that will ultimately proclaim America's next best drag superstar. However, before the show can fully commence, RuPaul silences the crowd and takes a minute to dedicate some words to her audience (S11, E14, 00:04:28, emphasis added):[1]

> To the millions of fans watching, on VH1 and around the globe, I want to say thank you. Because of you, our little drag show has become a cultural phenomenon. Because of you, 140 Ru Girls are spreading their charisma, uniqueness, nerve and talent for all the world to see.

And because of you, *a TV show of queer people, by queer people, and for queer people*[2] has won nine Emmy awards. Can you believe it?

If it were possible to travel back in time several decades before that night, one would be shocked at a very different event to be witnessed. Exactly 60 years before, in May 1959, just a few blocks away from the Orpheum Theater, one of the first LGBTQ+ uprisings in the US was taking place (Faderman and Timmons, 2009). Transgender women, lesbian women, gay men and drag queens were rioting against police harassment and mistreatment at the 24-hour Cooper's Donuts café: the police patrols had asked some of the guests for their IDs – a usual habit for police officers at that time, aimed at arresting men who were 'masquerading' as women.

The shift from events at Cooper's Donuts to the majestic show at the Orpheum Theater unveils a profound metamorphosis in the societal response to LGBTQ+ instances, which has developed through a myriad of facts, events, policies and social transformations within the last 60 years, and whose complexity and intersections go beyond the aim of this chapter.

Yet, what will be presented here is an interpretative analysis of a small segment of such development. Specifically, the story of how a queer-oriented TV show – a drag queen competition – has succeeded in crossing the boundaries of the gay community, captivating a more general and widespread audience,[3] allowing the drag world to gain an impressive visibility and ultimately being able to have an impact on pop culture (Brennan and Gudelunas, 2017a) and integrate drag into the mainstream.

RuPaul's Drag Race and a theoretical background for its analysis

It has been suggested that television has played a pre-eminent role in presenting a renewed image of queerness in the last decades (Lovelock, 2019), also leading to new occasions of visibility for the drag world. In this regard, *RuPaul's Drag Race* (RPDR) has been recognized by many as one of the main contributors to recent changes in representation, expectations and the fruition of drag (see Crookston, 2021b). It has consequently attracted much attention from scholars, fostering the development of numerous analyses (Daems, 2014; Brennan and Gudelunas, 2017b; Crookston, 2021a; just to mention the monographs).

In a very concise description, RPDR is a US reality TV competition whose aim is to proclaim, each year, America's next drag superstar. First aired in 2009 on the US channel Logo TV (specifically oriented to an LGBTQ+ audience), in 2017 it passed to VH1 (general-interest TV) and ultimately landed on international broadcasts and platforms, such as Netflix and WOW Presents Plus, which contributed to making its audience global.

By February 2024, the show was in its 16th season (with over 200 episodes in total). It is named after its host and creator RuPaul: an American singer, actor, presenter and performer, widely known as a drag queen (or 'the Queen of Drag', as she prefers to be called; Street, 2020). RuPaul is also the main coach and judge of the competition, in which the contestants show their entertaining and performing talents in several challenges. Each weekly episode usually ends with the elimination of one performer, until three or four are left for the Grand Finale, a final episode in which the winner is proclaimed. This drag superstar is assured of a cash prize, plus complementary rewards such as jewellery, show-business contracts, and yearly supplies of cosmetics. RPDR has also given origin to a constellation of spin-offs in the US (*RuPaul's Drag U*, *Drag Race All Stars*, *RuPaul's Drag Race: Untucked*) and international versions (such as in Chile, Thailand, UK, Canada, Netherlands, Oceania, Spain, Italy and so on), turning itself into a worldwide phenomenon, as declared by RuPaul herself (S10, E14, 00:00:35).

The growing success of the programme has set the presence of drag in show business with the creation of a fully fledged cultural brand (Campana and Duffy, 2021) that provides a powerful reference for the LGBTQ+ community (Whitworth, 2017) and connects with market dynamics, ultimately boosting the visibility of the 'Ru-niverse' through collaborations with mainstream commercial brands and the sponsorship of internationally renowned events. As a consequence, the show has been able to bring 'the subversive art of drag into the living rooms of millions of Americans' (Whitworth, 2017: 139), inaugurating 'the golden age of drag into the zeitgeist' (Brennan and Gudelunas, 2017a: 1).

It has been noted, however, that RPDR sells 'a commercially viable and politically simplified version of drag' (Crookston, 2021b: 3), with all the consequences that commodification brings to the original disruptive potential of drag with respect to social, political and anthropological issues. The over-representation of drag through the show's format, together with the pedagogical attitude of the host towards the contestants, has inevitably intertwined the concept of what constitutes drag with a set of normative behaviours strictly related to market and the nature of reality TV. As powerfully noted by Yudelman (2017: 27), the media strategies enacted through the show 'have less to do with how the series *reflects* drag culture, and more to do with how RPDR actively *transforms* drag culture by way of shaping its subjects' (emphasis in original).

Moving on from these considerations, the approach of this chapter is positioned on the Foucauldian line of studies on media production, relying on the latent connection that Couldry (2008) proposes between reality TV and neoliberalism.[4]

According to the Foucauldian perspective, in fact, the dynamics of power supporting neoliberalism do not originate from institutions by means of imposition or repression. Rather, individuals are induced to play an active and productive role in building, consolidating and renewing the power relations in which they are involved and to which, at the same time, they are subject, by taking part in the process of constructing themselves as neoliberal *subjects*. It is fundamental to underline that, according to this approach, citizens choose freely to cooperate with such a system and to construct their subjectivity according to its parameters, since it appears to be structured on a *regime of truth*. This concept refers to a set of constructs that individuals recognize as objectively true and grounded in common sense (Foucault, 2000). Foucault (2006) calls this form of power *governmentality*, and it can be generally interpreted as a systematic regulation and guidance of the everyday conduct of each individual by means of shared knowledge, norms or actions[5] (Ong, 2006) disseminated through a variety of different governmental dispositives.[6]

Approaches of this kind interpret reality TV as one of such dispositives enhancing neoliberal thinking, with the ultimate goal of showing citizens how to be successful in the era of the 'roll back' of the state[7] by proposing models that foster the values of self-discipline, self-entrepreneurship and competitiveness (Rose, 1996; Hay, 2000; Andrejevic, 2003; Murray and Ouellette, 2004; Ouellette and Hay, 2008a; Ouellette, 2014). Within such a frame, success is connected to social agreeableness and acceptance: a critical issue when it comes to the integration of queer instances within society.

Building on these assumptions, the analysis here will consider some elements of the US primigenial version of RPDR that can be interpreted as examples of compliance to contemporary neoliberal norms, in terms of both pedagogical and performative acts. The chapter will then discuss how and why such dynamics can play an important role in facilitating the acceptance of new drag models within mainstream culture.

Methodology

The methodology of the present analysis follows a qualitative approach within the classical interpretative paradigm of social sciences (see Wilson, 1970; Corbetta, 2003), by adopting the Foucauldian lens of discourse[8] analysis (Arribas-Ayllon and Walkerdine, 2008) to frame the concepts inductively derived from observation.

Specifically, by initially watching RDPR, I became aware that, on several occasions, the show would present dialogues and behaviours that reflected some typical features of the neoliberal discourse already identified within media production (Couldry, 2008; Türken et al, 2015), such as the celebration of individualism, self-confidence and productivity. As in other qualitative studies on RPDR (see Jenkins, 2017), a second attentive scrutiny of the episodes was performed, supported by note-taking, in order to outline a set of situational and dialogical patterns highlighting the earlier-mentioned features and pointing to the governmental dynamics of the show, whose elements will be fully analysed in the next section. Finally, in order to systematically study the show's discourse, the identification of specific situations and excerpts, as well as their analysis in context, has been supported by the interrogation of the entire corpus of RPDR dialogues through textual searches based on keywords, since corpus-based investigations exploiting keywords or textual patterns have proved to be a powerful tool for discourse analysis (Flowerdew, 2012), especially in Foucauldian approaches (Baker, 2006).[9]

This study, in fact, exploits a textual corpus of approximately 2.5 million words, composed of the English subtitles from all the episodes of the first 14 seasons of the show. Subtitle files have been collected from the opensubtitles. org database,[10] which represents a prominent open resource for subtitles in the contemporary entertaining audio-visual market. The reliability of the resource, in terms of both text timing and correct transcriptions, has been tested by spot-checking the files and comparing their content with the view of the corresponding episodes. The same process has been applied to all textual excerpts mentioned in this chapter. Indeed, the integration of textual data with their contextual visual information is fundamental in order to grasp non-verbal communication, as well as the editing techniques applied to the situations, which can also contribute to providing an exhaustive picture for the analysis.

For this chapter, all subtitle files have been kept in their original *srt* format,[11] and queries made via a *bash*[12] command-line interface through the use of the *grep*[13] command in combination with specific search patterns. Further details on the commands aimed at extracting specific information from the corpus are provided in the next section for each textual query made.

Evidence from the data

It is possible to recognize at least three themes running through the RPDR series declinable within the neoliberal frame: individualism, self-confidence and condemnation of idleness. This set of concepts is not an exhaustive list but rather an essential categorization arising from the most evident examples that were identified through the analysis: they can be thought as a first-order approximation of a wider range of more specific features identifiable in future investigations. In the following, each of these themes will be considered in relation to some relevant programme excerpts that exhibit them.

Individualism

Individualism is one of the key features of neoliberal thinking (Howard, 2007; Springer, 2016) as it places a strong emphasis on the autonomy and agency of individuals within market-driven societies. Neoliberal citizens, in fact, should pursue their own self-interests and maximize their potential through entrepreneurialism, personal responsibility and self-reliance (Lemke, 2001). It is possible to attest that, in RPDR, such a perspective is not only present, but strongly encouraged.

At the end of the Season 10 episode 'Tap That App', contestant Mayhem Miller stands together with her peers in front of the judges, receiving her critiques. Judge Michelle Visage complains about Miller not being convincing in her group performance and is spurring on Miller to admit that she was uncertain from the beginning about the results of the joke her team had been so determined in preparing. The dialogue ends up as follows (S10, E3, 00:48:16, emphasis added):

Michelle Visage:	Did you say something to your team?
Mayhem Miller:	Um, no, because I wanted to be a team player.
	…
Michelle Visage:	On this show, *you didn't come to make friends. You came to win a competition.*

This kind of exchange is not an isolated one. By searching for the collocation 'make friends'[14] and its variations within the entire corpus of RPDR subtitles, ten more occurrences appear, as listed in Table 2.1.

Excluding case 6 (S12), in which contestant Jackie Cox uses such an expression without any reference to the competition dynamics, only cases 3, 9, and 11 seem to convey a genuine validation of friendship. However, case 3 (S5) refers to a situation in which Ivy Winters has just been eliminated: in her case, the celebration of friendship cannot impact any more her path through the competition. Cases 9 and 11 (S13) are both utterances pronounced by contestant Kandy Muse. It has to be noted that, in the latter case, after celebrating friendship, Kandy Muse quickly shifts attention to herself in a sort of late correction following RuPaul's unconvinced expression (S13, E16, 00:17:45, emphasis added):

RuPaul:	Now, what's been your favorite part in this experience?
Kandy Muse:	Oh my God, I think *my favorite part,* number one, *is making the amazing friends that I've made on the show.* Me and the top four, I think we're the closest …
RuPaul:	I heard that.
Kandy Muse:	… ever. Ever.
RuPaul looks at her, incredulous.	
Kandy Muse:	But, honestly, just all the memes, and just showing the world who Kandy Muse is, because I wanted this for so long.

RuPaul: *(nodding)* Uh-uh.
Kandy Muse: And now being on this platform, *this is my favorite part.*
                   'Cause like I said: I'm delusional and self-centered.
RuPaul laughs.

Apart from case 2 (S4), in which Sharon Needles mentions friendship as the counterpart of the enemies she has made along the way, the remaining five cases exhibit the use of 'make friends' in accordance with Visage's perspective cited earlier. As inferable by the transcriptions, friendship is set up in opposition to the concepts of winning or prevailing on others, explicating that social bonding is allowed as long as it does not interfere with individual goals and success.

It is emblematic that contestant Rosé proposes a sort of shared [5] understanding of the concept when interviewed in the episode 'Reunited' (case 10 – S13, E15, 00:17:44). In response to the voiceover query, 'What's a phrase drag queens use way too much?', she quotes, '"I did not come here to make friends."' It seems, then, that the statement has become a sort of mantra, proposed 'way too much' by drag performers. Interestingly, Rosé is also the contestant who exhibits most occurrences of the use of 'make friends' in terms of burden against one's success. Finally, although uttered in the show's spin-off *Untucked*, it is worth mentioning that Season 4 contestant Lashauwn Beyond also provided a classical *golden quote* for the RPDR world while arguing with her peer Jiggly Caliente, as she polemically stated in Episode 1 (emphasis added): 'I'm not here to make best buddies, bitch! I'm not here to be your friend. … I'm here to … win $100,000, not be nobody's friend. … I don't have to be your friend to win this show. *This is not RuPaul's best friend race!*'

It must be noted that the individualistic perspective present in the six cases in which friendship is opposed to winning (1, 4, 5, 7, 8, 10) is primarily proposed by the contestants alone (4, 7, 8, 10), or in interaction with the host (1); only in one case (5) it is part of an explicit sanctioning act by a judge. Yet, the hypothesis that such an individualistic view is connected only to an unfiltered representation of the values of specific contestants – or judges – with a strong personality, with no reference to more general dynamics of the show, may be weakened by further cases.

In complete accordance with Visage's sanction to Mayhem Miller, for example, the following excerpt is powerfully impactful in showing how individualism is not only represented on screen by spontaneous points of view but also proposed as the only moral conviction leading to success.

In 'The Last Ball on Earth' (S10, E4), contestant Asia O'Hara stands in front of the judges (RuPaul, Michelle Visage, Tisha Campbell Martin), in tears because of the mediocre results she has achieved in producing the three outfits required for a design challenge. O'Hara, who is an expert sewer,

Table 2.1: Occurrences of 'make friends' and its variations in the corpus of *RuPaul's Drag Race* subtitles

#	When	Dialogue	Situation
1	S3, E13, 00:14:11	RuPaul:	So, it is safe to say you didn't come to the competition to *make friends*, you came to win.	RuPaul visits contestant Manila Luzon's table in the workroom to discuss her motivation.
		Manila Luzon:	Uh, well, both. I love meeting new people, so I'm gonna *make* a lot of *friends*, but if I have to stab them in the back … I mean, whatever. *(RuPaul laughs.)*	
2	S4, E13, 00:24:57	Sharon Needles:	There's just been ups and downs. I've made enemies. I've *made best friends*.	Contestant Sharon Needles is commenting on her experience on the show.
3	S5, E8, 00:41:12	Ivy Winters:	I *made* amazing *friends* along the way.	Contestant Ivy Winters is giving her final comments in the workroom after being eliminated.
4	S10, E1, 00:34:58	Aquaria:	I am in it to win it, and I did not come here to *make friends*, bitch.	Contestant Aquaria is complaining in the confessional about her peer Miz Cracker copying her make-up.
5	S10, E3, 00:48:16	Michelle Visage:	On this show, you didn't come to *make friends*. You came to win a competition.	Judge Visage is giving her critiques to contestant Mayhem Miller.
6	S12, E6, 00:12:58	Jackie Cox:	Well, you know, I'm a taken man back home. But we're, you know, always down to *make friends*.	Former contestant Miss Vanjie is with RuPaul at Cox's table in the workroom, flirting with her.
7	S13, E3, 00:33:02	Rosé:	The sisterhood and the friends that I'm making here, it's so lovely. But I did not come here to *make friends*.	Contestant Rosé is talking in the confessional about her motivation.
8	S13, E14, 00:02:33	Rosé:	As much as I love these bitches, athletes don't go to the Olympics to *make friendship* bracelets.	Contestant Rosé is talking in the confessional about her motivation.
9	S13, E14, 00:29:51	Kandy Muse:	It's interesting because coming here, I didn't think I was gonna *make*, like, any *friends*. But, like, y'all are like my good Judies, my little besties, my best friends from this point on.	Contestant Kandy Muse is opening up with her peers in the workroom while putting on her make-up.
10	S13, E15, 00:17:46	Rosé:	I did not come here to *make friends*.	Interview during the presentation of contestants of the ritual 'Reunited' episode.
11	S13, E16, 00:17:51	Kandy Muse:	I think my favourite part, number one, is *making* the amazing *friends* that I've made on the show.	Interview with RuPaul during the Grand Finale.

declares that she spent a lot of time helping her peers with their dresses and in the end had little time left to work on her personal creations. The dialogue proceeds as follows (S10, E4, 00:49:16, emphasis added):

RuPaul: How many of the girls did you help with their sewing?

Asia O'Hara: Um ... I helped everybody with their looks.

Two other contestants nod, saying: Everyone!
A third contestant remarks: Every single person!

Michelle Visage: Did that take time away from you doing yours?
                 O'Hara hesitates.

Asia O'Hara: It did, but I felt like my time was spent ... *(exhales, holding back tears)* my time was spent better helping them.

Tisha C. Martin: It's so sweet of you, but, just like when you're on an airplane, you have to put the oxygen on first.

RuPaul: You have to put the mask on your face before you put it on your child's face. Asia, *you need to take care of yourself first.*

As attested by the data discussed earlier, the show seems to reproduce the conviction that, whenever juxtaposed, the pursuit of self-interest should take precedence over social bonding. This individualistic perspective is reinforced by the judges through acts of validation – such as laughing[15] – and sanctioning, promoting a narrative that prioritizes personal gain and recognition over communal support.

Self-confidence

The concept of self-confidence holds significant relevance within the framework of neoliberal thinking as it generally fosters the belief in one's ability to succeed and thrive in competitive environments (Bröckling, 2016).

In RPDR, the display of self-confidence often appears as a duty to be always exhibited, and a lack of which challenges the right to remain in the competition. In 'Draggily Ever After' (S9, E3), for example, contestant Aja comments on the elimination of Jaymes Mansfield, a queen who struggled with showing herself as a strong competitor (S9, E3, 00:00:16, emphasis added): 'I mean, Jaymes was very insecure, and she wasn't sure of herself. And this is such a high-pressure competition. *You have to be sure of yourself.*'

The show provides numerous occasions to let the contestants express how much they believe in themselves and in their suitability to be the favourite for the win. One of the most evident moments in which the display of self-confidence is revealed is the runway. While the contestants walk the catwalk in front of the judges, their voiceovers often narrate how much they worked on their outfits and how stunning their results are. For each performer, the display of self-confidence, when firmly expressing that they are serving the best performance in the group, is palpable.

Self-confidence is the proper attitude to be shown even if the contestant is aware of the mediocre results obtained for her outfit. In the case of Asia O'Hara, mentioned in the previous section, we come to know by her own admission to the judges that her 'two first looks were things that weren't finished when I got here' (S10, E4, 00:49:09). Nevertheless, just minutes before, her voiceover on the presentation of her first outfit on the runway dedicated to 'Alaskan Winter Realness', was: 'I'm gonna turn heads on the beach. I am serving Alaskan tuna. Whatever fish live in Alaska, that's the fish I am, and the judges are eating every drop of it' (S10, E4, 00:35:31). O'Hara's voiceover for her second outfit, within the category 'Miami Summer Realness', is self-acclaiming with no less emphasis (S10, E4, 00:40:01): 'I've chosen to be very modern, fashion forward, futuristic, snow leopard neon bunny. Yes, it's the end of the world, but a bitch is still gonna look good!'

Another recurrent situation of the show can also reveal the importance of self-confidence, specifically in relation to the construction of the neoliberal subject. After the judges' critiques, or occasionally in the workroom, RuPaul can challenge the contestants to nominate someone as the worst performer, thus *deserving* to be eliminated from the show. Embracing a *mors tua vita mea* approach, contestants usually utter the name of a peer since, even when they are aware of having performed badly, in the words of contestant Heidi N Closet (S12, E13, 00:15:29): 'Of course I'm not going to say myself!'

By looking at all the occasions in which RuPaul asks the contestants who should go home,[16] 19 situations can be retrieved throughout all 14 seasons. In 17 of these, contestants nominate one of their peers for elimination. On two occasions – namely, the cases of Delta Work (S3, E3) and Nicky Doll (S12, E5) – the contestants nominate themselves as the worst performers, indicating that they feel they deserve to go home. Both contestants do end up having to *lip-sync for their lives*, that is, to perform the final challenge of each episode in which they execute a playback performance which then lets RuPaul declare who is saved and who is eliminated. However, while Delta Work's admission of deserving to be eliminated goes almost unnoticed and she eventually wins the lip-sync, Nicky Doll goes through a more intense elaboration of her behaviour.[17]

Right after Nicky nominates herself (S12, E5, 00:49:58), we see contestants Crystal Methyd and Jaida Essence Hall looking at her with shocked expressions, while judge Michelle Visage points her eyes down in what can possibly be read as disapproval. RuPaul herself seems disappointed, and after a few seconds interrupts Nicky's explanations to force her to nominate someone else. Eventually, after her lip-sync performance, Nicky Doll will *sashay away.*[18]

It is very interesting to report an excerpt from another episode in Season 12 – 'Reunited: Alone Together' – in which the dynamic of transformation and subjectification becomes more explicit thanks to Nicky's case. While chatting with all the contestants about their experiences in the show, RuPaul and Nicky have the following exchange (S12, E13, 00:15:30):

RuPaul: Hey, Nicky, what's the biggest lesson you learned from your time actually on the set?

Nicky Doll: If there's one thing that the show gave me, it's more confidence. Maybe a little bit more delusion, but more confidence when it comes to backing myself up … and, uh, yeah, if someone else says my name another time, I'll say their name too.

RuPaul laughs.

It is clear, here, that the acquisition of an increased self-confidence is the result of a lesson learned, and the outcome is explicitly appreciated.

Along the same line, another episode identified through the same search (S13, E13, 'Henny, I Shrunk the Drag Queens!') shows quite clearly the expectation in terms of exhibiting self-confidence. When asked by RuPaul about who should go home, contestant Olivia Lux looks very hesitant: 'When asked who I believe should go home tonight, I'm conflicted because I cannot say myself, and I cannot say any of them' (S13, E13, 00:47:25).

After 11 seconds of silence (as edited in the episode), RuPaul urges Olivia to say a name, but she still hesitates, while peers and judges show discomfort towards her behaviour. Eventually, her choice would go to Kandy Muse. It is very interesting to report the following comment about Olivia made by guest judge Cynthia Erivo to RuPaul, after all the queens have left the stage (S13, E13, 00:50:49, emphasis added):

When you asked her who she thought should go home and she decided not to say anyone for a second, I was a little bit disappointed that she couldn't say someone or say a name. Because, *if you're not gonna fight for yourself, who else is going to fight for you?*

This data shows that self-confidence is presented as a necessary condition to remain in the competition and to earn the esteem of judges and peers. In particular, the last example shows also how self-confidence is related to individualism within the general frame of the neoliberal reading of the show.

Condemnation of idleness

Productivity is a fundamental aspect of the neoliberal citizenship as it reflects one's ability to optimize resources and maximize outcomes by insisting on personal effort, initiative and the capability to generate value through work. As recalled by Lemke (2001: 203), the neoliberal system can function only if 'individuals "optimize" their relation to themselves and to work'. In this regard, the condemnation of idleness in favour of continuous production seems to be one more feature that RPDR is active in proposing.

During the second episode of Season 2, 'Starrbootylicious', contestant Tyra Sanchez is found asleep on a couch as RuPaul enters the workroom for her regular advisory talks during preparation. The host first approaches Sahara Davenport, the leader of the group in which Tyra Sanchez is included (S2, E2, 00:15:51):

RuPaul:	Do you feel as though you've been an effective leader for your team?
Sahara Davenport:	Most definitely. I think the end result will show that as well.
RuPaul:	So, you're ok that one of your team members is over there sleeping?

RuPaul looks at Tyra Sanchez.

Sahara Davenport:	I am worried. I am worried.
RuPaul:	Hm-mhh.
Sahara Davenport:	What am I to do?
RuPaul:	Well, it's, you know, hard out there for a pimp …

A few seconds later, RuPaul turns towards Tyra (S2, E2, 00:16:18):

RuPaul:	Tyra, sweetie. Darling? Sweetie pie.

Tyra Sanchez wakes up.

Tyra Sanchez:	Tired!
RuPaul:	You're tired?
Tyra Sanchez:	Yeah.
RuPaul:	Why you so tired?
Tyra Sanchez:	I don't know.

The image switches for a moment to the confessional, reporting Tyra Sanchez saying:

	When Ru woke me up I'm like, "Shit!"
RuPaul:	Now, why do you think everybody else is so busy, but you have time to nap?
Tyra Sanchez:	Um … *(referring to her peers)* they're hot-gluing.
RuPaul:	Uh-huh.

Tyra Sanchez:	And I sewed, and it took me, like, five minutes to make my costume.
RuPaul:	You know, you will be judged on not only your individual, but how well you work with the group.[19]
Tyra Sanchez:	I'm good. I'm perfectly fine. I don't have any doubt.
RuPaul:	(*seems hopeless*) Alright, get back to bed.

It is evident here that RuPaul tries to discuss the fact that being idle is inappropriate and must be explicitly sanctioned, regardless of the fact that the necessary individual work has already been done. In the first interaction with Sahara Davenport, we see that the contestant reveals a sudden shift in her certainties after RuPaul's considerations, turning her initial self-confidence about being an effective leader into the concern of her second reply, as in a performative pedagogical act guiding her (and the audience) towards awareness of idleness as a problem. On the contrary, Tyra Sanchez's firmness in rejecting RuPaul's critiques depicts her as a 'tough nut to crack'. Nevertheless, Tyra will eventually show a strong evolution throughout the season by accepting RuPaul's guidance later on in addressing her limitations and transforming her subjectivity, ultimately leading her to win Season 2.

Finally, it is worth noting that idleness can be perceived with discomfort by contestants themselves. In 'The Michelle Visage Roast' (S9, E8), contestant Valentina is complaining about herself not being able to write the jokes requested by the challenge, thus spending idle time, on which her peer Shea Couleé gives a clear-cut judgement (S9, E8, 00:10:04):

Valentina:	So, I have my pen in one hand, and I have my hand on a piece of paper, and I just think. And ... nothing. Oh ... *(looks desperate)* Virgen de Guadalupe, por favor, ayúdame en este momento porque no tengo nada.[20]
Shea Couleé:	*(from the confessional, annoyed)* Girl, Guadalupe ain't gonna write these jokes for you. You gotta do it for your own self, girl. So, get to work![21]

These examples can also attest that the judges and the contestants are involved in proposing a narrative that is fully adherent to the neoliberal ethos; namely, that idleness should be condemned in favour of an expected commitment to continuous production.

Discussion

The examples reported here unveil an implicit dynamic of the show aimed at exploiting selected individual behaviours and mixing them with sanctioning or pedagogical acts to produce an 'array of techniques that exercise power' and which can indirectly 'conduct, guide and enable a queen's action over the course of a season' (Yudelman, 2017: 27). From a Foucauldian point of view, this can be interpreted as a governmental dynamic that appears to be specifically oriented to the creation and reproduction of neoliberal subjects. In fact, individualism, imperative expression of self-confidence, and continuous production are proposed as the only favourable moral convictions: an ensemble which is tremendously adherent to the precepts of the contemporary neoliberal worker-citizen (Rose, 1999).

The data included here show that several techniques are used to both shape the contestants' subjectivities and let them corroborate their ethical positioning. Apart from tactics already identified in previous studies, such as 'discussions with Ru'[22] and 'well-placed reactions from other queens'[23] (Yudelman, 2017: 27), the production of neoliberal subjectivities is also fostered through autonomous statements of the queens[24] and explicit condemnations of unacceptable behaviours.[25] In line with the fact that governmentality calls for self-governance in the exercise of power, requiring individuals to internalize the dominant societal expectations, in the dialogue between RuPaul and Nicky Doll (in the section 'Self-confidence') we also see an explicit example of a contestant admitting to have learned what is best for her thanks to the show.

One should take into account, however, that the show's governmental dynamic goes beyond the characters appearing on screen. Studies such as those by Ouellette (2004) and Ouellette and Hay (2008b) have shown that what is transposed on reality shows can resonate with everyday experiences of individuals within neoliberal societies. As noted by Couldry (2008: 11): 'the "as if" of reality TV tracks with striking fidelity the dynamics of the neoliberal workplace'. With regards to RPDR, the consonance between the show and neoliberal citizenship experienced in the outside world is sometimes made explicit. In the Grand Finale of Season 13, for example, Kandy Muse answers RuPaul's question, 'Where does your fighting spirit come from?' with (S13, E16, 00:17:26, emphasis added): 'It comes from growing up in the hood. ... In the hood, you have no choice but to fight to get to the goal that you want to get to. *And coming in the competition, it was no different.*' Since the discourse of neoliberal thinking is by now taken for granted as common sense in the Western world (Harvey, 2005; Couldry, 2008; Hall et al, 2015), the consonance of shows like RPDR with the neoliberal framework translates into an adherence to, in RuPaul's words, 'the narrative that's already implanted in people's consciousness'.[26] The specificity of RPDR, though, is that the production of subjects compliant with the neoliberal 'common sense' is performed through drag identities, and this process is not neutral with respect to how queerness relates to mainstream imagery. My thesis, in fact, is that this process actually contributes to integrating queer instances within the mainstream, as well as to providing the basis for the mounting success of the show, as discussed in the following.

On a first level, showing that queer people impersonate the neoliberal dominant values, and are educated to do so, may point at disempowering one of the necessary conditions that Blumer (1958: 4) classically identifies as the basis of prejudice, discrimination and exclusion operated by societal dominant groups – the 'feeling that the subordinate group[27] is intrinsically different and alien'. With regards to the queer realm, studies such as those by Evans (1993), Bell and Binnie (2000) and Cooper (2004) have 'pointed to … support for and adherence to dominant cultural norms and values as key mechanisms for social inclusion' (Richardson, 2005: 521). Richardson (2005), in particular, discusses that, within the neoliberal framework, the politics of normalization of gay and lesbian instances are often based on the concept of *sameness*, intending that non-conforming individuals are constructed to be as good and valid neoliberal citizens as their heterosexual counterparts since they all share the *same* values and behave in the *same* way when involved in similar economic and professional contexts. By projecting such considerations onto the drag world as presented (and *produced*) by RPDR, we can similarly argue that the commonality of neoliberal values between the Ru girls and the dominant culture may represent a factor of normalization for the historically stigmatized subculture embodied by drag personae. Consequently, 'neoliberal drag' has higher chances to foster acceptance and recognition of queer inputs within the mainstream culture.

At the same time, Foucauldian-informed studies such as those by Engel (2007, 2011) and Ludwig (2016) have argued that the neoliberal role model is not only embraceable by all individuals, independently from their collocation with respect to a given normed lifestyle, but also particularly exalted through non-conforming identities. In fact, just as the neoliberal society is 'not orientated toward … the uniformity of the commodity, but toward the multiplicity and differentiation of enterprises' (Foucault, 2008: 149, cited in Ludwig, 2016: 421), so the differences in expressions and lifestyle of marketized subjects are seen as 'employable cultural capital' (Ludwig, 2016: 420). In other words, in a competitive, individualistic and privatized environment, where each individual should think of themselves as a 'sort of permanent and multiple enterprise' (Foucault, 2008: 241), 'everybody is expected to find ways of expressing difference as particularity and specialness' (Engel, 2011: 75) in order to capitalize on them.

It is evident that the non-conformity of drag is able to perfectly fit in with this perspective. However, neoliberal subjects are also required to constantly 'balance the precarious threshold between difference as promise and difference as threat' (Engel, 2011: 75). In this regard, the governmental dynamic of RPDR discussed earlier can act as a stabilizing factor. In fact, by firmly anchoring its subjects to the desirable neoliberal expectations of their self-reliant entrepreneurial behaviour, the show can orient the reading of drag differences in terms of neoliberal-consonant enhancement of specialness, rather than incitement to subversiveness. In this regard, Morrison (2014) had already noted that the *entertaining* queens from RPDR are positioned to 'contain the threat that their drag might entail', with the show 'promoting the history of the homophile movements and their call *to assimilate rather than to agitate* as the only queer history worth bringing back through camp practices' (Morrison, 2014: 141; emphasis added). This can ultimately allow the uniqueness of drag identities and the enrichment that drag brings to pop culture to be celebrated without fearing any destabilization from queer inputs. In this way, as long as its queerness is filtered through the lens of neoliberal values, RPDR is able to frame drag as one of the privileged domains in which the novelty of different – and marketable – cultural stimuli can foster interest, appreciation and success.[28]

Conclusion

This chapter has proposed an interpretive path aimed at unveiling further perspectives of analysis on RPDR, in order to account for its success in elevating drag to a worldwide cultural phenomenon and ultimately integrating queer instances into pop culture.

Following a Foucauldian approach, neoliberal governmentality has been identified as a seminal frame structuring the show's discourse to allow for a hybridization of the representation of drag non-conformity with the (re)production of neoliberal citizenship. The system of values proposed by the show is thus able to appear consonant with what has currently become common sense within neoliberal societies, providing a fundamental prerequisite of compatibility between queer and mainstream. By exploiting concepts deriving from Foucauldian analyses on media and queer issues, this chapter has discussed how the neoliberal 'Ru-presentation' of drag can be analysed as both a device pointing at disempowering the perception of otherness of queer individuals and a way to let drag be celebrated for its marketable specialness rather than its cultural subversiveness.

In conclusion, RPDR has proven to be a privileged case able to show how marketization and adherence to the values of neoliberal citizenship can foster a discourse of integration, in addition to that of exclusion of queer citizens as analysed in different contexts (see Peterson, 2011). It must not go unnoticed, however, that the cultural integration driven by the show appears inextricably connected to queer homologation and normativization, thus becoming one more example of the implicit power relationships, expressed by cultural phenomena, that pervade social dynamics.

Notes

[1] References to the episodes of the show are indicated in the format 'S00, E00, hh:mm:ss' where S stands for season and E for episode; the time format of hours, minutes and seconds is indicated wherever a dialogue is cited, and reports the temporal indication of the excerpt, according to the data available in the subtitle database.

[2] In this excerpt, RuPaul uses 'queer' as an umbrella term to refer to the broad variety of non-heterosexual life experiences, rather than solely focusing on those associated with non-cisgender identities (as primarily attested by the diverse range of identities publicly disclosed by the contestants throughout the series). In the following, such broader understanding of the term will be maintained, acknowledging that 'queer' can inclusively encompass the array of identities that transcend heteronormativity.

[3] Fenton Bailey, co-founder of the production company of RPDR, World of Wonders, has attested that, in 2018, 60 per cent of the people watching the show were women, and half of them were heterosexual (Jordan, 2018).

[4] As vastly analysed in literature (Drucker, 1988; Hall, 1988; Thrift, 2005; Sapelli, 2007), neoliberalism has represented a fundamental shift in the evolution of capitalism, leading to its 'new spirit' (Boltanski and Chiapello, 1999) characterized by the celebration of personal freedom and agency, the exaltation of economic interest as the only common good and the predominance of a pervasive and highly competitive market over the rigid rules of state bureaucracy (Magatti, 2009). The neoliberal perspective has become dominant 'in the major economic, political and social forums of the developed capitalistic countries and in the international agencies they influence' (Navarro, 2007: 47).

[5] Within this framework, neoliberalism is not interpreted as an ideological superstructure of capitalism but as a discursive practice; a system of meanings able to structure individual identities (Larner, 2000), oriented towards specific goals and self-regulating through a continuous reflection (Foucault, 2008).

[6] The definition of *dispositive* in Foucault's philosophy is broad and can include 'a thoroughly heterogeneous ensemble consisting of discourses, institutions, architectural forms, regulatory decisions, laws, administrative measures, scientific statements, philosophical, moral and philanthropic propositions – in short, the said as much as the unsaid' (Foucault, 1980: 194).

[7] As proposed by Peck and Tickell (2002), the *roll back* is a specific phase in the institutionalization of the neoliberal policies – whose initial deployment dates back to the 1980s – characterized by an 'active destruction' of the Keynesian welfare state. The reduction of the active role of the state requires citizens to be considered independent agents of their own destiny (in terms of both fortunes and misfortunes), who should thus become self-mastery people within an *ownership* society (Moini, 2012).

[8] *Discourse* is intended here as a system of statements and practices that shapes knowledge, truth, power and social reality (Foucault, 1972). It is a crucial element in understanding how power operates in society and how social norms and identities are constructed and maintained.

[9] Specifically, they have been effectively used in the analysis of the LGBTQ+ public discourse, including the representation of gay (Baker, 2005), queer (Bailey, 2019) and transgender subjectivities (Zottola, 2018) in media production, as well as to investigate governmental dynamics involved in the construction of the neoliberal subject (Mısır and Işık-Güler, 2022).

[10] opensubtitles.org/it/ssearch/sublanguageid-eng/idmovie-171453 (accessed 11 November 2022).

[11] The *srt* format is a plain-text file containing transcripts with their sequential number, as well as their start and end timecodes.

[12] gnu.org/software/bash (accessed 11 November 2022).

[13] 'Given one or more patterns, grep searches input files for matches to the patterns. When it finds a match in a line, it copies the line to standard output' (gnu.org/software/grep/ manual/grep.html, accessed 17 November 2022).

[14] The search has been performed assigning to grep the regular expression 'ma(k|d).* friends', to look for all inflections of the verb *make* followed by the string *friends,* allowing for possible intervening words, as long as *make* and *friends* still appear on the same line of text.

[15] Making the judges laugh is often presented as a sign of validation and approval in the show. As stated by contestant Monét X Change (S10), while commenting on her successful performance that saved her from elimination in a *lip-sync for your life*: 'So I was like, I need to really turn it out and do something crazy *to make RuPaul laugh*' (S10, E13, 00:06:36, emphasis added).

[16] The search has been initially performed by associating to the grep command the regular expression 'go.* home' to allow for the maximum recall. This search pattern outputs all occurrences of any inflection of the verb *go* followed by the string *home,* with any intervening word, as long as *go* and *home* appear on the same line. Such a broad search pattern is due to the great variability of ways in which RuPaul asks his question to the contestant, using different constructs such as *Who deserves to go home?, Who should be the one who goes home tonight and why?* and so on. After a manual filtering of the output to isolate only true occurrences of the targeted situation, it was possible to redefine the following grammar of variations identifying exact matches for the wanted search pattern, according to the regular expression syntax to be used with grep: 'who ((deserves|you want) to|(do you think)? should) (go|be (going|the one who goes)) home (tonight (and why)?)?'.

Data have been finally counter-checked with the footage from the different episodes, in order to filter out any occurrences of those sequences that are reported twice due to their inclusion in previews of the following episode or recaps from past episodes.

[17] This can also suggest a change in the intensity of the subjectification dynamics proposed by the show, which may have increased over the seasons and needs to be investigated in future research.

[18] It is worth mentioning that Nicky Doll is French: the degree of socialization of contestants to US culture and its dominant values may play a role in exhibiting this kind of behaviour and can be analysed in future studies. Although not included in the present analysis, in Season 5 of the *All Stars* spin-off, Filipino queen Ongina also nominated herself before then being eliminated. Unsurprisingly, her behaviour is heavily sanctioned by her peers in the next episode (E3) as we hear Alexis Mateo saying, 'I am still angry with her, because she just gave up' and Blair St Clair adding, 'If I went home and found out that someone else gave up, I'd be devastated.'

[19] Here we can identify another key topic of the neoliberal governmentality that Couldry (2008) recognizes in reality shows, that is, the promotion of team conformity through the imperative of making teamwork compulsory.

[20] 'Holy Virgin of Guadalupe, please, help me in this moment because I have nothing.'

[21] It is possible also to read here a reference to the Protestant perspective on the value of work, whose cultural setting, according to the classical Weberian analysis (1904), stands behind the flourishing of modern capitalism (and, indirectly, of neoliberalism). What Shea Coulée does here is condemn a *Catholic prayer,* performed to beg for something, as opposed to a *Protestant prayer,* which is only uttered to thank God for what the believer has already obtained as the result of their own work.

[22] As in the conversation between RuPaul and Nicky Doll from S12, E13 (in the section 'Self-confidence').

[23] As in the montage involving Valentina and Shea Couleé from S9, E8 (earlier in 'Condemnation of idleness').

[24] See, for example, cases 4 and 7 in Table 2.1.

[25] See, for example, case 5 in Table 2.1.

[26] The quote comes from the online trailer of the course 'RuPaul Teaches Self-Expression and Authenticity' (masterclass.com, June 2020), in which RuPaul states: 'You wanna make more money? You like money? Wear a suit. Put yourself together, people respond to it. [It] has nothing to do with you, it has to do with the narrative that's already implanted in people's consciousness. You don't wanna swim upstream. You want to work with what people already know. You can use that tool to get what you want out of this life.'

[27] Queer people in our case.

[28] Not surprisingly, RPDR positions itself as the only queer-oriented TV show in the top ten of all-time Emmy Award-winning programmes (7th place, with 26 Emmy awards – emmys.com/awards, accessed 23 November 2022).

References

Andrejevic, M. (2003) *Reality TV: The Work of Being Watched*, Lanham, MA: Rowman & Littlefield.

Arribas-Ayllon, M. and Walkerdine, V. (2008) 'Foucauldian Discourse Analysis', in C. Willig and W. Stainton Rogers (eds) *The Sage Handbook of Qualitative Research in Psychology*, London: Sage.

Bailey, A. (2019) '"Girl-on-girl culture": Constructing normative identities in a corpus of sex advice for queer women', *Journal of Language and Sexuality*, 8(2): 195–220.

Baker, P. (2005) *Public Discourses of Gay Men*, London: Routledge.

Baker, P. (2006) *Using Corpora in Discourse Analysis*, London: Continuum.

Bell, D. and Binnie, J. (2000) *The Sexual Citizen: Queer Politics and Beyond*, Oxford: Polity Press.

Blumer, H. (1958) 'Race Prejudice as a Sense of Group Position', *The Pacific Sociological Review*, 1(1): 3–7.

Boltanski, L. and Chiapello, E. (1999) *Le nouvel esprit du capitalism* [The New Spirit of Capitalism], Paris: Gallimard.

Brennan, N. and Gudelunas, D. (2017a) 'Drag Culture, Global Participation and RuPaul's Drag Race', in N. Brennan and D. Gudelunas (eds) *RuPaul's Drag Race and the Shifting Visibility of Drag Culture*, Cham/ Basingstoke: Palgrave Macmillan, pp 1–11.

Brennan, N. and Gudelunas, D. (eds) (2017b) *RuPaul's Drag Race and the Shifting Visibility of Drag Culture: The Boundaries of Reality TV*, Cham/ Basingstoke: Palgrave Macmillan.

Bröckling, U. (2016) *The Enterpreneurial Self: Fabricating a New Type of Subject*, London: Sage.

Campana, M. and Duffy, K. (2021) '*RuPaul's Drag Race*: Between cultural branding and consumer culture', in C. Crookston (ed) *The Cultural Impact of RuPaul's Drag Race: Why Are We All Gagging?*, Bristol/Chicago: Intellect, pp 108–130.

Cooper, D. (2004) *Challenging Diversity: Rethinking Equality and the Value of Difference*, Cambridge: Cambridge University Press.

Corbetta, P. (2003) *La ricerca sociale: metodologia e tecniche, I: I paradigmi di riferimento [Social Research: Methods and Techniques, Volume I]*, Bologna: Il Mulino.

Couldry, N. (2008) 'Reality TV, or the Secret Theater of Neoliberalism', *The Review of Education, Pedagogy and Cultural Studies*, 30(1): 3–13.

Crookston, C. (ed) (2021a) *The Cultural Impact of RuPaul's Drag Race: Why Are We All Gagging?*, Bristol/Chicago: Intellect.

Crookston, C. (2021b) 'Why Are We All Gagging? Unpacking the cultural impact of RuPaul's Drag Race', in C. Crookston (ed) *The Cultural Impact of RuPaul's Drag Race: Why Are We All Gagging?*, Bristol/Chicago: Intellect, pp 1–10.

Daems, J. (ed) (2014) *The Makeup of RuPaul's Drag Race*, Jefferson, NC: McFarland.

Drucker, P. (1988) 'The Coming of a New Organization', *Harvard Business Review*, 88: 5–53.

Engel, A. (2007) 'No Sex, No Crime, No Shame: Privatized care and the seduction into responsibility', *Nordic Journal of Women's Studies*, 15(3): 114–132.

Engel, A. (2011) 'Tender Tensions – Antagonistic Struggles – Becoming-Bird: Queer-political interventions into neoliberal hegemony', in M. Castro Varela, M.N. Dhawan and A. Engel (eds) *Hegemony and Heteronormativity: Revisiting 'the Political' in Queer Politics*, Aldershot: Ashgate.

Evans, D. (1993) *Sexual Citizenship: The Material Construction of Sexualities*, London: Routledge.

Faderman, L. and Timmons, S. (2009) *Gay L.A.: A History of Sexual Outlaws, Power Politics and Lipstick Lesbians*, Berkeley: University of California Press.

Foucault, M. (1972) *The Archaeology of Knowledge*, New York: Pantheon Books.

Foucault, M. (1980) *Power/Knowledge: Selected Interviews and Other Writings 1972–1977* (ed C. Gordon), New York: Pantheon Books.

Foucault, M. (2000) 'Truth and Power', in P. Rabinow (series ed) *Essential Works of Michel Foucault 1954–1984*: Volume 3, Power (ed J.B. Faubion), New York: The New Press.

Foucault, M. (2006) 'Governmentality', in A. Sharma and A. Gupta (eds) *The Anthropology of the State: A Reader*, Malden, MA/Oxford: Blackwell.

Foucault, M. (2008) *The Birth of Biopolitics: Lectures at the Collège de France 1978–1979*, New York: Palgrave Macmillan.

Flowerdew, L. (2012) 'Corpus-based Discourse Analysis', in M. Handford and J.P. Gee (eds) *The Routledge Handbook of Discourse Analysis*, London: Routledge, pp 174–187.

Hall, S. (1988) 'The Great Moving Right Show', in S. Hall and M. Jacques (eds) *The Politics of Thatcherism*, London: Lawrence and Wishart.

Hall, S., Massey, D. and Rustin, M. (2015) *After Neoliberalism? The Kilburn Manifesto*, London: Lawrence and Wishart.

Harvey, D. (2005) *A Brief History of Neoliberalism*, Oxford: Oxford University Press.

Hay, J. (2000) 'Unaided Virtues: The (neo-)liberalization of the domestic sphere', *Television and New Media*, 1(1): 53–73.

Howard, C. (2007) 'Introducing Individualization', in C. Howard (ed) *Contested Individualization*, Cham: Palgrave Macmillan, pp 1–23.

Jenkins, S.T. (2017) 'Spicy. Exotic. Creature. Representations of racial and ethnic minorities on *RuPaul's Drag Race*', in N. Brennan and D. Gudelunas (eds) *RuPaul's Drag Race and the Shifting Visibility of Drag Culture*, Cham: Palgrave Macmillan, pp 77–90.

Jordan, D. (2018) 'Why RuPaul's Drag Race is Big Business', BBC News, [online] 1 June, Available from: bbc.com/news/business-44335007 [Accessed 28 March 2020].

Larner, W. (2000) 'Neo-liberalism: Policy, ideology, governmentality', *Studies in Political Economy*, 63: 5–25.

Lemke, T. (2001) 'The Birth of Bio-politics: Michel Foucault's lecture at the Collège de France on neo-liberal governmentality', *Economy and Society*, 30(2): 190–207.

Lovelock, M. (2019) *Reality TV and Queer Identities: Sexuality, Authenticity, Celebrity*, Cham: Palgrave Macmillan.

Ludwig, G. (2016) 'Desiring Neoliberalism', *Sexuality Research and Social Policy*, 13: 417–427.

Magatti, M. (2009) *Libertà immaginaria: Le illusioni del capitalismo tecno-nichilista [Imaginary Freedom: The Illusions of Techno-Nihilistic Capitalism]*, Milan: Feltrinelli.

Mısır, H. and Işık-Güler, H. (2022) '"Be a Better Version of You!": A corpus-driven critical discourse analysis of MOOC platforms' marketing communication', *Linguistics and Education*, 69: 1–12.

Moini, G. (2012) *Teoria critica della partecipazione [Critical Theory of Participation]*, Milan: Franco Angeli.

Morrison, J. (2014) 'Draguating to Normal: Camp and homonormative politics', in J. Daems (ed) *The Makeup of RuPaul's Drag Race*, Jefferson, NC: McFarland.

Murray, S. and Ouellette, L. (eds) (2004) *Reality TV: Remaking Television Culture*, New York: New York University Press.

Navarro, V. (2007) 'Neoliberalism as a Class Ideology; Or, the Political Causes of the Growth of Inequalities', *International Journal of Health Services*, 37(1): 47–62.

Ong, A. (2006) *Neoliberalism as Exception: Mutations in Citizenship and Sovereignty*, Durham, NC/London: Duke University Press.

Ouellette, L. (2004) 'Take Responsibility for Yourself: Judge Judy and the neoliberal citizen', in S. Murray and L. Ouellette (eds) *Reality TV: Remaking Television Culture*, New York: New York University Press, pp 231–250.

Ouellette, L. (2014) *A Companion to Reality Television*, New York: Wiley-Blackwell.

Ouellette, L. and Hay, J. (2008a) *Better Living Through Reality TV: Television and Post-Welfare Citizenship*, Malden, MA: Blackwell.

Ouellette, L. and Hay, J. (2008b) 'Makeover Television, Governmentality and the Good Citizen', *Journal of Media & Cultural Studies*, 22(4): 471–484.

Peck, J. and Tickell, A. (2002) 'Neoliberalizing Space', *Antipode*, 34(3): 380–404.

Peterson, D. (2011) 'Neoliberal Homophobic Discourse: Heteronormative human capital and the exclusion of queer citizens', *Journal of Homosexuality*, 58: 742–757.

Richardson, D. (2005) 'Desiring Sameness? The rise of a neoliberal politics of normalisation', *Antipode*, 37(3): 515–535.

Rose, N. (1996) 'Governing "Advanced" Liberal Democracies', in A. Barry, T. Osbourne and N. Rose (eds) *Foucault and Political Reason: Liberalism, Neoliberalism and Rationalities of Government*, Chicago: University of Chicago Press.

Rose, N. (1999) *Governing the Soul: The Shaping of the Private Self* (2nd edn), London: Free Association Books.

Sapelli, G. (2007) *La democrazia trasformata [Democracy Transformed]*, Milan: Mondadori.

Springer, S. (2016) *The Discourse of Neoliberalism*, Lanham, MA: Rowman and Littlefield.

Street, M. (2020) 'Do Not Call RuPaul a Drag Queen – This Will Happen to You', *Out Magazine*, [online] 8 February, Available from: out.com/television/2020/2/08/do-not-call-rupaul-drag-queen-will-happen-you [Accessed 8 May 2023].

Thrift, N. (2005) *Knowing Capitalism*, London: Sage.

Türken, S., Nafstad, H.E., Blakar, R.M. and Roen, K. (2015) 'Making Sense of Neoliberal Subjectivity: A discourse analysis of media language on self-development', *Globalizations*, 13(1): 32–46.

Weber, M. (1904) 'Die protestantische Ethik und der Geist des Kapitalismus', *Archiv für Sozialwissenschaft und Sozialpolitik*, 20: 1–54.

Whitworth, C. (2017) 'Sissy That Performance Script! The queer pedagogy of *RuPaul's Drag Race*', in N. Brennan and D. Gudelunas (eds) *RuPaul's Drag Race and the Shifting Visibility of Drag Culture*, Cham: Palgrave Macmillan, pp 137–151.

Wilson, T.P. (1970) 'Normative and Interpretive Paradigms in Sociology', in J.D. Douglas (ed) *Understanding Everyday Life: Towards a Reconstruction of Sociological Knowledge*, Chicago: Aldine Publishing.

Yudelman, J. (2017) 'The "RuPaulitics" of Subjectification in RuPaul's Drag Race', in N. Brennan and D. Gudelunas (eds) *RuPaul's Drag Race and the Shifting Visibility of Drag Culture*, Cham/Basingstoke: Palgrave Macmillan, pp 15–28.

Zottola, A. (2018) 'Transgender Identity Labels in the British Press: A corpus-based discourse analysis', *Journal of Language and Sexuality*, 7(2): 237–262.

3

Drag Is Not Womanface

Paul Haynes

The role of broad categories of identity such as gender, sexuality, social class and ethnicity in identity performance for drag kings and queens is a central question in understanding if such performances challenge or reinscribe the identities they imitate or indeed the identities that are used to define the performer. This is not an idle question as, for some critics of drag, the performances have consequences for the perceived target of their imitations. As with other forms of identity appropriation, drag has implications. For some critics, the implications are detrimental and disempowering to women. Drag and other female impersonation performances 'may be glamorous or comic, and presented by gay men or straight men. Nonetheless, all of them represent a continuing insult to women, as is apparent from the parallels between these performances and those of white performers of blackface minstrelsy' (Kleiman, 2000: 669).

Kelly Kleiman notes that there are striking parallels between drag and blackface and there are certainly several obvious similarities. I will make the following twin observations to encapsulate the irony of these parallels, particularly in relation to contemporary attitudes towards forms of imitation, appropriation and identity:

Blackface is outrageous – it was never about someone white attempting to pass as someone from a different ethnicity; it is about applying a mask to represent the other in a ludicrous way for cheap laughs. It is meant as a type of unadulterated mockery, accompanied as it is by flamboyant gestures, and especially when 'characteristic' music is part of the performance. White people, who, after all, occupy a dominant position in society, might find it amusing to adopt an exaggerated, stereotypical persona of someone from a different, less socially powerful ethnicity for the purpose of ridicule and comedic effect, but there are serious social implications, as reflected in changing attitudes to its acceptability. Indeed, people who think it is in some way acceptable should be educated about how prejudice is at the basis of their (conservative and anti-progressive) opinion, as it is ultimately designed to be disempowering.

Drag is outrageous – it was never about someone male attempting to pass as someone from a different gender; it is about applying a mask to represent the other in a ludicrous way for cheap laughs. It is meant as a type of unadulterated mockery, accompanied as it is by flamboyant gestures, and especially when 'characteristic' music is part of the performance. Males, who after all, occupy a dominant position in society, might find it amusing to adopt an exaggerated, stereotypical persona of someone from a different, less socially powerful gender for the purpose of ridicule and comedic effect, but there are serious social implications, as reflected in changing attitudes to its acceptability. Indeed, people who think it is in some way unacceptable should be educated about how prejudice is at the basis of their (conservative and anti-progressive) opinion, as it is ultimately designed to be empowering.

This contrast, though not quite a consensus as the quote from Kleiman attests, reflects a sense that issues of cultural appropriation and identity representation are complex and need to be examined in much more detail. The difference between the reception of blackface and drag noted in this parallel might seem to be somewhat ironic, or perhaps puzzling, but the reason that there are contrasting attitudes regarding these examples is at the heart of the emerging debate concerning the identity narratives that shape the self and cultural appropriation that shapes group identity. One key consideration is that identity and cultural appropriation are often approached through predetermined notions of culture and power. A useful lens for evaluating the relevance of such complex socio-cultural patterns can be drawn from Deleuze and Guattari's (1986) concept of minor literature, in particular the focus on the implications of exchange and expression across cultures. This chapter will examine drag in terms of the difference between the features of identity narrative and cultural appropriation derived from perceptions of social exclusion and inequality. It will focus on the way identity performance encompasses multiplicity in both empowering and disempowering ways, which will offer a clearer evaluation of identity appropriation underpinning all forms of drag performance.

Identity appropriation

According to Matthes (2016: 343), cultural appropriation includes 'occurrences as varied as (1) the *representation* of cultural practices or experiences by cultural "outsiders" (sometimes called "voice appropriation"); (2) the *use* of artistic styles distinctive of cultural groups by nonmembers;

and (3) the procurement or continued *possession* of cultural objects by nonmembers or culturally distant institutions' (emphasis in original). Cultural appropriation is a theme that has attracted much discussion, in particular in charting the territory between empowering forms of reciprocal exchange and the commercial exploitation of the powerless by the powerful. Such discussion has been particularly vocal in denouncing the commodification of the artefacts of another culture's traditions and heritage: 'Today's issues are about minority groups and subjects (the disempowered, colonized, peripheral, or subordinate) who are seeking to claim and protect rights to a cultural heritage' (Ziff and Rao, 1997: 8).

While much of the popular debate on cultural appropriation is broadly concerned with issues of preserving authentic cultural heritage, a more focused understanding of cultural appropriation emphasizes the unauthorized use or imitation of characteristics, symbols, artefacts and so on from their cultural setting and contextualizing purpose, which includes identity appropriation – an unacknowledged adoption of elements from another heritage's cultural identity. It is clear that appropriating marginalized cultural heritage for exploitative commercial purposes is difficult to justify and exposes companies and brands to negative publicity or even legal action. In addition, forms of identity appropriation, though more complex, are potentially more pernicious or, in contrast, may provide opportunities or new contexts for subversion. Evaluating identity appropriation therefore presents a challenge, particularly if there are clashes of interpretation or there are competing identity narratives at stake. We might be asked to 'walk a mile in someone else's shoes' to truly empathize with the experience of others, but what if these shoes are stilettos or moccasins and deemed 'inappropriate' for the wearer?

While appropriation of cultural identity might hinge on the details of truthful representation and authenticity, the themes of blackface and drag performance do not. It is instead how they depart from the identities they 'imitate' that is crucial. In popular discourse of cultural appropriation, the word 'blackface' is used to describe examples of white people colouring their face black in order to imitate some aspect of cultural heritage originating in, or relating to, Africa, the Caribbean or other indigenous 'ethnic identity', or referring to specific individuals embodying such heritage, notably in reference to skin colour. It often involves exaggeration in both appearance and performance and reproducing stereotypes of 'black' behaviour or values. These range from white vaudeville-type (ersatz) African American 'minstrel' music, dressing as a 'black' celebrity, a white performer in the role of a character of a different ethnicity, to white influencers using dark make-up to 'pass' for a member of a different ethnicity. In a similar way, but to a very different reception, 'drag' is typically used to describe examples where a man adopts the intentionally exaggerated appearance and persona of a woman as part of a public performance, such as singing, dancing or comedy, although drag is also used to refer to more generic cross-dressing. Drag performers and performances also occupy a variety of personae – pageant female-illusionist queens, camp queens, androgynous or bearded queens, cis female drag kings and faux queens, tranimal/alien queens, transdrags and other, more fluid drag personae – presented in a variety of entertainment contexts, such as performance art or comedy. The difference in acceptability between drag and blackface performance can be explained by the relationship between the performance and identity. The difference is not as obvious as it might first appear and will need to be established.

Womanface: appropriation of womanhood

Before turning to identity performance through the lens of minor literature (Deleuze and Guattari, 1986), it will be helpful to address some of the core assumptions about performing drag in relation to the broader issue of the appropriation of womanhood. It is, of course, rather an understatement to assert that the notion of womanhood is a contested concept, and the relationship between gender and sex is complex and far beyond the scope of this chapter; however, a few observations are worth making, particularly to foreshadow the discussion presented later in the chapter.

The debate concerning the relationship between gender identity and biological sex turns on the question of how permeable the binary categories are that are used to assign 'male' and 'female' to individuals. Gender-critical feminists assert that these categories are impermeable: biological sex is immutable and different from gender identity; that is, sex categories (defined by chromosomes, hormones, internal reproductive organs, genitalia) are essentialist groupings to which constructed gender identity and gender expression imperfectly align (Stock, 2021). Alternatively, non-essentialist definitions have more permeable boundaries between female, male, alternative and non-binary categories. These suggest that gender identification based on self-perception or performativity, for example, enables those that have been assigned to one category (determined by biological 'markers') to transition towards or be reassigned to a different gender category, or to reject such classification altogether. Though there is disagreement concerning its application and its mutability, the notion of womanhood, as conceptualized in this chapter, converges on a type of gender construction shaped by biological, historical and mythological narratives. These gender narratives are, as Simone de Beauvoir (1961: 66) observes, adaptive: 'Woman is not a completed reality, but rather a becoming, and it is in her becoming that she should be compared with man; that is to say, her possibilities should be defined.' This emphasis on becoming is useful, not least that becoming-*woman* is identified by Deleuze and Guattari as a means to subvert fixed social and sexual roles through challenging majoritarian identity and anthropocentrism, as will be discussed later in the chapter.

Conceptualizing womanhood in this way means that the context within which it is appropriated matters, pivoting on the observation that such appropriation can be applied in order to define female roles. These range from attempts to prescribe or insult 'female' aesthetics or find humour in misogynistic bullying by invoking male power and thus: 'represent institutionalized male hostility to women on a spectrum running from prescription of desired behaviour to simple ridicule' (Kleiman, 2000: 669). A similar argument is deployed by Nicola Evans (1998: 199), who observes that drag can be a vehicle for appropriating womanhood in order to revive and promote undesirable gender stereotypes: 'under the cover of drag's new transgressive status, some very old-fashioned notions about race and gender are being smuggled back into popular culture'. Similarly, Stephen Schacht (2002: 174–175) asserts that, rather than subverting existing gender power relations, drag enacts them: 'In no way do those doing female drag realistically subvert existing gender hierarchies; instead, they still enact gender as dichotomous practice, although typically inverted in appearance, where images of the feminine are still employed to realize male dominance.'

Commercial costumes and other carnivalesque cross-dressing outfits effectively illustrate this argument. Popular cross-dressing costumes include French maid, cheerleader, schoolgirl, Hooter's waitress, nurse – 'compliant' female characters frequently encountered in (male) sexual fantasy. There are also cross-dressing costumes advertised using pejorative terms like 'ladyboy' and 'tranny' and modelled in transphobic and demeaning poses. If blackface is racist then, by extension, isn't drag sexist and misogynistic?

There is no reason why the appropriation of womanhood should not be immune from such criticism. There are many examples of films, TV shows and live performances featuring male comedians dressing as stock female characters – the dumb blonde, nagging wife, damsel in distress and so on – principally in order to mock the 'women' they portray. It is revealing that, although David Walliams and Matt Lucas, the creators and main actors in the popular UK TV comedy *Little Britain*, apologized in 2017 for performing in blackface and for their transphobic depiction of characters, they did not apologize for any depictions of female characters (racist old lady, dim working-class petty criminal, pushy stage mother), many of whom were typically just the stooge or punchline of a joke representing old-fashioned gender stereotypes through newer, but equally offensive, tropes. Many such contexts of cross-dressing and appropriation of womanhood seem at face value to be misogynistic depictions and imitations; however, recognizing that appropriation can be offensive under a variety of circumstances does not mean categorizing the drag performance context as itself offensive (see Cracker, 2015).

Drag performers might present stereotypical female identities, but they often play with them and develop a persona that draws from this depiction a facet that overturns expectations. A drag performance might exaggerate not to ensure conformity to established identities but in order to indicate the very thing that such established identities repress, notably the strict gender binaries, which the exaggeration serves to destabilize. A counter-argument, however, is that performing a drag identity might seem to be complicit with institutions that police or profit from compliance to specific gender norms. For example, drag-queen influencers are often sponsored by the cosmetics industry and so reinforce expectations of cosmetically enhanced standards of beauty. But, even when drag seems implicated, its presence often subverts the very assumptions on which it was engaged to promote. The cosmetics industry, for example, relies on concealing that such beauty outcomes are a myth; however, using a drag queen as an influencer illustrates that portrayals and images created by cosmetics are as fake as the woman that the drag artist creates: a drag-queen influencer is not dressing as a woman, but as a drag queen. This dissonance is further illustrated by the growing number of faux drag queens – women who dress as drag queens and use the drag scene to go beyond the limits of female identity (and its performance) and, as a corollary, play with the implications of being a drag queen. Drag might therefore be used as a vehicle for raising the very questions about female identity and representation that those critiquing drag express as their priorities, such as addressing gender-defined 'subordination' (Schacht, 2002: 175) or being able to challenge disempowering gender narratives (Kleiman, 2000).

The issue concerning the appropriation of womanhood (and its potential reappropriation through draghood) is therefore not framed in the same way that questions are typically posed within appropriation discourse, such as when unauthorized imitation threatens members' income or presents a value context that threatens a perception of authenticity, or that distorted portrayals threaten to erase what makes a cultural heritage distinct (Heyd, 2003). There are, however, clear examples and contexts within which the appropriation of female identity *is* insulting and misogynistic and the analogy with blackface *is* an accurate comparison. These portrayals are, it would seem, the exception to the broader ethos of drag performance, but to clarify why the ethos of drag is so very different from the examples that are meant to demean and disempower (and share more in common with blackface), we need to consider a clearer framework for assessing appropriative representation and strategies. It is for this reason that we now turn to the notion of minor literature.

The 'minor' in minor literature

Minor literature is a form of writing that expresses socio-political forces in innovative ways, as exemplified by the focus of Franz Kafka's writing on external forces, such as a minority struggle with bureaucracy and legislative structures (Deleuze and Guattari, 1986). To define the 'minor' in minor literature and examine its relevance to identity and performance it will be worthwhile to clarify a number of relevant relationships to avoid confusion later. Deleuze and Guattari's discussion of 'minor' begins by framing a distinction between minoritarian and majoritarian. These are not oppositional for Deleuze and Guattari, but are terms based on how group identity is shaped. In this way, minoritarian is not a reference to someone being part of a cultural minority or ethnic or identity minority but is instead characterized by being different from an embodiment or approximation of a benchmark or standard that is used in order to *define* a majority. It is in its difference from the abstract standard that separates, and sets apart, the minority. Majority thus assumes a state of power and domination as the standard measure (Deleuze and Guattari 1988). Woman or 'becoming-woman' is used by Deleuze and Guattari to clarify minoritarian identity. As Claire Colebrook (2002: 104) clarifies in her evaluation of Deleuze and Guattari's majoritarian/minoritarian distinction, a majoritarian classification approach:

presents the opposition as already given and based on a privileged and original term. So, 'man' is a majoritarian term; we imagine that there is some general being – the human that then has local variations [and in this way, the] opposition between man and woman is majoritarian: we think of woman as other than, or different from, man. A minoritarian mode of difference does not ground the distinction on a privileged term, and does not see the distinction as an already-given order.

In other words, the majoritarian character (in this example 'man') is a constant homogeneous entity or system in contrast with minorities as subsystems dependent on, but invisible within, the system. Thus, it is the minoritarians (woman or becoming-woman) who are seen as the source of 'a potential, creative and created, becoming' (Deleuze and Guattari, 1988: 105–106). In this regard, majority is expressive of identity: inert and invariable. As such, becoming-majoritarian is an oxymoron: becoming is *always* minoritarian. It is here that minor enters into consideration, as Deleuze and Guattari go beyond a majority-minority duality, adding a third category or state: 'becoming-minor' – a creative process of becoming different or diverging from the abstract standard that defines majority. As Colebrook (2002: 104) continues: 'If we really acknowledge the possibility that there is something like becoming-woman, then we acknowledge that there is something truly other than man: that human life is not defined by the male ideals of reason, strength, dominance and activity. "Woman" opens the human to new possibilities.' It is in this regard that drag and blackface diverge, and different meanings of identity appropriation emerge from this conceptual relationship.

Navigating the implications of these borders and boundaries returns us to Deleuze and Guattari's notion of minor literature. In contrast to established 'major' literature, minor literature does not attempt to meet a predefined standard but instead attempts to disrupt or modify the standard itself: 'minor no longer designates specific literatures but the revolutionary conditions for every literature within the heart of what is called great (or established) literature' (Deleuze and Guattari, 1986: 17–18). In this regard, all great literature is minor literature in that it creates its own standard. By extension, the minor appropriation of identity, a type of appropriation found with drag but not blackface, creates its own identity paradigm or standard as a reversal of the conventional interpretation of narrative construction. In order to clarify this process in relation to their analysis, Deleuze and Guattari identify three key characteristics of minor literature, which will be appropriated here for examining the possibility of minor-gender, with relevant illustrations.

The first characteristic describes the case in which 'language is affected with a high coefficient of deterritorialization' (Deleuze and Guattari, 1986: 16). By this, they mean that those perspectives that are typically suppressed or marginalized become repositioned as the focus of emphasis and they operate to challenge dominant codes and conventions. As a consequence, the dominant codes and customs become rendered foreign, weird or incoherent. Drag embodies this characterization in repositioning forms of derided male, gay, sexual mannerisms as an empowered mock female (hetero)sexual charisma through the guise of a liberated drag artist. A drag performance often uses its platform to present perspectives that are often invisible and otherwise suppressed, while rendering ordinary codes and conventions around gender as unfamiliar and distorted. Someone singing or telling jokes in a way that is indistinguishable from a popular female singer or a conventional male comedian would be confusing, and it would not be drag performance if it failed to disclose the performer as a drag king or queen.

The second characteristic emphasizes social and political forces rather than focusing primarily on the personal experiences of individuals, as occurs in major literature. Deleuze and Guattari (1986: 17) observe that, in minor literature: "[The] cramped spaces force each individual intrigue to connect immediately to politics. The individual concern thus becomes all the more necessary, indispensable, magnified because a whole other story is vibrating within it." Throughout the history of drag, its performers have risked violence, abuse, imprisonment and social ostracism, but, even where drag performance poses less of a risk for the performer, the way it challenges preconceived ideas and how it breaks out of the confinement of its predesignated spaces make it more political still. Sometimes, even which bathroom to use or issues of the inclusion, comparison and discourse concerning 'transfeminine' or non-binary contestants on *RuPaul's Drag Race* (Brennan, 2022: 373) become significant political inflection points.

The third characteristic stresses the adoption of collective value. Deleuze and Guattari (1986: 17) explain the implications of this characteristic in the following way:

Indeed, precisely because talent isn't abundant in a minor literature, there are no possibilities for an individuated enunciation that would belong to this or that 'master' and that could be separated from a collective enunciation. Indeed scarcity of talent is in fact beneficial and allows the concept of something other than a literature of masters; what each author says individually already constitutes a common action, and what he or she says or does is necessarily political, even if others are not in agreement.

With the different types of drag performance, the notion of talent changes in accordance with themes, styles and objectives that characterize the performance context, although passing for a professionally trained female singer is entirely unnecessary. Being able to sing in tune, or project a little humour into a song chosen for its ironic appeal, or even merely competently lip-synching helps the drag artist to amplify the other features of the performance, providing the conditions for a collective enunciation in forging 'the means for another consciousness and another sensibility' (Deleuze and Guattari, 1986: 17). Writing, as minor literature, repeats the process of great writing as literary becoming: influenced by great writing, but as a freedom to write, *not* as a constraint. By the same logic, a drag performer appropriates a female persona not to repeat the female identity but to repeat the *force* of performing a female identity and to rethink identity performance in general. This can be extended to animal, monstrous or alien drag personae, as exemplified by *The Boulet Brothers' Dragula* TV show. By not being 'real', a monstrous or alien persona provides the 'perfect place for queer performers to locate their own sense of rebellion from the homonormalizing forces of "realness"' (Prins, 2021: 52).

These characteristics collectively describe 'the literature a minority make in a major language' (Deleuze and Guattari, 1986: 16) or, in the case of identity, the expression of identity that a minority make (those that do *not* aspire to be like James Bond!) in the heteronormative game of roles. Drag, unlike blackface, expresses identity in a way that subverts a key component of majoritarian identity; deconstructing, destabilizing or deterritorializing established expressions of gender (or, indeed, anthropocentric) difference. Blackface, however, is an expression of a feature of majoritarian identity itself, a performance that reinscribes majoritarian standards and norms. This is made clearer by contrasting the way majoritarian identity is formed in relation to the shaping of minoritarian identity.

Majoritarian identity is based on representing an established measure; it is an 'extensive multiplicity' – additional examples do not change the identity but conform to it. With additional examples of blackface there is no change concerning what the multiplicity is. Instead, each new example reinforces existing culturally racist archetypes and comic stereotypes as embodied in the stock characters of blackface. Even when it is part of an attempt to appreciate or celebrate people with African or Caribbean heritage or culture, it does so through a distorted lens of cultural representations, often appropriating the very constructs that were used to justify colonialism or dehumanize entire populations. As Domenick Scudera (2017, np), theatre professor and drag performer, observes: 'Minstrel show audiences reinforced their perceived superiority over others. If they were celebrating anything, it was their white privilege.'

In contrast, minoritarian identity has no such pre-established measure; it is an 'intensive multiplicity' – additional examples add to the collective identity, transforming it. With a drag persona, each individual performer creates and explores a different sense of identity; exploring sexual orientation, gender identity or multiple aspects of culture (ethnicity, nationality, class and so on) or indeed sources of identity beyond an anthropocentric basis (cyborg, animal, monster, alien). In addition, drag performance is not limited to men. Drag kings, female drag queens and non-binary or trans performers are adding to and redefining the appearance that a drag persona is able to take, and, as such, drag is emerging in new and unexpected guises. In this way, drag offers opportunities to explore the implications of rethinking any gender identity derived from different experiences (a point that will be further unpacked in the conclusion to this chapter). Indeed, for much of its history, drag performance offered an avenue for expressing alternatives to binary gender and heteronormativity during periods when such expression was – and in some places still is – otherwise illegal and severely punishable: 'transgenderism, same-sex sexuality, and theatrical performance are central to the personal identities of these drag queens, who use drag to forge personal and collective identities that are neither masculine nor feminine, but rather their own complex genders' (Taylor and Rupp, 2004: 114).

The margins of identity

Drag is still evolving as a performance and identity-shaping space, with each additional wave of drag performers reflecting and feeding back into the collective experiences from which it emerges. Brewis et al (1997) attempt to operationalize distinctions between transvestitism, power dressing, transsexuality and drag, but, a quarter of a century later, these divisions seem much more porous than originally postulated, particularly as drag has evolved and mutated with greater penetration of public attention, although perhaps these distinctions were always somewhat contrived. In this way, drag exemplifies how 'experiments' originally confined to the margin do not remain marginal but inevitably find a line of flight to the centre. As Niall Brennan argues, drag initially works most effectively from the margins. Representations of drag are able to engage their audience in response to the expression of the drag performers' experience as a gendered other, 'conditioned by the marginality of gay men [and] further marginalized by transgressing a cisgender, homonormative universe in becoming women' (Brennan, 2022: 379). To quote Sasha Velour, former winner of *RuPaul's Drag Race*: 'My drag was born in a community full of trans women, trans men, and gender non-conforming folks doing drag. ... From the second there was drag, trans people were doing it. And when cis women started being allowed in theaters, then cis women doing drag was part of theater' (quoted in Leighton-Dore, 2018).

Within this performative context and derived from its unconventional gender-cognisant communities, pejorative labels and insulting words are never quite what they seem, with irony woven into each component of the drag assemblage as a performer's concealed layer of protection. To return to the insightful Domenick Scudera, in societies where failure to conform to specific narrow characteristics of masculinity is met with shame and humiliation, it is often through a drag identity that a performer acquires their initial experience of appreciation and self-worth, finding

strength in her and wear[ing] her like a shield. Drag is some of the best parts of who he is, magnified and impervious. A blackface performer is dressing up the ugliest parts of himself: the racist, belittling, superior parts of himself. This ugliness is worn on his face for the amusement of others like him. (Scudera, 2017, np)

This is not to say that the appropriation of womanhood is fine because it serves the interest of males who are themselves marginalized and therefore have a priority over other groups of superior numbers and presumably are less marginalized in some way. There is nothing in the appropriation of female identity that is inherently 'enlightened' – drag could have evolved to be womanface, and perhaps has been or continues to be so in specific circumstances despite the non-conformist sexuality of the performer. However, as the lens of minor literature illustrates, drag does not restrain gender possibilities; instead it affords a multiplicity of 'minor-genders' able to reveal the distortion in treating established gender roles as though they were defining limits of identity options. In this way, rather than producing an imitative womanface appropriation, drag operates as minor literature in producing an inappropriate performance of womanhood – which I term 'inappropriation' – in order to reveal and subvert key aspects of the given identity of the performer. At the same time, it reveals and subverts corresponding aspects of the given identity that is being performed.

Focusing on the beneficiaries of appropriative/inappropriative practices is thus a useful device in ensuring that standards remain an opportunity to enhance appreciation of perspectives derived from a variety of cultures and to enrich artistic creation. The negative issues identified with blackface's cultural appropriation cannot be addressed by majoritarian strategies. Minoritarian approaches, such as inappropriation, are required to reflect an appropriate measure of responsibility and cultural awareness in defining an approach to identity that contests and disturbs the order. In this way, inappropriation creates uncertainty, where gender *certainty* is often a contributory factor to disempowerment, for example where there are attempts to define, name and classify in order to make gender exceptions fit a predetermined taxonomy, such as in applying terms like 'gender dysphoria' or 'gender incongruence' as defined by the World Health Organization's *International Classification of Diseases* (2022). Drag is therefore, in this sense at least, a 'dangerous supplement' to binary gender classification – 'It adds only to replace. It intervenes or insinuates itself in-the-place-of; if it fills, it is as if one fills a void' (Derrida, 1976: 145).

Inappropriate selling

The notion of 'minor-gender' and focusing on the use of 'gender-inappropriate' body language, clothing, hair and accessories in entertainment performance may seem somewhat loaded in assumptions, but they highlight that the implications of identity appropriation are not distinct from authority – who has it and who lacks it. The lens of minor literature therefore helps in clarifying the different implications of identity performance. Using this lens enables a distinction to be applied to gender engagement and related identity performance based on its implied multiplicity: appropriation/ misappropriation of identity diminishes, dispossesses or disempowers members that share the identity. Alternatively, *inappropriation* of identity refers to the repurposing of the narratives, techniques, symbols and artefacts so as to enhance the performativity of identity, creating new categories or providing opportunities to subvert or highlight prejudice and inequality. This is because appropriation and inappropriation are not neutral processes – they depend on factors beyond the immediate goals of identity performance. Instances of identity appropriation predominantly serving majoritarian interests are thus ethically implicated. This is because the exploitation of cultural identities developed by marginalized groups to serve the interests of dominant social groups coercively reshapes and redefines these identities in terms of interests that diverge from the cultural forms they exploit. As with cultural appropriation, identity appropriation 'harvests' marginalized cultures in order to support the interest of established power relations (see Haynes, 2021).

In contrast, instances of inappropriation occur when creativity associated with marginal cultures or dominated social groups is produced in accordance with cultural and identity resources developed by these social groups in order to challenge the standards that maintain and legitimize forms of cultural dominance. The inappropriate use of gender identities, unlike 'appropriate' gender performance in service to the interests of dominant cultural forms, is thus able to highlight exclusion and inequality. As a consequence, it provides a variety of opportunities for re-examining these standards. In cultural terms, this encounter equates to Richard Rogers' (2006) category of 'transculturation'. This is conceptualized as a hybridization of different cultural elements from multiple sources, in which the product of the relationship represents a new form. Drag's inappropriation in this regard destabilizes aspects of gender identity, in much the same way that 'transculturation is not always or only degradation or homogenization; it can also be constitutive of cultural particularity, agency, identity, inventiveness, and resistance' (Rogers, 2006: 497).

There are, in addition, marketing and commercialization implications. The cultural appropriation/inappropriation division identified through the lens of minor literature helps to position different aspects of cultural exchange and identity performance, ethically and politically. This distinction has often represented a challenge for marketers and advertisers unsure where such borderlines are to be drawn. The implications of the majoritarian/minoritarian distinction helps in identifying the principle underpinning the form of appropriation. A majoritarian usage involves taking ownership of cultural phenomena or aspects of identity without questioning the image or essence of its own sense of cultural identity. As clarified in the previous section, such a majoritarian standard, even when it does not express a numerical majority, expresses extensive multiplicity, in that adding more instances does not change the nature of its identity. In this way, it appropriates by disempowering, and exposes commercial interests to accusations of being manipulative.

In contrast, a minoritarian usage expresses intensive multiplicity: it doesn't just match features already established; each additional example alters the composition of the group. In this way, minoritarian practices will take cultural identity, practices, content or styles and use them in ways that help to shape the possibilities of their identity and make connections, which in turn shape other identities. These are therefore seen as more accessible and inclusive of marginalized identities, which is an easier narrative for commercial companies to 'sell' to customers as ethical marketing. This is particularly the case where the 'identities' of products, ambassadors and promotional strategies resonate with customer values and present relevant and coherent identity narratives (see Holt, 2004). The commercialization and marketization of drag – as evidenced by popular TV shows and its centrality to Pride month and measured by drag performer/influencer analytics and the growth of live shows and events such as drag brunches, drag bingo and drag-queen story hours – creates as many challenges as opportunities. An example of such a challenge is the apparent dissonance of Dylan Mulvaney as a Bud Light commercial partner (and as part of a more general coordinated 'conservative backlash'). The reduction of sales and the visible campaign against Mulvaney within the context of a Bud Light paid promoter illustrate the challenges that commercial interests face in their engagement with gender-non-conformist individuals (Aratani, 2023). An alternative challenge is for commercial businesses to police the drag influencers with whom they form promotional 'partnerships' in order to ensure that they meet the expectations required of them as commercial investments: non-threatening, unobjectionable and entirely intelligible. In regulating what drag performance should be – as an expression of identity – these rules set a new standard for drag performance, one that 'personifies' and defines drag's essential qualities. In being managed (and standardized) in this way, 'drag identity' would become majoritarian and, as a consequence, betray the very traits that make it subversive and appealing in the first place. As will be examined in the final section, however, minor-gender identity remains in many ways positively inappropriate for commercialization.

Conclusion

To return to selling performance rather than products, the minoritarian appropriation underpinning drag becomes a type of immersive-identity fan fiction, inappropriately inserting a character or identity into entertaining relationships so that new aspects of their identity or setting can be elaborated and extended beyond their established world. In this way, the (lip-synched!) voices repeated within the drag performance are intermediaries, (re)writing the event that opens up new possibilities for spectators. The inappropriate gender performance repeats by imitation in order to transform the gender it reproduces: repeating the power of difference by repeating the conditions from which the identity is entangled. It therefore works, as Judith Butler suggests (2013: 336–337), by requiring the observer not to take appearance nor the binarism of imitation/imitated at face value: 'Drag says "my 'outside' appearance is feminine, but my essence 'inside' is masculine." At the same time, it symbolizes the opposite inversion: "my appearance 'outside' is masculine but my essence 'inside' myself is feminine."'

As drag has evolved to be a more inclusive mode of performance and expression, as evidenced by the diversity of stories that underpin contemporary drag culture, it becomes clearer that attempts to capture an essence of drag and draw it into mainstream entertainment face resistance from the very performers and performances it hopes to commandeer. This occurs through drag's ability to transform itself and evade imposed conditions of what it is and by subverting the logic of established standards of what drag must be, even in the most welcoming of spaces (see Strings and Bui, 2014). It is perhaps the way drag stages transgression as a characteristic element of an 'inappropriately appropriate' performance that enhances its standing as a 'spectacularization of its core stigma' (Campana et al, 2022). It also affords drag a campaigning platform (for example, the Black Trans Lives Matter campaign) and 'provides a contested site and complex semiotic space for dealing with sensitive matters of race/ ethnicity' (Strings and Bui, 2014: 822) and allows individual performers to express an 'unwillingness to relinquish her agency as disruptive' (Brennan, 2022: 379) even when the reward structure is favourable for compliance, banal camaraderie, confected personal rivalry between individuals and stereotypical femininity.

Drag performance perceived as minor-gender, as opposed to the appropriation of another established (and stable) gender identity, sets drag apart from other forms of cultural appropriation, and seems empirically to be ethically justified when examining the role of performance as shaping the identity of the performers themselves: 'transgenderism, same-sex sexuality, and theatrical performance are central to the personal identities of these drag queens, who use drag to forge personal and collective identities that are neither masculine nor feminine, but rather their own complex genders' (Taylor and Rupp, 2004: 114).

Considering the persistence of discrimination, prejudice and hostility directed towards those expressing non-conformist gender identity and sexuality, it seems reasonable to celebrate the individuals who confront this intimidation by turning their exploration into public expression. This is, of course, the main reason why drag is not aligned in the public perception with blackface or 'fauxmosexual' ridicule. If we look deeper into the implications of drag and its continued evolution, it becomes clear that much more is at stake in the inappropriation of clothing, posing and performing than mere amusement. Prime among these is the uncertainty of who is really the source of ridicule that the performance embodies.

References

Aratani, L. (2023) 'As the US Becomes More Divided, Companies Find They Can't Appeal to Everyone', The Guardian, [online], 12 June, Available from: theguardian.com/business/2023/jun/12/bud-light-target-lgbtq-pride-business [Accessed 19 May 2023].

Brennan, N. (2022) 'Performing Drag in a Pandemic: Affect in theory, practice and (potential) political mobilization', *Consumption Markets & Culture*, 25(4): 369–381.

Brewis, J., Hampton, M.P. and Linstead, S. (1997) 'Unpacking Priscilla: Subjectivity and identity in the organization of gendered appearance', *Human Relations*, 50(10): 1275–1304.

Butler, J. (2013) Gender Trouble, Feminist Theory, and Psychoanalytic Discourse', in L. Nicholson (ed) *Feminism/Postmodernism*, London: Routledge, pp 324–340.

Campana, M., Duffy, K. and Micheli, M.R. (2022) '"We're All Born Naked and the Rest is Drag": Spectacularization of core stigma in RuPaul's Drag Race', *Journal of Management Studies*, 59(8): 1950–1986.

Colebrook, C. (2002) *Gilles Deleuze*, London: Routledge.

Cracker, M. (2015) 'Drag Isn't Like Blackface. But that doesn't mean it's always kind to women', *Slate*, [online] Available from: slate.com/human-interest/2015/02/is-mary-cheney-right-about-drag-being-like-blackface.html [Accessed 15 December 2022].

De Beauvoir, S. (1961) *The Second Sex*, New York: Bantam.

Deleuze, G. and Guattari, F. (1986) *Kafka: Towards a Minor Literature*, Minneapolis: University of Minnesota Press.

Deleuze, G. and Guattari, F. (1988) *A Thousand Plateaus*, London: The Athlone Press.

Derrida, J. (1976) *Of Grammatology*, Baltimore: Johns Hopkins University Press.

Evans, N. (1998) 'Games of Hide and Seek: Race, gender and drag in *The Crying Game* and *The Birdcage*', *Text and Performance Quarterly*, 18(3): 199–216.

Haynes, P. (2021) 'The Ethics and Aesthetics of Intertextual Writing: Cultural appropriation and minor literature', *The British Journal of Aesthetics*, 61(3): 291–306.

Heyd, T. (2003) 'Rock Art Aesthetics and Cultural Appropriation', *The Journal of Aesthetics and Art Criticism*, 61(1): 37–46.

Holt, D. (2004) *How Brands Become Icons*, Boston, MA: Harvard Business School Press.

Kleiman, K. (2000) 'Drag = Blackface', *Chicago Law Review*, 75(3): 669–696.

Leighton-Dore, S. (2018) 'Sasha Velour has More to Say on RuPaul's Trans Comments', *SBS*, [online] 16 March, Available from: sbs.com.au/topics/pride/fast-lane/article/2018/03/16/sasha-velour-has-more-say-rupauls-trans-comments [Accessed 30 March 2021].

Matthes, E.H. (2016) 'Cultural Appropriation Without Cultural Essentialism?', *Social Theory and Practice*, 42(2): 343–366.

Prins, K. (2021) 'Monsters Outside of the Closet: Reading the queer art of winning in *The Boulet Brothers' Dragula*', *QED: A Journal in GLBTQ Worldmaking*, 8(2): 43–68.

Rogers, R.A (2006) 'From Cultural Exchange to Transculturation: A review and reconceptualization of cultural appropriation', *Communication Theory*, 16: 474–503.

Schacht, S.P. (2002) 'Four Renditions of Doing Female Drag: Feminine appearing conceptual variations of a masculine theme', *Gendered Sexualities*, 6: 157–180.

Scudera, D. (2017) 'Dear Mary Cheney: Here are reasons why drag is socially acceptable and blackface is not', Huffpost, [online] 6 December, Available from: huffpost.com/entry/dear-mary-cheney-here-are_b_6589910 [Accessed 6 June 2024].

Stock, K. (2021) *Material Girls: Why Reality Matters for Feminism*, London: Fleet.

Strings, S. and Bui, L.T. (2014) '"She Is Not Acting, She Is": The conflict between gender and racial realness on RuPaul's Drag Race', *Feminist Media Studies*, 14(5): 822–836.

Taylor, V. and Rupp, L.J. (2004) 'Chicks with Dicks, Men in Dresses: What it means to be a drag queen', *Journal of Homosexuality*, 46(3–4): 113–133.

World Health Organization (2022) *International Classification of Diseases (ICD-11)*, Geneva: World Health Organization.

Ziff, B.H. and Rao, P.V. (1997) *Borrowed Power: Essays on Cultural Appropriation*, New Brunswick: Rutgers University Press.

PART II

Marketizing Drag

4

Crafty Queens: Meaning Co-Creation by Drag Performers and Brands through Artisanal Framing

Alina Both, Raian Razal and Rohan Venkatraman

Ever since the mid-2010's, mainstream popular culture has witnessed a steady increase in the visibility of cultural diversity, including a stronger presence of sexual minorities. LGBTQ+ and queer culture has now firmly established its presence in Western media. This presents an attractive new opportunity for marketers in the fashion and beauty industries in particular – not only by establishing LGBTQ+ as a target market (see Nölke, 2018) but also by examining the active production of LGBTQ+ professionals in shaping marketing communications (Ciszek and Pounders, 2020; Frankel and Ha, 2020).

This development is in no small part due to the rapid rise in popularity of one particular art form traditionally connected to the LGBTQ+ community and culture – drag. Drag has, in recent years, advanced far beyond LGBTQ+ audiences and subcultures, with performers becoming celebrities to vast international audiences, driven by reality TV shows such as *RuPaul's Drag Race* (RPDR) and the wide reach enabled by social media platforms. Yet, the entry of drag into mainstream cultural consciousness has been largely unaccounted for in both sociological and marketing research (McCormack and Wignall, 2022).

As an art form, drag entails a number of practices, rituals, competencies and even vocabulary that both emerge from and are embedded in its culture. These material and cultural cues are increasingly being used as signifiers by brands. This becomes visible through partnerships of beauty brands collaborating and including drag performers' names on new products (such as

Kim Chi Sugarpill Cosmetics) or splashing their drag persona on marketing campaigns (Shangela fuelling 'fierceness' at McDonald's).

This chapter explores how drag performers employ artisanal practices to shape brand meanings. Artisanship is a term often used by anthropologists to describe skilled craftsmanship. Traditional artisans own both the material aspects of their work and possess knowledge in craft production (Dickie and Frank, 1996). Moreover, they make decisions autonomously, engage actively in the production process and take pride in the quality of their work. In doing so, they imbue the artefact that results from their work with a certain aura, a notion of the extraordinary that may create a relationship with a certain audience of followers (Spencer, 1973; Joy and Belk, 2020). Thus, by creating meaning and order out of a set of raw materials, artisans tap into and create potential value-orders that have the power to shape consumption practices in a marketplace setting – a mechanism well known and used by modern brands (see Leissle, 2017; Mulholland et al, 2022).

Overall, this chapter seeks to contribute to expanding knowledge on drag as a subcultural phenomenon that shapes brand meanings through a signification of artisanal practice. We thus theorize the artisanal signalling surrounding the performance of drag with a view towards the marketplace mechanism of branding. After outlining our key theoretical pillars, we draw methodological inspiration from Kozinets (2022), implementing an immersive netnographic approach. Given that technology usually mediates brand-drag performances, which are often shared on social networks, netnography offers an appropriate method for capturing this cultural phenomenon. We collect archival data based on brand-owned media and social media accounts of drag performers and pay attention to the visual elements of presentation. This approach combines visual methodologies to generate semiotic readings and thus elucidates deeper structures of meaning (see Rose, 2001). Finally, a thematic analysis and discussion of the signifiers and codes emergent from the data establishes and theorizes drag queens as cultural artisans of the marketplace, shaping both brand meanings and mainstream cultural consciousness.

Theoretical framework
Artisanship and branding

Subcultures have, in the past, often been read and understood in terms of their resistance to another more dominant culture – a view to which the academic examination of drag has certainly also subscribed (Jones, 2021; McCormack and Wignall, 2022; Baldwin et al, 2004). Drag's rapid and ongoing shift into the mainstream limelight also warrants a closer investigation of how aspects of identity and the performance(s) of the self are reflected in a diverse range of activities, practices and signals shared and perpetuated not just by the drag community but by all sorts of marketplace actors that surround drag culture, such as brands and celebrities. Since sociological accounts of drag's entry into the mainstream cultural consciousness are scarce (McCormack and Wignall, 2022), invoking theoretical concepts connected to artisanship – and thus a view of drag artists as artisans – may help us understand drag's multifaceted contributions to brand meanings.

The terms 'craft' and 'artisan' are widely used by brands today in order to signal a certain level of quality and authenticity to their audiences. This trend has become so ubiquitously employed that researchers speak of a trend of 'craft-washing' even for clearly mass-produced goods such as frozen pizza (Mulholland et al, 2022). On the other hand, a special emphasis on artisanship is also to be found within the luxury goods sector, a context which has drawn considerable research interest (for instance Manlow, 2021). Here, the figures of artisan and artist tend to become blurred, merging into one mythical persona the consumer is meant to connect to by purchasing an artisanal product (Dion and Arnould, 2011; Gerosa, 2022; Mulholland et al, 2022). Thus, the individual figure becomes central for the artisan economy, with the decisive purchase criterion no longer being a matter of price or even quality but rather the relationship between artisan and consumer (Mulholland et al, 2022). The terminology of 'artisanal' and 'craft' seems to be used interchangeably in both colloquial and academic contexts. Even etymologically, art and craft have long been regarded as synonymous. We shall therefore follow this example for the purpose of this chapter.

The concept of artisanship has been defined as knowing how to work with certain materials and transforming them through an appropriate technique, thus using one's knowledge to yield a desired result (Ostrom, 1980). The artisan, therefore, has a specialized set of skills and expertise and a vision, a concept, of what they are creating, along with a sense of judgement and authority as to what constitutes high quality within their field of expertise (Ostrom, 1980). Through the creation of artefacts, artisans help to invoke a sense of identity, belonging, authenticity and community. For brands, these associations can imbue brand meaning in several important ways. Similar to the figure of the artist, artisanship provides a certain aura of uniqueness and, by emphasizing the human factor in the production of the artefact, establishes a relationship to the source of creation (Mulholland et al, 2022). Further, artisanal branding establishes a link between the product and works of art, again in line with the blurring of artist and artisan (Dion and Arnould, 2011; Leissle, 2017). Brands may also add a dimension of sincerity to their image by associating with the artist-as-maker or craftsperson, thereby attempting to build a more stable and ongoing relationship with consumers. This social dimension may even lead to consumers' participation within a community of like-minded individuals (Mulholland et al, 2022). Thus, the artisan brand ultimately becomes a quasi-religious icon around which an ideology of consumption revolves, complete with its own aesthetics, rituals and language signifiers (Willis, 1990; Baldwin et al, 2004; Mulholland et al, 2022).

With these notions in mind, a point can be made for examining drag queens as icons and emissaries of drag and LGBTQ+ culture through the distinct lens of their role as artisan figures within the marketplace. As such, not only do they imbue brands and products with their unmistakable aura by providing a visual link between their art and the endorsed product, but they equally appear as possessing the expertise and level of judgement associated with artisan roles. Moreover, they are uniquely able to communicate a sense of sincerity and vulnerability for an audience to connect with. Ultimately, it is this human factor, this centrality of the relationship between craftsperson and consumer, that gives drag personalities a special role within the shaping of brand meanings. Competence, in the form of knowledge and experience, remains a prized resource by these performers. Therefore, this investigation sheds a light on the drag artisan's role as a cultural intermediary (Gerosa, 2022) characterized by transformation and exuding a charm that companies and brands attempt to capitalize on (Mulholland et al, 2022), but which also entails the possibility of launching a genuine dialogue about one of humanity's master binaries through the mouthpiece of branding, consumption and popular culture.

Charisma and aura

We follow the definition of charisma as 'a social mechanism through which individuals inspire devotion and followership in others' (Wieser et al, 2021: 732). The abilities ascribed to an individual through charisma are also often likened to supernatural properties or some special powers. In a secular sense, the term tends to denote a certain feeling of awe towards groups, roles or objects – in other words, something extraordinary (Spencer, 1973). In his essay on charisma, Martin E. Spencer (1973) highlights mastery and the ability to create meaning and order from a seemingly chaotic reality as key dimensions of charisma. Thus, a charismatic figure is described as providing guides for action and an outlook for the future. In doing so, charismatic figures create and structure 'a universe of values for [their] followers that satisfies deep-felt needs' (Spencer, 1973: 347). This, in turn, results in the followers' awe and enthusiasm. Thus, charisma is also understood as being inextricably linked with representation and the relationship between the charismatic figure and their followers and/or fans. The ultimate instance of charisma through representation, then, is to be found in the realm of artists, who create symbols or aesthetic visions of value-filled order and, if taken to an extreme, tap into new aesthetic possibilities that transcend the classical standards of the time (Spencer, 1973).

Charisma in consumer research has often been examined in the context of luxury retailing (Dion and Arnould, 2011; Semaan et al, 2019), or as residing among authoritative leaders (Wieser et al, 2021). In Dion and Arnould (2011), this charisma is located in an artistic brand director that draws followers through the mobilization of their aura. However, we aim to explore an alternative, non-mainstream account of charisma that emanates from drag performers, who arguably come from a more-marginalized position, far from the luxury retail space.

Hence, given that charisma is one of the qualities that are often actively sought in being the next drag superstar, along with uniqueness, nerve and talent (Simmons, 2014), or considered one of the virtues for drag queens, our context is ripe for examining other sites where charisma may be at work. Moreover, based on Spencer's dimensions of charisma, it can be argued that drag performers represent a case of charisma creation through representation of a contemporary artistic figure who constantly questions and reinvents the aesthetic standards of their time as an expression of a more fundamental challenging of binary social norms (see also Butler, 1990). If seen as such, it follows that drag queens as charismatic figures also create a certain 'universe of value' (Spencer 1973: 347) for their admirers, a universe that is based on a certain idea of beauty and which flows into a certain ideology of consumption.

Furthermore, the idea of charisma as presented here is closely interlinked with the notion of an aura as the result or outcome of charisma. Thus, the concept of charisma has previously been used to theorize the emergence of a certain aura from products that are part of an artist's or designer's vision (Alexander, 2009; Dion and Arnould, 2011). Aura, in turn, has also been closely linked to the conceptualization and perception of beauty and aesthetic, giving rise to the concept's growing popularity in branding research (Dion and Arnould, 2011; Joy and Belk, 2020). Especially in terms of artisan brands, exuding an aura fulfils a central role in ascribing authenticity to such brands while, at the same time, retaining their mystical properties (Mulholland et al, 2022). So, the idea of representational charisma and a certain resulting aura that evokes awe and enthusiasm and provides a universe of values aligns well with the notion of artisan creators just outlined. Both concepts deal with a figure's ability to raise meaning and order from a chaotic assembly of raw materials and thereby communicate a certain set of values that have the potential to shape actions within the market. Brands aligning themselves with such figures make active use of these abilities in order to adapt to marketplace changes and gain legitimacy and authenticity with new or evolving audiences (Joy and Belk, 2020; Eagar et al, 2022).

Hence, by examining the imbued properties of charisma and aura through the signalling of artisanship and craftsmanship, we use these theoretical lenses to elaborate on the specific mechanisms of how drag queens, in their partnership with brands, emerge as cultural artisans within the marketplace.

Methodology

This chapter leans into an interpretive approach sympathetic to the consumer culture theory, drawing inspiration from earlier work on drag fandom (Canavan, 2021) where the researcher is a key instrument in constructing meaning from the performances and digital traces of the drag performers as they collaborate with brands. Methodologically, the netnographic method (Kozinets, 2012) was applied, where the first two authors of this chapter immersed themselves in the rich digital context of drag, placing particular focus on drag queens that have the widest reach in social media. We chose this focus as such queens can provide us with the greatest theoretical insight into the activities and materials involved in their collaborations with brands in industries such as beverages, make-up, transportation and other services.

By seeking out drag queens with high numbers of followers, we identified our sample purposively (Bryman, 2016), in that the profiles included belong to the top 20 most followed queens on Instagram (Statista, 2022). Having a strong base of followers is an important benchmark for brands and marketers, who use followership as a heuristic for reach (De Veirman et al, 2017). Therefore, social media reach provided our key selection criterion, along with ethnic diversity. Specifically, we looked at three digital spaces that document the myriad forms of drag queen and brand collaborations: PR-related posts, Instagram posts and YouTube channels. We then implemented a thematic analysis (Braun and Clarke, 2006) by first familiarizing ourselves with all the content and communications, identifying and aligning codes, constructing, generating and naming themes and, finally, engaging in the written preparation of the text.

Findings: drag performers as craftspeople

In examining branded content put out by – or in concert with – drag performers, it becomes clear that the queens themselves form the central artist figures, gaining iconic status both literally and by implication. Compositionally, brands tend to foreground the performers themselves rather than the product in photographic advertisements, even if that product is physically larger (see Shangela for BMW, Bob the Drag Queen for Delight, various queens for Toyota Aygo). Moreover, the queens' personalities are at the focus of accompanying advertising texts. Rather than emphasizing product features, as is often done in automotive advertising, BMW, for instance, chose to focus on the goal-getting personality and attitude of drag collaborator Shangela when partnering with her for a recent campaign. Through such compositional choices, brands attempt to establish the drag queen as artist and larger-than-life icon, thereby hoping to invoke their charisma and aura favourably, creating a personal connection and accessibility for LGBTQ+ and allied audience groups. The following sections take a closer look at the themes through which this iconic status of artisanship is established and embedded within an ideology of consumption.

Transformation through skill and expertise

One aspect continually stressed when drag performers pair up with brands is their mutability and uniqueness, all of which are presented as the result of a highly specialized set of skills possessed by each individual to different degrees. Such skills include very literal, manual abilities like make-up artistry (as seen in the case of, for instance, Trixie Mattel and Kim Chi) and fashion design and sewing (for example Monét X Change or Bianca del Rio), but also non-material competences such as resilience, a stringent work ethic or self-affirmation (Bob the Drag Queen, Shangela, Bianca del Rio). All of these abilities are portrayed as flowing into the queens' craft, providing them with an air of expertise and authority when it comes to shaping brand meanings.

Trixie Mattel, for example, reviews make-up produced by the popular UK brand Rimmel by recreating her signature drag look using only the brand's products. Thus, the artistic outcome, the signature drag look, is crafted using a specific set of branded tools, blending together Mattel's art with the Rimmel brand and simultaneously imbuing the brand's products with the queen's craft. Therefore, from the concept to the title 'Trixie gets the London Look', which utilizes the brand's slogan, brand meaning is being reframed and permeated with the drag performer's aura (an idea that will be further discussed in a later section). Along the way, Trixie tells the audience about her personal connection with the brand, including first encounters and vivid memories (00:30),[1] speaking with the authority of an experienced make-up artist throughout the promotional video, for example when commenting on how finely powder products should be milled (25:10). In doing so, she creates an air of relatability and authenticity as well as maintaining her role as an expert authority qualified to make informed judgements about the brand and its products. Having started her career as a make-up artist, this level of expertise puts Trixie on a par with many other beauty YouTubers; however, she goes a step further in giving additional advice for a drag-specific context as well as evaluating the products' general, everyday functionality. Thus, water-based foundation and lip primer are singled out as not being particularly useful for drag make-up, as they would not withstand the stresses of performing (6:18; 22:17), but are deemed serviceable in an everyday context. Similarly, when Violet Chachki endorses a hair-care product on her Instagram profile, it is on the basis of her expertise as a drag artist: 'years of tape, ponytails and wigs has put a lot of stress on my hairline. That's why I'm partnering with [brand] to help repair and strengthen my naturally luscious locks' (Instagram, 30 June, 2022). Both performers can therefore be seen as invoking their specific craft in order to imbue brand products with meaning and added value by way of association.

While make-up and hair products seem to be a natural fit for drag performers' artisanal and artistic endorsements, with many – such as Trixie Mattel or Kim Chi – having professional expertise as make-up artists, brands such as BMW or International Delight coffee also invoke the performers' non-material skills as a source of authority stemming specifically from their status as queens. Bob the Drag Queen, for example, is chosen as a partner for the coffee brand because, as claimed in the ad, 'Nobody does self-expression as well as Bob the Drag Queen', while Shangela's work ethic is framed in a BMW ad as a source of knowledge and authority when it comes to cars and technology: 'I'm an actor, a dancer, a community advocate, and an entrepreneur. I learned early on that dynamic performance is intentional excellence, baby.' Here, brands are invoking the performers' invisible, intangible charisma in order to add another layer of meaning to their products in an attempt to create a relationship with new audiences. Thus, whether they be material or non-material, drag performers' unique skill sets are continuously being framed as a source of their transformative power, affording them the expertise and authenticity to endorse brands and thereby shape brand meanings in a similar way to more traditional artists and craftspeople.

Charisma and vulnerability

As we have seen, invoking an artisan's charisma and creative spirit to enrich brand meaning is not a new phenomenon. With drag artisans, however, we can see a dimension of vulnerability entering the artisanal framing, creating meaning and authenticity by baring their own feelings. In a collaboration with Boots UK,[2] The Vivienne was involved in a make-up tutorial in which she frames her advice in the form of hacks and easy-to-follow tips and she invites viewers to 'take all my hacks and slay your way'. This indicates that, through the skills and expertise that The Vivienne possesses, the ideology of consumption is engaged in a shared space where the aura is transmitted from her own individuality to the viewer.

Drag performers impart a part of their charisma onto with the brands they collaborate with. Take, for example, the following quote, where we see that the direct elements (flowers, colours) that can be considered as part of Trixie Mattel's universe (music record) become infused artfully inside phone cases: 'I was like, well, let's take some of the design elements like the hearts and the flowers from the record, and let's make a case out of it because it just looks so beautiful together. So, this is original, but kind of shares DNA with the record.'[3] Hence, the product is described to possess a shared DNA with the Trixie Mattel brand in a way that harmonizes beautifully. This charisma, however, is not only maintained through a well-curated facade. An element of this charisma also emerges from taboo-breaking behaviour, such as profanity, and by engaging in the authentic campy vibe of the drag performer.

In a cooperation with Serv Vodka, Trixie emphasizes the product experience as enhanced with the magical sprinkling of glitter and colour: 'I serve my dinner party with Trixie's pink lemonade iced tea. ... Add a sprinkle of edible pink glitter because, yes, Serv the party.'[4] This ties into the general form of language markers that drag performers use when enacting their charisma. The language used by the drag performers, such as 'giving high-glam drama' (Violet Chachki), 'give you the full illusion' (Pearl) and 'I want like magic and fairy-dust' (Yara Sofia), suggest that charisma and aura are linked to the ability to create a powerful and fantastical image or persona by the drag performer.

Interestingly, this charisma also comes across through the drag performers' authentic and original stories that showcase their vulnerability. One rather common signifier of this vulnerability is a bare face, sometimes even a semi-nude body, showing the performer out of drag and actively highlighting what some may perceive as imperfections. For instance, Violet Chachki has her own YouTube channel where she showcases the preparation of getting ready, transforming her bare face into one that is fully made up. A heightened form of sharing this kind of vulnerability is elaborated in Kim Chi's interview for *Elle* magazine. During this account, she discusses her experience of coming out and the emotional distress associated with it, while appearing natural and without any make-up in front of a very neutral set. In addition, queens use social platforms to share stories about their marginalized position and, as performers, often become personal with their audience (for example addressing viewers in a familiar manner – 'you guys'). In another instance of signalling vulnerability, they frequently share stories about their own lives, or allow their audience a glimpse of their living spaces (Bob the Drag Queen, Trixie and Pearl), zooming out and granting viewers an image of the wider context, thereby blending the staged and the personal.

In these accounts, vulnerability allows drag performers to create a sense of charisma that emanates from their personal lives. Disclosing this as part of their artisanal aura allows their audience to gain the sense of a meaningful connection rather than a distant feeling of awe. Viewers are invited to take part in the perpetuation of the universe of values created by the performer, given that these messages are shared and relayed via social platforms. Thus, through a juxtaposition of the perfect and the imperfect, the artefact and its very constructedness, drag performers undo the illusion of completeness and totality. In this process, they create a much more meaningful allegory of beauty and self-image for their audience, invoking truth through a disruption of the aura of perfection.

Artisanal signalling and queering the brand

We now move on to some material and non-material means by which drag queens are framing themselves – and being framed by brands – as artistic craftspeople that utilize charisma and aura. We cannot overlook the vast and intricate nexus of signifiers contributing to this image and, in being picked up by both popular brands and mainstream audiences, transporting meaning, artisanship and charisma. In addition to invoking key elements of their individuality to imbue the brand with the drag performer's charisma and vulnerability, they are also able to queer the brand in some way by drawing on queer representations to disrupt assumptions of static heteronormativity that might be laid upon brands (Södergren and Vallström, 2021). Drag performers challenge more than the norm of what brands usually push for in terms of representation when it comes to terms of sexual orientation.

First, we can find a host of linguistic signifiers used by drag performers and their communities – from simple logographic and phonetic changes, as in the affirmative 'yaass' taken up by beauty brand Lush in its 2018 Christmas campaign (Prinzivalli, 2018), to proper slang vocabulary such as 'fish/ fishy' signifying an especially feminine-looking performer (see also Frankel and Ha, 2020; Simmons, 2014). Interestingly, many of these expressions are closely tied to themes of hard work, handicraft and artistry. The simple expression 'work' (sometimes spelled 'werk') alone takes on a central role in drag language, being used as an affirmative (such as 'yaass, work, bitch!'), a term for a great performance ('work that runway'), or a display of extraordinary effort to get the best effect out of some material ('working' an outfit). Work, or werk, is thus used to signify an indisputable level of talent and artistry in a drag performer. Often, this also goes hand in hand with a notion of adaptability, the idea of making do and creating something beautiful and extraordinary out of scarce or mundane raw materials. Bianca del Rio, for example, shows off thrift-store garments she has resewn into photoshoot looks on her Instagram profile and Trixie Mattel calls herself 'thrifty Mattel' as she gives out tips on Instagram on the clever use of make-up. This particular signification of artisanship also tends to accompany a certain self-deprecating humour through which the queens imply that their own, pre-transformation faces or bodies represent such 'scarce' or 'mundane' resources out of which something extraordinarily beautiful is created by means of their own craft and artistry. Katya Zamo, for example, frequently refers to herself in an unfavourable manner out of drag, calling her make-up session on Instagram a transformation 'from Voldemort into a San Diego bridesmaid' (27 May, 2022). Similarly, Trixie Mattel jokes in one of her make-up tutorials[5] that 'up close, I look like a homosexual kitchen sponge' (4:10). Thus, working hard in order to create an artful product out of simple or limited resources is a notion clearly reflected in a variety of linguistic signifiers and framings that are ubiquitous in drag.

In the same vein, a variety of terms suggesting artisanal handiwork are being used specifically in relation to drag make-up and styling. Leading the way is the simple fact that, among drag performers, doing one's make-up is commonly referred to as 'painting', implying both skilled labour and artistry. One veteran *Drag Race* contestant, for instance, hosts a social media series, *Painted with Raven*,[6] showcasing other make-up talents, and Shea Couleé asserts on Instagram (11 September, 2022) that people were constantly asking her about a certain highlighter she was using 'while I was painting'. Meanwhile, Trixie Mattel has made the expression 'painting for the back of the room' into a catchphrase. Kim Chi, using the same terminology in a portrait interview with *Elle* magazine, goes one step further by describing: 'I see my face as a blank canvas' (1:45).[7] Beyond the artisanal vocabulary of painting, drag language also invokes other forms of artistic skilled labour when, for example, contouring is referred to as 'pre-shaping the face' (Trixie on YouTube) or when the process of letting make-up and powder sit on the face is called 'baking' or 'cooking'. With her own make-up brand, Trixie Cosmetics, Trixie Mattel took the analogy with handicraft quite literally, launching a kit of 'beauty tools' made to look like workman's tools in the summer of 2022 under the slogan 'real tools, toy packaging' (Instagram, 15 August).

These are just a few examples of how drag performers' status as skilled craftspeople and artisans is being framed, established and perpetuated within social media and popular culture, granting them iconic status as both artists and proficient experts.

Beyond representation, queering the nature of the brand may be viewed in terms of the specific product-related work that the drag performer conducts. In her collaboration with Goose Island Beer Co, for instance, Shea Couleé has played a role as a partner though which the flavour of the wheat beer she is endorsing has been developed. On the beer can's design, we see that elements of drag merge with the brand assets (the goose wearing a crown) and take on Shea's name (Shea Coul-Alé), even donning the tagline 'drag a beer'. However, this queering effect can also transcend to a macro level, as drag queens distort and challenge the gender binaries through their drag performances.

Discussion: drag performers as cultural artisans

Drag performers' position, surrounded by a nexus of signifiers, both material and non-material, and the ways in which these create a certain cultural framing, allow drag performers to take on the role of charismatic artisanal figures when it comes to shaping brand meanings.

Depicted as experts within their fields (whether these be make-up artistry, fashion, a specific mindset or an amalgamation of all), they clearly share the theme of artistic transformation through unique skill with other artisanal branding efforts and brand communities (Dion and Arnould, 2011; Leissle, 2017; Sams et al, 2022). The artefact created in this case, however, can be described as non-material; a performance (Goebl, 2001). This artefact is so embedded within the sayings and doings surrounding drag artisanship that it attains iconic status and thereby the potential to create a connection, a lasting relationship with the audience.

As we have seen in the previous section, drag performers often use irony, self-deprecating humour and openness to exude a dimension of vulnerability and sincerity that has thus far rarely been discussed in connection with either artistic charisma or artisanal branding (Leissle, 2017; Arnould et al, 2021; Wieser et al, 2021). This kind of accessibility, which makes it possible to form social connections and attract a brand community of like-minded individuals, highlights the drag performer's role as the central, iconic figure around whom a unique ideology of consumption revolves and who has the potential to impart some of their charisma onto other brands and products (see Figure 4.1).

As discussed previously, the idea of charisma in this context seems to be as something shared with the audience. Drag performers do not frame themselves as lofty, untouchable artistic geniuses, as in other instances of charisma-based branding (Dion and Arnould, 2011). Instead, through the aforementioned self-ironic humour and vulnerability, they encourage their audience to partake in that charisma, share that iconic aura, or, as The Vivienne puts it, 'slay [their] way'.

Since drag performers communicate a specific idea of beauty subsumed within the ideology of consumption surrounding their persona, an idea that goes beyond the heteronormative master-binary, they may be seen as artisans taking on the role of cultural intermediaries within the marketplace. While feminist theorists have criticized drag performers for reproducing a certain type of sexualized femininity catering to the male gaze and thus merely reinforcing current, normalized ideas of desire and desirability (Coles, 2007), the variety of drag that has broken into mainstream consciousness highlights that this, as well as the gender parody referenced by Butler (see Coles, 2007), is arguably only one of many shapes that modern drag takes (see also Mundel et al, 2022). Highly successful performers such as Yvie Oddly and Sasha Velour (both RPDR winners), for instance, do not easily fall into a category, much less one describing hypersexualized femininity. Even classic 'pageant queens' who may be said to perpetuate this image, however, at least call attention to – and make overt the heteronormative thinking that structures much of our lives and consumption practices.

Figure 4.1: Drag performers as cultural artisans

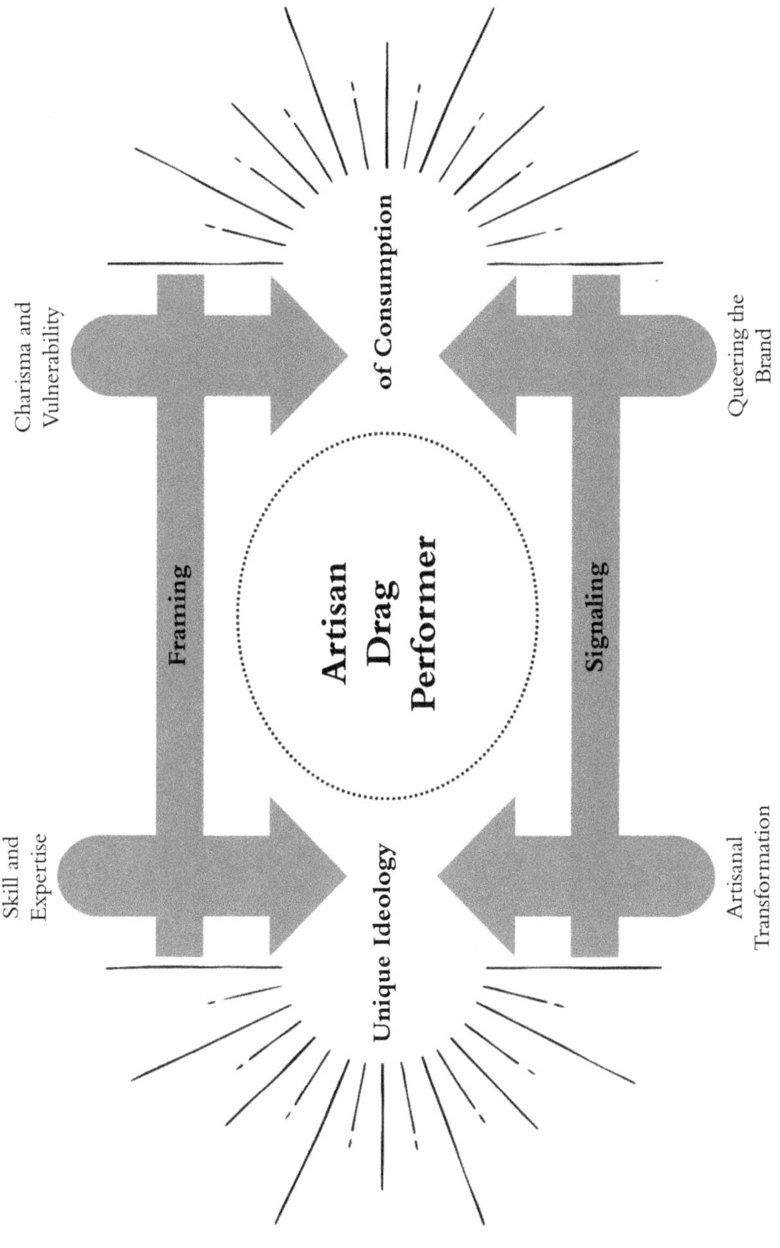

Charisma and Vulnerability

Queering the Brand

Skill and Expertise

Artisanal Transformation

of Consumption

Framing

Signaling

Unique Ideology

Artisan Drag Performer

Fourteen years after the advent of *RuPaul's Drag Race* and the concomitant widespread popularization of drag, the effects of drag performers as cultural artisans are keenly felt in a wide variety of industries (as illustrated by the examples discussed here), but especially within the realms of fashion and make-up. Here, in particular, a broader, younger and more diverse audience is adopting the tools, techniques, habits and language embedded in the ideology of consumption surrounding drag performers – sometimes without even associating them with queer culture. Says Trixie Mattel (on YouTube): 'They don't identify as drag queens but they are in the trappings of drag queens; it's pretty crazy!' (4:45).[8] Make-up artist Sarah Tanno puts it even more bluntly when reflecting on popular trends within the beauty industry: 'It's like you're basically doing drag, whether you know it or not' (0:43).[9]

In the end, it can be said that modern drag performers, by taking on the role of artisans and cultural intermediaries within the marketplace, are in a position that allows them to influence brand meanings and imbue brands and products with their specific, unique charisma and aura. In doing so, at the very least, they draw attention to – and make overt – normalized views of gender and beauty, thereby opening a space for questioning the male-female master-binary and queering the brand. However, the effects of this cultural artisanship becoming subsumed within brand meanings and branding strategies remain dubious. While this process might represent a chance to open up a dialogue about consumption practices informed by normalized views of gender and beauty, a mainstream commercialization and commodification of drag might equally lead to the aforementioned reinforcement of gender norms as the sayings and doings become more and more removed from their queer cultural context.

Theoretical implications

Overall, viewing drag performers as cultural artisans within the marketplace adds to several bodies of research literature. First and foremost, this chapter contributes to the growing body of literature concerned with queer and LGBTQ+ representation within marketing and branding strategies (Mundel et al, 2022) and addresses drag in light of its recent entry into the pop-cultural mainstream – a phenomenon that marketing research has thus far largely neglected (McCormack and Wignall, 2022).

Our findings further offer up an understanding of how drag performers conduct cultural artisanship as iconic figureheads and intermediaries within the marketplace. We theorize that they engage in cultural artisan-signalling by imbuing their charisma onto brands and inviting the audience to share in it.

Moreover, drag performers treat their work as a craft, allowing products and brands to become imprinted with their charisma. This charisma is built upon an underlying ideology of consumption that views beauty and the tools to achieve it as non-binary, inviting all audiences to partake in the language, rituals and ultimately the universe of the values displayed. In addition, by being vulnerable to the drag performers' individuality, charisma is thus democratized and shared.

Moreover, we expand on the literature and theorization concerned with charisma and aura by viewing drag charisma as a phenomenon that originates from the margins of society, identifying locales for its generation that differ from those of luxury and status, as can be found in other charisma-based fields of marketing (see, for example Semaan et al, 2019; Joy and Belk, 2020). Thus, we highlight that certain levels of irony and vulnerability constitute crucial parts of drag performers' charisma, giving them the ability to invite audiences in on a personal level and creating an air of transparency and authenticity that is somewhat atypical for the beauty and fashion industries, where an unattainable level of physical perfection tends to be communicated to a primarily female audience (Verrastro et al, 2020). In highlighting their transformation through skill, on the other hand, drag performers openly point out and share the specific techniques and materials it takes for them to achieve their looks. This transformative signalling highlights a queered, non-heteronormative view of beauty and charisma that is made possible by the performer-as-intermediary.

Within the context of modern drag and its emergence into mainstream cultural consciousness, we further emphasize drag being regarded as an artisanal practice, which encapsulates its unique position within the marketplace in a way that moves beyond gender parody or subversion (Butler, 1990; Coles, 2007). By viewing drag as a non-material cultural artefact and drag performers as artisans, we draw attention to the ways in which their networks of symbols, rituals and language become more and more normalized in the marketplace as brands and mainstream audiences adopt and reproduce them. This bears the potential of either reinforcing gender hierarchies or, by making overt the practices involved in a certain kind of gender performance, opening them up to a wider audience and inviting a dialogue about beauty and charisma that moves beyond heteronormativity.

Limitations and future research

Naturally, as this interpretive chapter deals in no small part with visual representations and the meanings they may convey, it needs to be pointed out that no visual imagery is ever innocent. Ways of seeing and interpreting are dependent on historical, geographical, cultural and social contexts (Rose, 2001), which is why the reader should be aware of the fact that, while both members of the research group identify as belonging to, or allied with, the LGBTQ+ community, neither identifies as a drag performer or, at the time of writing, as non-binary. Thus, subconscious and culturally ingrained white, heteronormative biases may still have found their way into this interpretation and we encourage the reader to critically process and engage with it on these terms.

Second, the realm of social media and advertising is only one of several channels and lenses through which to view representations of drag. What is more, within the history of this art form, these are what one might call more recent channels. It would therefore be interesting to see the practices, rituals and commercial meanings co-created and influenced by drag performers within different contexts and communication channels, such as live performances, fashion events and conventions such as DragCon. Moreover, many performers have become brands in their own right (Frankel and Ha, 2020), which is why further examining the interplay of personal and commercial branding might present an interesting concept to extend to this context. Our focus of investigation scopes the ideology of consumption that assumes the artisanal framing as subsumed within the ideology of brands in a more capitalistic sense. Hence, further investigation merits the question of whether the nature of drag through, for example, camp (Kates and Belk, 2001) and its more subversive elements clash with and are overshadowed by consumerist logics. Specifically, therefore, further research might look into the interplays between the individual personal brand and the capitalistic brand.

This chapter only addresses the site of the emergence and communication of certain images and language surrounding drag queens as artisans. Further studies on consumers' perceptions of, and reactions to, drag performers' brand endorsements and collaborations might be highly illuminating when it comes to aspects such as vulnerability, authenticity and queering a brand's image. Especially in the latter case, audience studies might help researchers gain a clearer image of whether we might be witnessing a mere commodification and repurposing of drag, or whether the normalization of queered advertising and branding might actually shift long-ingrained binary perceptions. Another interesting viewpoint that takes into consideration the understanding of the audience of drag performers is that of authenticity. Fans are essential in assessing authentic portrayals from the drag industry's most popular TV show (RPDR; Canavan, 2021), where frustrations over capturing the truth are negotiated in a complex manner. It is worth seeing this aspect cross over from the space of the show – which is heavily produced and specifically framed for the viewer – to the narratives emerging from brand-drag collaborations and exploring audience perceptions of authenticity.

Finally, our research and sampling, even though care was taken to capture a wide variety of performers, do not fully encapsulate the variety that exists within modern forms of drag. Between club kids, pageant queens, drag kings, non-binary drag performers, spooky queens or muscle queens, one could even raise the question of whether this chapter has not treated drag performers as too homogeneous a group. Modern drag's intersections with other cultural and subcultural influences, the concomitant understandings of beauty and charisma and the meanings disclosed as a result represents yet another avenue for future researchers engaging with drag performers as cultural artisans.

Conclusion

Drag queens have emerged as powerful figures in the LGBTQ+ community, using their craft to challenge traditional gender dualities. By examining the framings and signifiers intertwined with their emergence into mainstream popular culture and branding, this chapter has proposed that drag performers represent key roles as cultural artisans of the marketplace. Through their performances and personas, they have created a space for gender expression that is not limited by societal norms and expectations, posing an attractive influencing force in the scheme of cultural branding. This chapter has specifically explored the defining contours of drag performers' artisanship as embedded in the skills, expertise, charisma and aura that allow them to achieve their transformation and to queer the brand by imbuing it with the aura of their non-material artefact: the drag persona. The linking of the framings of drag to artisanal signification overall communicates an ideology of consumption that is inclusive, empowering and transformative – having gained such ubiquitousness that brands and consumer groups adopt parts of it almost unwittingly, blurring the boundaries of doing drag and potentially even divorcing these signifiers from that inclusive, empowering, non-binary realm of meaning. Thus, brand meaning, in the end, no longer resides with marketers' intentions but is ultimately transmitted across the drag queen as cultural artisan and the consumers invited to share her charismatic aura.

Notes

[1] 'Trixie Gets the London Look | Trixie Makeup with All Rimmel Products', youtube. com/watch?v=cAANPVm0knY

[2] 'Make-up Tutorial | Make-up Hacks with RuPaul's Drag Race UK's The Vivienne | BootsX | Boots UK', youtube.com/watch?v=oPmCx-CsM20

[3] 'Trixie Mattel x Wildflower Cases', https://www.wildflowercases.com/en-gb/collections/trixie-mattel-x-wildflower-cases-drag-elegance-fashion-trendy-limited-edition

[4] 'SERV Trixie Mattel Pink Lemonade Vodka Cocktail', https://www.youtube.com/watch?v=Rt3W8g4Owh4

[5] 'Trixie Gets the London Look | Trixie Makeup with All Rimmel Products', youtube. com/watch?v=cAANPVm0knY

[6] 'Painted with Raven: Makeup Tutorials – Ariana – Greyscale', youtube.com/watch?v=_CKA9SknWtc

[7] 'Drag Queen Kim Chi Transforms with Makeup | ELLE', youtube.com/watch?v=7dpBkN5yEhg

8 'Trixie Gets the London Look | Trixie Makeup with All Rimmel Products', youtube.com/watch?v=cAANPVm0knY
9 'BEAT. Contour. Snatched. How Drag Queens Shaped the Biggest Makeup Trends | ELLE', youtube.com/watch?v=g83SowqTi6c&t=171s

References

Alexander, N. (2009) 'Brand Authentication: Creating and maintaining brand auras', European Journal of Marketing, 43(3/4): 551–562.

Arnould, E.J., Arvidsson, A. and Eckhardt, G.M. (2021) 'Consumer Collectives: A history and reflections on their future', Journal of the Association for Consumer Research, 6(4): 415–428.

Baldwin, E., Longhurst, S., McCracken, S., Ogborn, M. and Smith, G. (2004) 'Subcultures: Reading, resistance and social divisions', in E. Baldwin, S. Longhurst, S. McCracken, M. Ogborn and G. Smith (eds) Introducing Cultural Studies (revised 1st edn), London: Pearson Education, pp 316–362.

Braun, V. and Clarke, V. (2006) 'Using Thematic Analysis in Psychology', Qualitative Research in Psychology, 3(2): 77–101.

Bryman, A. (2016) Social Research Methods, Oxford: Oxford University Press.

Butler, J. (1990) Gender Trouble: Feminism and the Subversion of Identity, New York: Routledge.

Canavan, B. (2021) 'Post-Postmodern Consumer Authenticity, Shantay You Stay or Sashay Away? A netnography of Rupaul's Drag Race fans', Marketing Theory, 21(2): 251–276.

Ciszek, E. and Pounders, K. (2020) 'The Bones Are the Same: An exploratory analysis of authentic communication with LGBTQ publics', Journal of Communication Management, 24(2): 103–117.

Coles, C. (2007) 'The Question of Power and Authority in Gender Performance: Judith Butler's drag strategy', Esharp: Electronic Social Sciences, Humanities, and Arts Review for Postgraduates, 9: 1–8, api.semanticscholar.org/CorpusID:54092893

De Veirman, M., Cauberghe, V. and Hudders, L. (2017) 'Marketing through Instagram Influencers: The impact of number of followers and product divergence on brand attitude', International Journal of Advertising, 36(5): 798–828.

Dickie, V. and Frank, G. (1996) 'Artisan Occupations in the Global Economy: A conceptual framework', Journal of Occupational Science, 3(2): 45–55.

Dion, D. and Arnould, E. (2011) 'Retail Luxury Strategy: Assembling charisma through art and magic', Journal of Retailing, 87(4): 502–520.

Eagar, T., Lindridge, A., and Martin, D. M. (2022). 'Ch-Ch-changes: the geology of artist brand evolutions', European Journal of Marketing, 56(12): 3617–3651.

Frankel, S. and Ha, S. (2020) 'Something Seems Fishy: Mainstream consumer response to drag queen imagery', Fashion and Textiles, 7(1).

Gerosa, A. (2022) 'The Resurgence of Craft Retailing: Marketing and branding strategies in the food and beverage sector', in J. Mulholland, M. Massi and A. Ricci (eds) The Artisan Brand, Cheltenham: Edward Elgar, pp 193–208.

Goebl, W. (2001) 'Melody Lead in Piano Performance: Expressive device or artifact?', The Journal of the Acoustical Society of America, 110(1): 563–572.

Jones, A. (2021) In Between Subjects: A Critical Genealogy of Queer Performance, London: Routledge.

Joy, A. and Belk, R.W. (2020) 'Why Luxury Brands Partner with Artists', in R.W. Belk (ed) The Oxford Handbook of Luxury Business, Oxford: Oxford University Press, pp 309–329.

Kates, S. and Belk, R. (2001) 'The Meanings of Lesbian and Gay Pride Day', Journal of Contemporary Ethnography, 30(4): 392–429.

Kozinets, R.V. (2012) 'Marketing Netnography: Prom/ot(ulgat)ing a new research method', Methodological Innovations, 7(1): 37–45.

Kozinets, R.V. (2022) 'Immersive Netnography: A novel method for service experience research in virtual reality, augmented reality and metaverse contexts', Journal of Service Management, 34(1): 100–125.

Leissle, K. (2017) '"Artisan" as Brand: Adding value in a craft chocolate community', Food, Culture & Society, 20(1): 37–57.

Manlow, V. (2021) 'Jewelry Design in the Luxury Sector: Artistry, craft, technology and sustainability', in I Coste-Manière and M.Á. Gardetti (eds) Sustainable Luxury and Jewelry: Environmental Footprints and Eco-design of Products and Processes, Singapore: Springer, pp 145–177.

McCormack, M. and Wignall, L. (2022) 'Drag Performers' Perspectives on the Mainstreaming of British Drag: Towards a sociology of contemporary drag', Sociology, 56(1): 3–20.

Mulholland, J., Massi, M. and Ricci, A. (2022) 'Introduction to the Artisan Brand', in J. Mulholland, M. Massi and A. Ricci (eds) The Artisan Brand, Cheltenham: Edward Elgar, pp 1–12.

Mundel, J., Close, S. and Sasiela, N. (2022) 'Drag Dollars: Making room for queens in advertising', in J. Mundel, S. Close and N. Sasiela (eds) Drag in the Global Digital Public Sphere, London: Routledge, pp 89–112.

Nölke, A.-I. (2018) 'Making Diversity Conform? An intersectional, longitudinal analysis of LGBT-specific mainstream media advertisements', Journal of Homosexuality, 65(2): 224–255.

Ostrom, V. (1980) 'Artisanship and Artifact', Public Administration Review, 40(4): 309–317.

Prinzivalli, L. (2018) 'Lush Rings in the Holidays with Campaign Starring Three Drag Race Queens', Allure, [online] 10 November, Available from: allure.com/story/lush-holiday-rupaul-drag-queens-campaign [Accessed 7 June 2024].

Rose, G. (2001) Visual Methodologies: An Introduction to the Interpretation of Visual Materials, London: Sage.

Sams, D.E., Rickard, M.K. and Sadasivan, A. (2022) 'The Perspective of Artisan Vendors' Resilience, Dedication to Product Authenticity, and the Role of Marketing and Community: 21st century', Arts and the Market, 12(1): 70–83.

Semaan, R.W., Ashill, N. and Williams, P. (2019) 'Sophisticated, Iconic and Magical: A qualitative analysis of brand charisma', Journal of Retailing and Consumer Services, 49: 102–113.

Simmons, N. (2014) 'Speaking Like a Queen in Rupaul's Drag Race: Towards a speech code of American drag queens', Sexuality & Culture, 18: 630–648.

Södergren, J. and Vallström, N. (2021) 'Seeing the Invisible: Brand authenticity and the cultural production of queer imagination', Arts and the Market, 11(3): 275–297.

Spencer, M.E. (1973) 'What is Charisma?', The British Journal of Sociology, 24(3): 341–354.

Statista (2022) Most-Followed Drag Queens from Rupaul's Drag Race on Instagram Worldwide as of June 2022, Available from: statista.com/statistics/1010019/most-followers-instagram-drag-queen-global [Accessed 7 July 2022].

Verrastro, V., Liga, F., Cuzzocrea, F. and Gugliandolo, M.C. (2020) 'Fear the Instagram: Beauty stereotypes, body image and Instagram use in a sample of male and female adolescents', QWERTY – Interdisciplinary Journal of Technology, Culture and Education, 15(1): 31–49.

Wieser, V.E., Luedicke, M.K. and Hemetsberger, A. (2021) 'Charismatic Entrainment: How brand leaders and consumers co-create charismatic authority in the marketplace', Journal of Consumer Research, 48(4): 731–751.

Willis, P. (1990) Common Culture, Milton Keynes: Open University Press.

5

Legitimation Spillover in the Berlin Drag Scene: From Conflict to Collaboration

Pia Seimetz and Jan-Hendrik Bucher

Legitimacy plays a crucial role in shaping the interactions and perceptions of various social groups within a community. In many contexts, groups may differ in their perceived legitimacy, resulting in dynamics of conflict, rivalry or marginalization. The process of legitimation is not fixed, however; it is dynamic and can evolve over time, allowing for legitimacy to spill over from one group to another. This chapter explores the fascinating case of the Berlin drag scene, where legitimacy spills over from a subgroup of more established and legitimate Drag Queens[1] to a previously less legitimate subgroup of Tunten. Tunten and Drag Queens are defined as members of the drag community who diverge in their aesthetics and attitude towards politics and commercialism. In short, Drag Queens perform as glamourous and commercial female personas, while Tunten prefer deliberately 'untidy' aesthetics and despise commercialism.

The drag community in Berlin has a rich history of changing legitimacy. In the 1970s, drag in Germany was not legitimate in relation to dominant social norms. At that time, presenting female as a man was instantly categorized as homosexual behaviour and thus undesirable (Rubin, 2018). Supported by prominent politicians, the general public tended to perceive homosexuality as a form of damage. Today, the public perspective on LGBTQ+ activities in Germany has changed, and the drag community is now legitimate in relation to dominant social norms (Feldman and Hakim, 2020; Workman, 2020). Some scholars even speak of this being a 'golden age' for drag (Brennan and Gudelunas, 2017). This can be observed in three instances. One example is the global commercial success of the TV series *RuPaul's Drag Race*. Its UK edition had over 12 million views at the end of 2019 (McCormack and Wignall, 2022), paving the way for the casting of the German edition in 2022. Second, Berlin's epicentre for drag shows, the club SchwuZ, grew to employ 100 people (Trott, 2020). Lastly, public institutions such as museums also started showing drag (McCormack and Wignall, 2022).

In Berlin, the drag scene encompasses various groups with different legitimacy statuses. One of them is the subgroup of Tunten. A performance by a Tunte is characterized by a political focus, messy expression and dismissive attitude towards commercialism. Naturally, this created a conflict when the US style of doing drag as a drag queen swept to Germany in the 1990s. In contrast to Tunten, the Drag Queens focused on entertaining the audience and marketing themselves, instead of spreading a political message. In recent decades, however, these two groups have collaborated, thus changing their legitimacy status.

While earlier research has highlighted that entities gain legitimacy from one or more authorities (Meyer and Scott, 1983), it does not explain what happens if there is more than one entity that is being legitimated. Additionally, research has found that legitimacy diffuses (Johnson et al, 2006), which creates a possibility for conflict, but these conflicts have not then been researched. This chapter shows that, through resolving the conflict between an illegitimate and legitimate group, the former can attain more legitimacy, and then the chapter maps out the legitimation process.

The chapter highlights three stages in this legitimation process. Stage 1 is characterized by conflict and rivalry between the two groups. Stage 2 is marked by collaboration and mutual acceptance, leading to legitimacy spillover. Stage 3, unity and diversity, is the current stage, at which the drag scene is more cohesive and inclusive.

The following sections review relevant literature on legitimation processes in both consumer culture theory and the context of the drag scene. They then delve into the three stages of the Berlin drag scene's legitimation spillover, exploring the challenges faced, the transformative events and the current state of collaboration and acceptance. The findings contribute to a deeper understanding of legitimation dynamics and offer valuable insights for researchers and practitioners seeking to foster inclusivity and acceptance within diverse communities.

Literature review

Current research on legitimation often relies on the definition by Suchman (1995), according to whom, legitimation is a perception that an entity acts in congruence with social norms. Other scholars prefer to approach legitimation by leaning on resource dependence or from an institutional perspective. Dowling and Pfeffer (1975) see legitimation as a resource that is extracted from an institutional environment. Scott (1995) defines legitimation as a condition that signifies congruence with rules, norms or cultural-cognitive frameworks. For this chapter, we lean on the definition by Suchman (1995). In contrast to Dowling and Pfeffer (1975) and Scott (1995), this definition allows us to examine legitimation as a process rather than a fixed resource or condition. Previous research has identified several ways in which the process of legitimation happens. The following sections review and summarize this research.

Meyer and Scott (1983) explain that entities are legitimated by one or more authorities. An entity can have various forms, such as an event, object, individual or organization. Because of the possible multiplicity of authorities, an entity can be legitimate according to one authority, but illegitimate in the eyes of another authority. An example for this can be found in Martin (1994). To explain the role of different authorities in the legitimation process, she uses the topic of salary inequalities: women earn less than men. In this scenario, the issue of salary inequality is the entity that is legitimated. Society at large and women in society act as authorities. Authorities assess the legitimacy of an entity. Here, larger society tolerates salary inequality and hence legitimates it. According to the authority of larger society, salary inequalities are legitimate. However, the group of women in society poses as another authority. According to them, salary inequalities are not legitimate. Here, we can see that different authorities can evaluate the legitimacy of entities in different ways. However, research has not covered how the legitimacy of two entities interacts.

Johnson et al (2006) identified a four-stage process of legitimation: innovation, local validation, diffusion and general validation. The first stage refers to the creation of a social innovation to address a need, purpose, goal or desire on the local level. Small groups, who develop new ways of thinking to accomplish their tasks, are an example of social innovation. In the second stage, the innovators work towards establishing their innovation as a valid social fact. Once validated, they assume that it will be accepted in other social contexts. In the third stage, they diffuse their innovation into new local situations. As the new social innovation spreads, it needs less justification and may arrive at the fourth stage of general validation. (Johnson et al, 2006) These stages touch on interesting themes, but the authors leave room to unpack more. In stage three, 'diffusion', legitimacy is transferred from the local to the global level and there may be conflict here, which has not been researched.

What has been researched, however, is the change from an illegitimate practice to a legitimate one. According to Coskuner-Balli and Thompson (2013), formerly illegitimate practices such as care work can be legitimated through capitalizing. In their study of stay-at-home-fathers, legitimacy is attained through entrepreneurial practices, emotional support, solidarity building and masculinizing domesticity. The stay-at-home-fathers attached a different value to their practices by framing them closer to already-established legitimate practices. In larger society, care work is much less legitimate than wage work. The stay-at-home-fathers legitimated their care work by making it seem more like wage work. This research highlights that an illegitimate entity can be legitimated by adopting the habit of a legitimate entity, but this process is actively controlled by the illegitimate entity. We do not know how the process unfolds if the legitimate actor takes action as well.

Scott (1995) shows how entities can be legitimated through congruence with regulative, normative and cultural-cognitive pillars. Regulative legitimation references the legal status of practices; defined as the degree to which a practice is congruent with government rules. Normative legitimation refers to the congruence of a practice with dominant norms, values and concepts of morality. Cultural-cognitive legitimation is defined as the level to which an entity is taken for granted in a society. These three pillars show us, just like the different authorities in Meyer and Scott (1983), that legitimacy is not universal. Different entities can have different levels of legitimacy according to different authorities. Likewise, an entity can be legitimate in one pillar, but not in another. For example, it can be a written law and legitimate to the first pillar, but not morally accepted or taken for granted, thus lacking the second and third pillars of legitimation. Although Scott (1995) defines categories for legitimacy, we do not know how the three pillars are connected and how transfer of legitimacy might happen.

Humphreys (2010), builds on the work of Scott (1995) and adds that legitimation can occur through territorialization: an entity can be legitimated by attaining a physical space. A casino, for example, which occupies a physical space in a city, is highly visible to the city's inhabitants and thus gains legitimation. The research by Humphreys (2010) shows us that legitimation can happen through exposure. Yet, in her study about casino gambling, she researches the creation of new spaces (casinos) that are entirely illegitimate at the point of their creation. It remains out of focus how the territorialization may resonate with an illegitimate entity that transfers to a legitimate space.

So far, we have reviewed existing research about the processes of legitimation. We are interested in whether those processes also apply in the drag scene. So, the following section focuses on research that looks at legitimation in the drag scene.

A vast body of literature has devoted itself to legitimation in the context of *RuPaul's Drag Race* (RPDR), but research about the legitimation of offline drag communities is very scarce. Generally, RPDR is seen as legitimate according to dominant social norms because it seeks congruence. Feldman and Hakim (2020: 397) explain that the show promotes 'entrepreneurial individualism and competitiveness, beauty/polish, hard work and a clearly articulated identity'. McCormack and Wignall (2022) summarize this as 'competition and consumption'. More critical scholars explain the series' legitimation with reference to the commodification and standardization of drag culture and repetition of homonormative ideals (Workman, 2020). This is closely connected to two shortcomings in current research about the legitimation of drag. First, most researchers focus on RPDR. As the series shows only a standardized version of drag, research about it neglects drag subgroups such as Tunten in Berlin. Those subcultures are an important part of drag culture. Second, drag as promoted by RuPaul has been legitimate since its inception, because it was created with the intention to cater to mainstream society (Feldman and Hakim, 2020). Consequently, authors who focus on the TV series can only discuss why it is legitimate and not map out the historical process. Yet, this process is interesting to research, as the Tunten subgroup, for example, has undergone a radical change from being illegitimate to being legitimate. This chapter aims to fill this gap by focusing on the question of how subgroups in the Berlin drag scene were legitimated.

Context: the Berlin drag scene

To research the processes of legitimation, we study the Berlin drag scene, the largest and most vibrant drag scene in Europe (Bryant, 2021). The Berlin drag scene constitutes a rich context in which to study legitimation processes as it has had a well-documented history of legitimation since 1980 (Balzer, 2005; Trott, 2020).

The origins of drag can be traced back to theatrical traditions in ancient civilizations where men would cross-dress and portray female characters. For many centuries, women were not allowed to perform on stage, so female roles were performed by men. Several folk etymology theories place the origins of the word drag in this context. Supposedly, playwrights used to write the acronym DRAG in the script margins for special roles written for women and enacted by men, from which comes the theory that claims drag is shorthand for 'DRess As Girl', while another suggests that the word drag comes from the movement of costume dresses being dragged carelessly across the floor by male performers (Scarlett Gasque, 2023). Although the first theory has been elucidated by famous drag queens such as RuPaul (Lewis, 2019), modern scholars debate its lack of representation of non-cis-male drag performances. In the 19th and early 20th centuries, drag performances gained popularity in vaudeville and burlesque shows. These often combined comedy, satire and risqué humour. Drag queens in these settings challenged gender norms and provided a form of entertainment that was both titillating and comical. Today, drag is a self-chosen label by individuals who partake in genderqueering performances. Most commonly used is 'drag queen': a gender-conservative person, typically male, who dresses in exaggerated feminine attire and often acts with exaggerated femininity (Balzer, 2004). Drag queens are performers who entertain audiences by singing or, more often, lip-syncing to songs, dancing and engaging in theatrical performances. They may also participate in various forms of artistic expression, such as comedy, acting, and fashion.

The term drag queen has became popular as a self-selected label by performers who follow the style of drag promoted by RuPaul since the 1990s. These drag queens do not seek subversiveness, but integration into mainstream society. They portray a glamourous version of femininity and sometimes perform with an attitude that plays with nobility. The term is often falsely used as an umbrella term for all subgroups of the drag scene, including Travestie, Tunten and drag kings. In fact, drag queens primarily represent a US style of doing drag. Meanwhile, in Berlin there is a subgroup of drag that has a long history of conflict with that US style: Tunten.

The word Tunte can be translated along the lines of 'faggot' or 'sissy'. It was used as a derogative term for effeminate men in the 1970s. At that time, social and cultural changes caused a generational conflict in Germany. During the '68' movement, the failure to come to terms with National Socialism and other controversies led to uprisings from the younger generation. Many students participated in the protests. In the spirit of these student revolts of 1968 in West Germany, radical gay men reclaimed the term Tunte. They explicitly called themselves Tunten while performing political drag at demonstrations (Balzer, 2005). In 1971, gay men founded the Homosexual Campaign West Berlin (HAW) and established the first gay centre, Schwulenzentrum (SchwuZ), in Berlin. In 1973, the HAW debated whether doing drag as a Tunte was emancipating or not, which came to be known as the Tunten Dispute (Tuntenstreit). Those in favour of the Tunten style of drag stayed and created many gay projects out of the SchwuZ centre (Balzer, 2004).

Doing drag as a Tunte is characterized by a certain kind of gender performance. Tunten do not present a polished version of femininity but rather portray the girl next door, with a little twist. There are different forms of presentation. If their key feature is incorrect make-up, they can be called a Trash-Tunte (Trümmer-Tunte). If they focus on their political engagement, they may call themselves Political Tunten (Polit-Tunten) and if they don't clearly belong to one of these categories but perform on a stage, they may be a Stage Tunte (Bühnen-Tunte). If one encounters a Tunte, one may remember her egalitarian attitude. Tunten are organized in communities with their own rituals, such as the Tunten baptism (Menze, 2023) and there is even a written Tunten law with several paragraphs. Within their rules and rituals, Tunten mock the establishment and perform as 'gender anarchists' (Balzer, 2004).

Compared with the collective identity of Tunten, Drag Queens have tended to show low solidarity and high competition (Balzer, 2004). Typically, a Drag Queen performs alone on stage, where she is the centre of attention. Other Drag Queens are seen as rivals rather than colleagues. This can be observed in the Drag Queen performance of 'roasting', where queens sharply criticize each other.

This kind of behaviour fits neatly into the shift in German youth culture after the fall of the Berlin wall in 1989. After the Second World War, Germany had been divided into Soviet-governed East Germany and Allies-governed West Germany. When the borders opened in 1989, inhabitants of East Germany came into contact with the 'joys' of a commercial capitalist system, in an atmosphere of excitement and indulgence. Where Tunten represent the activism-oriented spirit of the generation of 1968, Drag Queens mirror the 'heterogeneous, individualistic and more fun-and-consumption-oriented' atmosphere of Berlin after 1989 (Leggewie, 1995, quoted in Balzer, 2005: 125).

The popular American drag parties in Berlin coincided with the RuPaul's success in music. Born in 1960, RuPaul is a US drag queen, singer, actor and television host, who is one of the most well-known personalities in the drag scene (Workman, 2020). In 1993, two of her songs reached number one on Billboard's Hot Dance Music charts. In 2009, the first episode of *RuPaul's Drag Race* aired. It came to be a global success and made drag queens visible to mainstream society. In Berlin, the drag community gathered for streamings of the TV show and many oriented their style towards this Americanized version of drag (Berger, 1997). *Drag Race* started out with a focus on marginalized identities, but soon professionalized, with queens talking about their marketing strategies. Performing as a drag queen has grown into a viable career.

Although US-style drag queens are much more prominent in the media than Tunten, the Berlin drag scene encompasses both. As Balzer (2005: 127) puts it, 'one cannot point to a sole Drag Queen identity as suggested by the media hype'.

One important milestone in the history of both Drag Queens and Tunten in Berlin is the Christopher Street Day (CSD) parade. It is a commemoration of the Stonewall riots of 1969, where queer people drew attention to their dire living conditions and position in society. First established in 1979 in Berlin, the name refers to Christopher Street in New York, where the riots started. The parade consists of carnival-style wagons and participants walking and dancing behind them. Interestingly, the term CSD is mostly used in Germany; in other parts of the world, similar parades most commonly come under the Pride banner. As more and more Drag Queens took part in the CSD parade from the 1990s, politically active Tunten criticized it for becoming gradually more commercial. After an incident where the subversive wagon of the Tunten was stopped by police, the Tunten organized an alternative parade in the Kreuzberg district.

From 1998 until 2013, members of the drag scene had to decide whether to join the commercial CSD parade or the political one (Oloew, 2008). While the political parade then scattered into different rallies after 2013, the commercial parade grew even bigger and attracted corporate sponsors. In 2023, the organizers had to limit the wagons to 75 and registered about 500,000 walking participants.

This popularity provides a marked contrast to the attitude towards gay people right after the establishment of the parade. In 1981, the discovery of AIDS set off a moral panic (Lawrence, 2011). The illness spread quickly among members of the gay community and, as they were not valued by society, resources directed towards care or a cure were very scarce. At that time, members of the Tunten actively campaigned for funds and established aid organizations, benefit concerts and a mobile AIDS-homecare service (Balzer, 2004). The AIDS situation only improved, however, after celebrity involvement, which eventually led to the first major treatment options in the 1990s.

Another event in the 1990s significantly improved the lives of drag performers in Berlin: the abolishment in 1994 of the law that had made homosexual actions illegal (Paragraph 175, StGB: Verbot von Homosexualität in Deutschland). This enabled big events such as the Wigstöckel[2] drag festival to take place, starting in 1996. At first, the festival mainly attracted spectators from the drag scene. With increasing popularity, however, more and more interested participants from outside the scene joined as well.

The 2000s were characterized by the rise of the internet and the early days of social media. This heavily influenced the drag scene. Drag Queens in particular used the opportunity to market themselves to a wider audience. For example, famous Drag Queen Olivia Jones participated in the German *Dschungelcamp* (the German version of the mainstream TV show *I'm a Celebrity ... Get Me Out of Here!*). The audience enjoyed her performance in the show. In the wake of the positive mood regarding drag, Austrian Drag Queen Conchita Wurst even won the Eurovision Song Contest in 2014. Large media producers sensed an opportunity and German celebrity Heidi Klum launched her own series *Queen of Drags* in 2019.

Then the COVID-19 pandemic hit the drag scene hard. As venues were closed, many tried to switch to online shows but few were able to monetize them. However, through the confinement to their own apartments and free time, many young performers started doing drag following their online role models. In the safety of their own home, they could try out drag without the pressure of a physically present audience.

The year 2022 promised to be a particularly interesting one for research, as the Tunten and Drag Queens were very active. Tunten are able to perform again after COVID lockdowns and Drag Queens are excited by a casting call for a German edition of *RuPaul's Drag Race*.

Method

To explore the legitimation of Berlin's drag subcultures, we conducted 12 in-depth, semi-structured interviews. In order to be included, participants had to be connected to the Berlin drag scene (as a performer, organizer of events and so on) and describe this connection as meaningful. So, all participants lived in Berlin at the time of the interview and regularly engaged with the local drag scene.

Table 5.1 provides further information about the interviewees. All participants consented to the use of their drag name in this publication. For ethical reasons, their actual names have been replaced by aliases in this book chapter. The aliases use the same style and combination of words as often used in the drag scene and reference common phrases. The second column shows the participants' association to one or several drag subcultures, followed by the amount of time in which they have engaged in the Berlin drag scene. This ranges between 3 and 37 years (giving a mean of 15.4), not counting one participant who did not wish to disclose their age or time in the scene. The fourth column reports the participants' ages (between 25 and 61 years). Interviews lasted between 13 minutes and 1 hour 33 minutes (mean of 54 minutes).

We recruited the participants through purposive and snowball sampling via email, Instagram and our own personal networks. We started by reaching out

Table 5.1: Overview of the Berlin drag subculture interview participants

Drag name	Main drag subcultures	Time in the Berlin drag scene	Participant's age	Length of interview (h:m:s)
Mark Bridges	Drag Kings[3], Drag Queens	37 years	61	01:33:54
Amalia Socute	Drag Queens	32 years	57	01:06:35
Max	Drag Kings	22 years	49	00:45:00
Feey	Tunten	21 years	43	01:01:24
The Godmother	Drag Queens	18 years	42	00:47:42
Espresso Martina	Tunten	18 years	38	00:41:30
Rhonda Realness	Tunten	14 years	32	01:16:38
Draginator	Drag Queens	7 years	25	00:13:20
Cherish Chocolate	Drag Queens	5 years	36	00:45:15
Mistress Alice Viado	Drag Queens	4 years	28	00:40:52
Cherry Chapstick	Drag Queens	4 years	26	00:43:34
Shantay	Drag Queens	3 years	25	00:35:03

to organizations with publicly available contact details (Siegessäule, go drag!, Trash Deluxe). After that, we contacted queens who were new to the scene, arriving in the 2000s, as well as the first Berlin Drag Queens of the 1990s. We included participants from all major drag subgroups in Berlin: queens that follow the US style drag promoted by RuPaul and those who were part of the Tunten movement. We did not include performers who identify as doing Travestie as well as Ballroom activities, because those cultures have been described as separate from the drag scene by our participants.

Seven participants were interviewed online via Zoom; five preferred to have the interview at home. This offered additional insights into their lived realities. Interviews were conducted in German or English, depending on the preferred language of the participant. After opening the interview with 'grand-tour' questions (McCracken, 1988), we moved on to talk about the participant's path through drag culture. Finally, we asked for influential events and legitimation in Berlin. As our first themes emerged, we revised the interview guide accordingly to better fit the research question. All interviews were transcribed and later coded.

Our interview data is supplemented by ongoing engagement in queer cultural activities and personal interest by the first author. The first author has been a member of the audience at drag shows, engaging in a queer association and consuming drag-related media formats since 2015. This broader understanding serves as a fruitful base for data collection as well as analysis (McRobbie, 2016).

Data analysis

We analysed our data through a hermeneutic iterative approach (Belk et al, 2013). At first, each of us coded the data separately for important events in the drag scene. The results were 20 events that had significantly shaped the drag scene in Berlin. We included events that were connected to drag subcultures such as Tunten and Drag Queens, but not events in Ballroom or Travestie, as our interviewees reported them to be remote from the drag scene. In a second step, we took the identified events and complemented them with previous research. The result was a chronological timeline (Figure 5.1). In the third step, we were interested in the legitimation mechanism. For this focus, we took the chronological timeline with the interviews and coded for previously defined legitimation mechanisms (such as normative and cultural-cognitive) and for emerging mechanisms (conflict and rivalry, collaboration and acceptance, unity and diversity).

Findings

To understand legitimation processes in the Berlin drag scene, we studied the scene as it changed from 1977 to 2022. We found that legitimacy can spill

Figure 5.1: Significant events in the Berlin drag scene 1977–2022

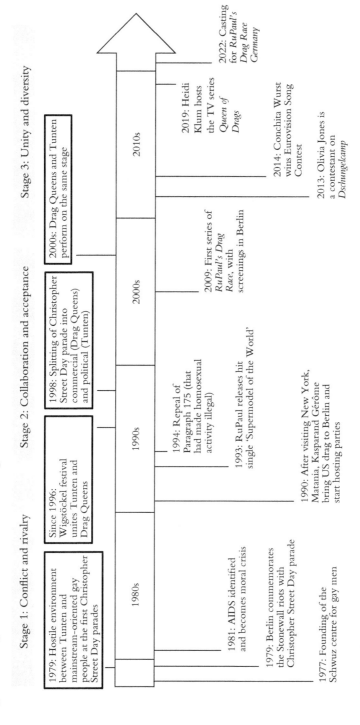

Note: The timeline is based on previous research and emerging themes from this study.

over from more legitimate to less legitimate actors, presented in an event timeline that includes three phases (Figure 5.1). In Stage 1, conflict and rivalry, the Berlin drag community is highly dived into the less legitimate Tunten and the more legitimate Drag Queens, who exist and perform separately from each other. In Stage 2, collaboration and acceptance, Tunten and Drag Queens perform together and legitimacy spills over. In Stage 3, unity and diversity, Tunten enjoy greater legitimacy, which continuously spills over from Drag Queens.

Stage 1: Conflict and rivalry – the clash between Drag Queens and Tunten

At this initial stage, the Berlin drag scene was scattered into different subgroups. The two largest were the less legitimate Tunten and the more legitimate Drag Queens. These two groups existed and performed separately from each other. The division between the groups was characterized by their different approaches to performance and aesthetics and their perceived alignment with the larger society. Drag Queens were known for their sophisticated commercial performances that followed traditional drag aesthetics. They enjoyed a higher level of legitimacy than Tunten due to their adherence to these traditional aesthetics, more refined performances and their reflection in mainstream media or entertainment spaces. In contrast, Tunten did not embody the typical highly glamorous and refined aesthetic. Instead, they were known for their bold appearances and politically charged performances that did not adhere to traditional glamorous aesthetics. Their make-up was considered untidy and their voices were loud and shrill and shook the audience. Feey, a Tunte, says: 'The idea of the Tunte is not to represent a woman, but simply to celebrate femininity in the male body. That is, the Tunte does not care that the make-up fits and that the hairstyle is always 100 per cent correctly styled!' Instead of solely entertaining the audience, Tunten used their performances to draw attention to pressing political issues. Thus, Tunten were regarded as more radical or subversive, which led to their marginalization within both the larger society and the drag scene itself.

The legitimacy divide between these two subgroups was exacerbated by the overarching goal of the Berlin gay community at the time. Many participants sought to gain legitimacy from the general public. They desired acceptance and wanted to be perceived as 'normal' individuals who happened to diverge from the average citizen only in their sexuality. 'The gay motto was: "We all want to be perceived as normal. We are gay, but apart from that, we are just like you!"' (Feey, Tunte). Many members of the Berlin gay community feared that the association with Tunten, who were seen as more radical and unconventional, would hinder the broader gay community's efforts to achieve this normalcy and societal acceptance. This perception arose because, in the eyes of the general public, Tunten were often associated with the broader gay community.

Fearing that this would cast the entire scene in an illegitimate light, the Berlin gay scene tried to suppress Tunten and keep a distance from them. This was especially evident in public appearances, such as at the Christopher Street Day celebrations. Many gay participants denounced Tunten as 'not normal' and shouted to ask them what they were even doing there. 'We were told, "Faggots out" and "Tunten shouldn't run along the parade"' (Feey, Tunte).

In response to this marginalization and desire for political expression, the Tunten organized a separate, more political version of the Christopher Street Day parade. This division between a more commercial parade (led by the Drag Queens) and a more political parade (led by the Tunten) reflected the broader split within the Berlin drag scene and the struggle for legitimacy and acceptance among its diverse subgroups. The Tunten parade was described as having a strong political emphasis. Participants used this platform to express their activism and draw attention to important social and political issues. Their parade activities were likely infused with provocative and subversive elements, reflecting their desire to challenge the status quo and push for societal change. The focus was not just on entertainment but also on making statements and advocating for marginalized communities.

The simultaneous occurrence of two parades, one led by Tunten and the other by Drag Queens, created a significant dilemma within the Berlin drag scene. Members of the drag scene were faced with the challenge of choosing between aligning themselves with the more political and radical Tunten or the glamorous and commercial Drag Queens. This divide not only separated them physically at different events, it also led to heated discussions and conflicts when they encountered each other.

The following quote from Rhonda Realness (who belongs to the Tunten) illustrates the tensions between the two groups: 'It used to be said that all the Tunten trannies stink; they all look like shit; and then we said back, "And you Drag Queens just don't have a message. I'd rather stink than let my whole scene down like that."' There was a perception by Drag Queens that Tunten did not uphold traditional drag aesthetics, while the criticism aimed at the Drag Queens was that they lacked a meaningful message and were more focused on entertainment without addressing pressing political issues.

This dilemma reflected a broader clash of ideologies and goals within the Berlin drag scene at that time. On one hand, Tunten sought to use their platform to advocate for social and political change, embracing a more provocative and confrontational approach. On the other hand, Drag Queens aimed for mainstream acceptance and legitimacy by adhering to conventional drag aesthetics and entertaining the audience. The conflict between these two groups was not just about the style of performance but also about the larger vision for the drag scene. The Tunten criticized the Drag Queens for being politically inactive and neglecting the community, whereas the Drag Queens found faults in Tunten's deliberately 'untidy' and esoteric artistic expressions. Some members of the drag community felt torn between the desire to push for societal change and political activism, even though it meant not conforming to mainstream beauty standards, and the aspiration to gain wider acceptance and recognition by adhering to traditional glamour and entertainment.

Although the more legitimate Drag Queens and the less legitimate Tunten usually attended different events at that time, they engaged in heated discussions when encountering one another. For instance, at the CSD parade in 1998, mainstream-oriented gays called the police over the Tunten truck at the parade in 1998. Subsequently, the Tunten left the parade. The tensions and debates between Tunten and Drag Queens created a complex and challenging environment for the Berlin drag scene, with individuals grappling with their identities as performers and activists in a changing socio-political landscape.

Stage 2: Collaboration and acceptance – the coming together of Drag Queens and Tunten

In this phase, collaboration between the previously divided subgroups of more legitimate Drag Queens and less legitimate Tunten began to grow. This sense of collaboration and mutual acceptance contributed to a more unified, but at the same time diverse, drag community in Berlin. Performers worked together towards common goals, leading to a legitimacy spillover from Drag Queens to Tunten. This section of the chapter outlines the development of the Berlin drag scene through the example of two events that were important for the growing-together of Tunten and Drag Queens: the Wigstöckel festival and developments at the SchwuZ club.

The first Wigstöckel in 1996 was a significant event in the history of the Berlin drag scene. It provided a space where all kinds of gender performances were welcomed and celebrated and so the festival became a symbol of inclusivity and acceptance, challenging traditional notions of drag and successively transcending earlier animosities. Drag performers, regardless of their style, approach or perceived legitimacy, were encouraged to participate and showcase their artistic expressions. The festival aimed to bring together different subgroups of drag performers on one stage, specifically the more legitimate Drag Queens and the less legitimate Tunten. In the climate of heated arguments between Tunten and Drag Queens, this was revolutionary.

For years, there were efforts to bring the two scenes of Tunten and Drag Queens together. I helped organizing a series of events called Wigstöckel. ... Basically, a couple of New York Drag Queens organized an open-air festival in America called Wigstock, where a lot of people, a lot of drags, from all over the world performed, and that was one of the first drag festivals; that was an event where we always tried to put different people together, the Drag Queens and the political Queens [Tunten], and the trans people and the non-binary performers. That was one of the events that brought a lot of people together that otherwise wouldn't be on stage together. (Feey, Tunte)

As Feey elaborates, the festival was established with the aim of breaking down the barriers that had previously separated the Drag Queens and the Tunten. For the first time, Tunten and Drag Queens shared the spotlight, performing side by side. These joint performances created opportunities for broader audiences to witness the diversity of drag and appreciate the different approaches to drag performance, breaking stereotypes and prejudices that had previously divided the drag scene. Thereby, the Wigstöckel festival created opportunities for mutual understanding and appreciation.

The active involvement of more established performers in events that showcased the diversity of drag helped to build bridges between the subgroups and foster a supportive atmosphere for less legitimate actors (such as Tunten) to gain wider recognition. As the definition of drag evolved, the boundaries between the subgroups started to blur, allowing for greater acceptance of different drag expressions. The once strictly separate subgroups began to engage in supportive and cooperative interactions. This created mutual understanding and appreciation, which ultimately led to a legitimacy spillover from Drag Queens to Tunten. This legitimacy spillover marked a shift in the dynamics of the drag scene, promoting further collaboration and cooperation between previously divided subgroups and contributing to a more inclusive and accepting drag community in Berlin. This was groundbreaking and revolutionary at the time, considering the historical division between the two subgroups. In summary, the festival played a crucial role in fostering unity, collaboration, and a legitimacy spillover between the two groups.

SchwuZ is another pivotal place that has significantly contributed to the legitimacy spillover from Drag Queens to Tunten. SchwuZ is one of Berlin's oldest and most important gay clubs (founded in 1977). According to interviewee Cherish Chocolate (Drag Queen), this venue has served as a vital epicentre for Berlin's drag community, providing a dedicated space where performers from different drag subgroups can come together and showcase their talents. SchwuZ's inclusive policy fosters an atmosphere of cooperation, cross-pollination of ideas, and a sense of community among drag artists. It thus represents another 'coming together' of the once divided subgroups.

The SchwuZ has been in Berlin for a very long time. It's the biggest gay club in Berlin, or maybe they would say queer club. I would describe it as an epicentre for Berlin's drag scene. It's the place where, when a famous drag queen is coming, where she would perform, but they also have a lot of local Tunten performers. I guess SchwuZ is a place where these two scenes meet. But it leans more towards the Tunten side because it's a Tunten establishment. It's an important place in the history of Berlin's modern drag scene, I think. (Cherish Chocolate, Drag Queen)

In SchwuZ, both sides of the drag divide began to collaborate and support each other's artistry, which was a groundbreaking shift considering the historical animosities and conflicts between the two subgroups. That organizers of the club allowed formerly despised Drag Queens to take to the stage in their safe space speaks for the genuine effort of Tunten to settle the argument and consolidate the scenes. By allowing Drag Queens to perform in their place, the Tunten demonstrated their commitment to inclusivity and acceptance, thus contributing to the legitimacy spillover. Drag Queen fans from the general public then increasingly visited the club to enjoy their favourite drag shows. So, through association with more legitimate Drag Queens and shared performances on the same stage, Tunten performers started to gain more legitimacy themselves.

As Drag Queens and Tunten performed together and shared resources at SchwuZ, the boundaries between the subgroups continued to blur. This cross-pollination of talents and experiences helped to challenge traditional drag norms, expand the understanding of drag performances and foster greater acceptance of different drag expressions. Audiences witnessed the diversity of the drag scene first-hand, breaking down stereotypes and prejudices that had previously divided the drag community.

So, the opening of SchwuZ to Drag Queens was a transformative event that played a significant role in the growing-together of Tunten and Drag Queens in Stage 2 of the legitimation process in the Berlin drag scene. By providing a space where the subgroups could perform side by side and share their unique artistic expressions, SchwuZ fostered a sense of community, cooperation and legitimacy spillover. The club's inclusive policy and the willingness of both sides to embrace each other's performances marked a revolutionary shift in the dynamics of the drag scene, promoting collaboration and acceptance between previously divided subgroups. By performing alongside Drag Queens, Tunten were able to associate themselves with established performers who already enjoyed mainstream acceptance and popularity. This association helped blur the lines between the subgroups and contributed to elevating the status of Tunten within the drag scene and for the general public. Where they had argued and denounced each other's legitimacy in Stage 1, the groups now shared stages and resources, such as at the SchwuZ club and the Wigstöckel festival and thus legitimacy.

According to Suchmann (1995), legitimation is a perception that an entity acts in congruence with social norms. The events described here exemplify the growing-together of Tunten and Drag Queens in Stage 2, collaboration and acceptance, and led to a more inclusive and accepting drag community in Berlin. Less legitimate Tunten were able to associate themselves with the more established Drag Queens, and, in turn, benefit from their legitimacy. Tunten, in turn, opened their venue, the SchwuZ club, to Drag Queens, whereby additional legitimacy gradually spilled over from the Drag Queens to the Tunten. The Tunten gained more recognition and acceptance within the drag scene, and their unique contributions were increasingly valued and appreciated. This spillover of legitimacy marked a significant shift in the Berlin drag scene, leading to a more diverse community of performers working together towards common goals.

As Stage 2 progressed, the Berlin drag scene became more cohesive, with performers recognizing the strength in their diversity. The once-heated debates and tensions between Tunten and Drag Queens gradually subsided as they learned to appreciate each other's unique contributions to the drag scene. This newfound unity set the stage for the next phase in the evolution of the Berlin drag scene, where the legitimacy spillover would continue to play a significant role.

Stage 3: Unity and diversity – the fusion of Drag Queens and Tunten

Unity and diversity describe the current atmosphere in the Berlin drag scene, which is characterized by collaboration and mutual acceptance between Tunten and Drag Queens. In Stage 3, the efforts to bring together the two groups have been successful. Drag Queens and Tunten respect and accept each other. Collaborations are not exceptions, but the norm. Instead of insulting each other, Tunten and Drag Queens praise each other's performances. They watch each other's shows and take part in parades together. Coherent with this close contact, Tunten and Drag Queens take elements of each other's style and integrate it into their own aesthetics. This indicates a significant shift from the situation in Stage 1, where both groups openly insulted each other. Some performers have even changed their identification to not being exclusively Tunte or Drag Queen, but a mix of both.

> We have always had the political claim that the Drag Queens did not have. So, I may not deny the Drag Queens completely. Barbie Breakout [a Drag Queen] is a very big HIV activist, but others take no position publicly. I would say, in any case, I started as a trash-Tunte and I don't really want to give up this trash, because I think it still has a twist. I also still have this claim that you should see that it's a man, even if I have evolved a lot in the direction of glamour, because I don't see myself

like that. I don't disguise my voice, I don't have breasts, I don't shave my legs that often, I don't tape my eyebrows, I don't do padding. So, I would say I'm a glamour Tunte, the Tunte is still there. (Rhonda Realness, Tunte)

Rhonda gives us details about the mix of Tunten and Drag Queen styles in the modern drag scene. She talks about the Drag Queen Barbie Breakout, who chose to be politically active and campaign on HIV issues. Previously, Drag Queens did not express political opinions because it might be a threat to their wider acceptance and commercial success. Currently, many commercial companies hire LGBTQ+ performers for marketing campaigns, especially during Pride Month, a celebration of visibility for the LGBTQ+ scene. Thus, a Drag Queen's decision to be politically active does not necessarily, today, stand against their goal of being commercial.

In the new climate of exchange and mutual inspiration, Tunten have borrowed elements from Drag Queen performances too. Rhonda explains that, influenced by Drag Queens, her performances are more glamorous than before, but she makes a point of retaining many elements that connect her with her identity as a Tunte. This includes using her own voice, instead of changing it to a tone that the audience would connect more with a woman. Additionally, she does not use prosthetics, such as breasts or padding. Padding, in the drag scene, is a filling material with which performers emulate their chosen body structure. Most commonly, padding is used to create a rounder figure around the hips. Drag Queens often shave their legs and usually tape their eyebrows and draw over them. Rhonda chooses not to do these things, in order to still look like a man. Even though she has changed elements of her style towards a more glamorous version, she is still rooted in her identity as a Tunte. She calls herself a glamour Tunte, signifying the combination of features. This reveals the result of the spillover process in Stage 2, collaboration and acceptance. Whereas in Stage 1, there were aesthetic rules for performers of either Tunten or Drag Queens, now there is a free field to play with inspirations. Instead of rigid structures, there is fluidity. This diverse style of doing drag is encouraged by organizers of drag events. For example, Drag Queens that organize drag shows explicitly seek a diverse line-up. Cherish Chocolate, Drag Queen and hostess, describes how she encourages diverse styles of drag:

In Berlin, the freedom of being or doing drag any way you want is pretty much alive and well and very much encouraged. I definitely want to encourage it in my shows, because I am a cis white gay man in a dress and I invite other performers – I don't want to see only white drag performers.

Where in the first stage, there were clear categories of doing drag that were conflicting with each other, now performers have the freedom to integrate whatever they want into their performances. Drag Queens may add a political element, and Tunten may lean towards the commercial side. Additionally, Cherish Chocolate talks about her own identity as a cis white gay man in a dress. (Cisgender is defined as the identification with the gender that was assigned at birth. The contrasting concept is transgender.) Cherish explicitly talks about not just inviting other cis white male performers. Thus, other performers could belong to Tunten or Drag Queens; they might be cis or transgender, white or people of colour; male, female or have a non-binary gender identity. They do not represent different factions of a rigid scene, rather an ever-evolving mix that makes the drag scene very interesting. Although individual styles may be ephemeral, the cohesion between all groups is very strong: 'I find we have gone from different camps to one big community, of course there are still the different camps but they work more with each other than against each other now' (Rhonda Realness, Tunte).

Although the boundaries between the different groups of the drag scene have not dissolved fully, the situation widely differs from the conflict and rivalry of Stage 1. Drag Queens and Tunten collaborate closely. Their identification as one community makes obsolete any efforts to denounce each other. Instead of actively working against each other, they can now share resources and achieve a better situation for all members of the scene. Most importantly, the legitimacy of Tunten has changed drastically since Stage 1. Although sometimes appearing in mainstream media, they used to be laughed at, not laughed along with. Through the collaboration with legitimate Drag Queens, Tunten have experienced a shift towards higher legitimacy themselves. Instead of being the laughing matter, Tunten can take centre stage and throw the best punchlines themselves: 'What's actually happening is that Tunten are no longer the laughing matter. That's what's tipped over. When drag performers appear on TV, they are now the style icons or the ones with the best lines' (Feey, Tunte).

In summary, the Tunten subgroup has experienced a large shift in legitimacy in recent decades. Prior to the 1990s, political Tunten were not legitimate. After the appearance of commercial and legitimate Drag Queens, the two subgroups fought each other (Stage 1: conflict and rivalry). In the early 2000s, efforts were made to bring the two groups together (Stage 2: collaboration and acceptance), which resulted in a spillover of the Drag Queens' legitimation. Tunten started to perform together with Drag Queens in the same spaces and they were associated more with each other. This led to Stage 3, unity and diversity, where both perform together and enjoy legitimacy. Drag Queens exploit the Drag Queen hype and generate large revenue by taking opportunities for commercial campaigns. This allows them to organize events at which they invite Tunten on stage as well. Through this, a large audience comes into contact with Tunten. The audience can enjoy the Tuntens' subversive performances embedded into Drag Queens' entertainment schedule and are more likely to enjoy it. Thereby, legitimacy from Drag Queens spills over and Tunten performers become more legitimate themselves.

Discussion and conclusion

Earlier scholars have identified several processes on how legitimation happens. Entities can be legitimated by one or more authorities (Meyer and Scott, 1983), through a four-stage process (Johnson et al, 2006), through capitalizing (Coskuner-Balli and Thompson, 2013), through congruence with regulative, normative and cultural-cognitive frameworks (Scott, 1995), and through territorialization (Humphreys, 2010). Our analysis reveals that, inside the Berlin drag scene, the interaction between the subgroups of Tunten and Drag Queens is directly linked to their legitimacy. While previous research has highlighted that entities are legitimated by one or more authorities (Meyer and Scott, 1983), it does not explain what happens if there is more than one entity that is being legitimated. This chapter shows that legitimacy from closely related groups can spill over. We further show that legitimation can occur through resolving a conflict between a legitimate and illegitimate group. While earlier research has found that legitimacy diffuses (Johnson et al, 2006), which creates a possibility for conflicts, these conflicts have not been researched. Through resolution of a conflict between an illegitimate and a legitimate group, the former can attain more legitimacy. Coskuner-Balli and Thompson (2013) found that formerly illegitimate practices can become legitimate, but they do not put the illegitimate actor in an active role. Our analysis reveals that an illegitimate actor can attain more legitimacy by growing closer to legitimate actors. Thus, our study shows, the illegitimate actor can start the process of legitimation through collaboration with legitimate actors. We call this transfer of legitimacy from the more legitimate actor to the less legitimate one spillover.

Our analysis also reveals that legitimation can happen through an illegitimate entity that transfers into a legitimate space. Other research has shown what happens when an illegitimate actor takes up space that they did not before – this is what Humphreys (2010) calls territorialization. However, we did not know what might happen when legitimate spaces were frequented by illegitimate actors. Our study shows that legitimacy can spill over from legitimate spaces to less legitimate actors.

This chapter has explored the processes of legitimation in the Berlin drag scene. The findings from our study shed light on the complex dynamics of legitimation within the scene, where legitimacy has spilled over from a more legitimate group – Drag Queens – to a previously less legitimate subgroup – Tunten. The chapter highlights three stages in this legitimation process: Stage 1, conflict and rivalry; Stage 2, collaboration and acceptance, leading to legitimacy spillover, and Stage 3, unity and diversity – the current stage, in which the drag scene is more cohesive and inclusive.

In Stage 1 the Berlin drag scene had distinct subgroups, with Drag Queens enjoying higher legitimacy due to their adherence to traditional, mainstream aesthetics and commercial performances, while Tunten were perceived as more radical, unconventional and politically charged, leading to their marginalization. The broader gay community's desire for mainstream acceptance contributed to the marginalization of Tunten, and the groups invested in working against each other, further lowering Tunten legitimacy in larger society.

In Stage 2, the drag scene experienced a transformation as collaboration between Drag Queens and Tunten grew, leading to a legitimacy spillover from the former to the latter. Events like the Wigstöckel festival and the opening up of the SchwuZ club played vital roles in fostering unity, cooperation and acceptance between the two subgroups. As Drag Queens and Tunten performed together, shared resources and exchanged ideas, the boundaries between the subgroups blurred, challenging traditional drag norms and expanding the understanding of drag performances. This legitimation spillover marked a significant shift in the dynamics of the drag scene, promoting a more inclusive and accepting community.

In Stage 3, the drag scene reached its current state of cohesiveness and mutual acceptance. Tunten and Drag Queens now respect and collaborate with each other, with different styles of drag performances being encouraged and embraced. Performers have the freedom to use elements from both subgroups and create unique expressions of drag. This reflects a marked departure from the rigid divisions of Stage 1, with the drag scene evolving into a more fluid and diverse community.

The legitimation process observed in the Berlin drag scene has broader implications for understanding legitimation dynamics in other contexts as well. By choosing to lean on Suchman's (1995) definition of legitimation as a process rather than a fixed resource or condition, our study provides insights into how legitimacy can be acquired and transferred between groups in different settings.

Our findings contribute to the existing literature on legitimation processes in consumer culture theory and the context of the drag scene. This chapter demonstrates that legitimation is not a static phenomenon but a dynamic process that can change over time. It also highlights the role of collaboration, mutual acceptance and shared experiences in fostering legitimacy spillover between groups.

In conclusion, our study adds to the understanding of legitimation processes by revealing how legitimacy can spill over from one group to another. The case of the Berlin drag scene illustrates the transformation from conflict and division to collaboration and inclusivity. By examining the stages of this legitimation process, we have highlighted the importance of cooperation, acceptance and embracing diversity in creating a more cohesive and legitimate community. The findings offer valuable insights for researchers and practitioners interested in understanding and fostering legitimation processes in various social and cultural contexts.

Limitations

It is important to note that the information provided here is specific to the historical context of the Berlin drag scene until 2022. Drag scenes in different cities and regions may have their own unique dynamics and divisions. Additionally, the landscape of drag and LGBTQ+ acceptance has evolved significantly over the years, and what may have been perceived as legitimate or illegitimate in the past might not hold the same significance in contemporary contexts.

For the study in this chapter, performers and organizers from various backgrounds have been interviewed. Although they are diverse and represent different times and groups of the Berlin drag scene, more interviews may uncover new emerging themes related to legitimacy. Another limitation may be the first author's involvement in the Berlin LGBTQ+ scene. This proved to be an advantage when it came to finding interview partners and understanding the context, but yields potential for personal bias. The second author was not involved in the LGBTQ+ scene and therefore challenged these assumptions. Additionally, this study focuses on the conflict between Tunten and Drag Queens in Berlin. Future research may be dedicated to other groups such as Drag Kings or Travestie performers, or emerging styles such as creature drag or the intersection of drag and the Ballroom scene.

Notes

[1] "Drag Queen" is capitalized in this chapter in order to emphasize Drag as part of the moniker and self-image of one subgroup of performers. Whereas "drag", without the capitalization, refers to the act of doing drag, encompassing all drag styles.

[2] The name is a combination of Wigstock, a popular US drag festival that parodied the iconic Woodstock music festival, and the German word Stöckel, which means stiletto heels.

[3] A Drag King is defined as an individual who engages in genderqueering performances that play with masculine identities. This is in contrast to Drag Queens or Tunten, who focus on embodying female identities.

References

Balzer, C. (2004) 'The Beauty and the Beast: Reflections about the socio-historical and subcultural context of Drag Queens and "Tunten" in Berlin', *Journal of Homosexuality*, 46(3–4), 55–71, doi.org/10.1300/J082v46n03_04

Balzer, C. (2005) 'The Great Drag Queen Hype: Thoughts on cultural globalisation and autochthony', *Paideuma: Mitteilungen Zur Kulturkunde*, 51: 111–131, jstor.org/stable/40341889

Belk, R., Fischer, E. and Kozinets, R. (2013) *Qualitative Consumer and Marketing Research*, London: Sage.

Berger, P.L. (1997) 'The Four Faces of Global Culture', National Interest, 49: 23–30.

Brennan, N. and Gudelunas, D. (eds) (2017) Rupaul's Drag Race and the Shifting Visibility of Drag Culture: The Boundaries of Reality TV, Cham: Palgrave MacMillan.

Bryant, R. (2021) 'Which City has the Best Drag Culture?', Quora [online forum post], Available from: quora.com/Which-city-has-the-best-drag-culture [Accessed 9 June 2024].

Coskuner-Balli, G. and Thompson, C. (2013) 'The Status Costs of Subordinate Cultural Capital: At-home fathers' collective pursuit of cultural legitimacy through capitalizing consumption practices', *Journal of Consumer Research*, 40(1): 19–41, doi.org/10.1086/668640

Dowling, J. and Pfeffer, J. (1975) 'Organizational Legitimation: Social values and organizational behavior', *Pacific Sociological Review*, 18(1): 122–136.

Feldman, Z. and Hakim, J. (2020) 'From Paris is Burning to #dragrace: Social media and the celebrification of drag culture', Celebrity Studies, 11(4), 386–401, doi.org/10.1080/19392397.2020.1765080

Humphreys, A. (2010) 'Semiotic Structure and the Legitimation of Consumption Practices: The case of casino gambling', *Journal of Consumer Research*, 37(3): 490–510, doi.org/10.1086/652464

Johnson, C., Dowd, T. and Ridgeway, C.L. (2006) 'Legitimation as a Social Process', *Annual Review of Sociology*, 32: 53–78.

Lawrence, T. (2011) 'Listen, and You Will Hear All the Houses that Walked There Before: A history of drag balls, houses and the culture of voguing', in S. Baker (ed) *Voguing and the House Ballroom Scene of New York City 1989–92*, London: Soul Jazz Books.

Lewis, R. (2019) 'RuPaul reveals history of the term "drag" proving every day is a school day', Metro, [online] 28 September, Available from: metro.co.uk/2019/09/28/rupaul-reveals-history-term-drag-proving-every-day-school-day-10823869 [Accessed 13 March 2024].

Martin, J. (1994) 'The Organization of Exclusion: The institutionalization of sex inequality, gendered faculty jobs, and gendered knowledge in organizational theory and research', *Organization*, 1(2): 1–431.

McCormack, M. and Wignall, L. (2022) 'Drag Performers' Perspectives on the Mainstreaming of British Drag: Towards a sociology of contemporary drag', *Sociology*, 56(1): 3–20, doi.org/10.1177/00380385211008387

McCracken, G. (1988) *The Long Interview*, London: Sage.

McRobbie, A. (2016) 'Towards a Sociology of Fashion Micro-enterprises', *Sociology*, 50(5): 934–948.

Menze, N. (2023) *Ökonomisches Handeln in der Drag- und Tunten-Szene*, Münster/New York: Waxmann.

Meyer, J.W. and Scott, W.R. (1983) 'Centralization and the Legitimation Problems of Local Government', in J.W. Meyer and W.R. Scott, *Organizational Environments: Ritual and Rationality*, Beverly Hills: Sage, pp 199–215.

Oloew, M. (2008) 'Christopher Street Day: Erinnern, demonstrieren und feiern', Tagesspiegel, [online] 27 June, Available from: tagesspiegel.de/berlin/erinnern-demonstrieren-und-feiern-1669450.html [Accessed 10 June 2024].

Rubin, G. (2018) 'Esther Newton Made Me a Gay Anthropologist', *American Anthropologist*, 120(4): 852–853.

Scarlett Gasque (2023) 'The Intertwined History of Drag and Burlesque', Scarlett Gasque [blog], Available from: scarlettgasque.com/blogs/blog/the-intertwined-history-of-drag-and-burlesque [Accessed 13 March 2024].

Scott, W.R. (1995) *Institutions and Organizations: Ideas and Interests*, Thousand Oaks, CA: Sage.

Suchman, M.C. (1995) 'Managing Legitimacy: Strategic and institutional approaches', *The Academy of Management Review*, 20(3), 571–610, doi.org/10.2307/258788

Trott, B. (2020) 'Queer Berlin and the Covid-19 Crisis: Politics of contact and ethics of care', *Interface: A Journal for and About Social Movements*, 12(1): 88–108.

Workman, N.T. (2020) Drag Incorporated: The Homonormative Brand Culture of RuPaul's Drag Race [Master's thesis], Old Dominion University.

6

Non-Fan Perception and Behaviour towards Cosmetics Endorsed by Drag Celebrities in Japan

Bình Nghiêm-Phú

Celebrities are people whose names and images are recognized by many audiences in their fields of expertise. Due to their famousness and popularity, celebrities are paid or invited to participate in business and prosocial activities as endorsers to spread information to their audiences and to affect the audiences' behaviours (Brooks, 2021). Fans' trust in and relationship with a celebrity can positively affect their perception of, and intention and loyalty towards a business (Kim et al, 2014; Chung and Cho, 2017).

Celebrities, however, are people. In addition to the fans and lovers, there are anti-fans and haters of celebrities (Liew, 2019) who are driven by their anger, hatred, jealousy and ethical standpoint. They may condemn or boycott the celebrities and their endorsed businesses (Braunsberger and Buckler, 2011). Celebrities often avoid these attacks rather than engage in responding activities (Kilvington and Price, 2019), and rarely is a celebrity's involvement with their anti-fans investigated (Chin, 2019). In addition, the relationship between fans and anti-fans is hardly examined as these two groups are often separate (Hill, 2015).

Although there are small gaps in the literature, researchers have thoroughly examined the celebrity/fan/anti-fan triangle. They have largely neglected, however, the non-fans or the neutral and ordinary consumers (Gray, 2003). Noticeably, the attitudes of non-fans differ from those of fans and probably anti-fans (Gamboa and Gonçalves, 2014; Delmar et al, 2018), and together the non-fans can form a desirable and influenceable market segment of potential consumers (Duffett, 2013). So, it is necessary to expand the current research portfolio to non-fan consumers, especially their attitudes toward celebrities, fans, anti-fans and endorsed businesses.

Non-fan consumers' coexistence with fans and anti-fans can be observed with regards to any celebrity, from the more conventional and acceptable ones, such as pretty female singers, to more modern and controversial ones, such as drag performers (Ellis, 2022). The controversy often comes from the public's diverse and sometimes opposite interpretations and acceptance, or not, of what is generally considered (non)stereotypical (Campana et al, 2022). Drag-queen figures, having gone against conventional norms about the male gender, cannot avoid some of this fuss. Such controversies may affect the drag queens' inducing prowess and the non-fan consumers' purchasing intentions. Nonetheless, although researchers have carefully investigated drag-related issues from a socio-psychological standpoint (Campana et al, 2022; Ellis, 2022), studies about the commercial aspects of drag queens are limited (Frankel and Ha, 2020; Mundel et al, 2022). From both the socio-psychological and commercial perspectives, drag-related topics are little known about in Japan (Lunsing, 2002; Mitsuhashi [Hasegawa], 2006). In addition, studies about drag-related beauty products and activities (Plante, 2016; Hall and de Sousa Araújo, 2019) are very scarce in this country. The gap concerning drag-related beauty products, celebrities, fans, anti-fans and non-fans, especially in Japan, needs to be addressed.

This chapter examines Japanese non-fan consumers' perceptions of drag celebrities and their behavioural intentions toward the beauty products (particularly cosmetics) that these celebrities endorse, considering the coexistence of the fans and anti-fans. Grounded in consumer psychology and supported by psychology theories in other fields, such as family psychology and educational psychology, this chapter will help enrich the literature on non-fan consumer study and provide practical implications for managing and marketing drag-endorsed beauty products.

Literature review

Drag celebrities and drag-endorsed businesses in Japan

A drag queen is often a male person who wears clothes and make-up to imitate the female figure for entertainment. The drag queen phenomenon could be seen, for example, in the early 1700s in England and become prominent in the 1960s, especially in the US (Moncrieff and Lienard, 2017). Drag queen culture was introduced to Japan in the 1990s (Tomohisa, 2008), but Japan already has a long history of female impersonation, with Kabuki male actors performing as female characters for more than three centuries (Petkova, 2019).

Many drag figures work as fashionistas and make-up artists (Willson and McCartney, 2017; Hall and de Sousa Araújo, 2019). They have fabulous outfits, pretty faces, and beautifully styled hair; some also have charming physiques (Carretta et al, 2019). Such positive images, emboldened and promoted by social media (Feldman and Hakim, 2020), enable certain drag figures to become the celebrity endorsers of several products or services, such as cosmetics (Mundel et al, 2022). For example, Trixie Mattel, a former winner of *RuPaul's Drag Race*, has her own product lines under the Trixie Cosmetics brand. Similarly, Durian Lollobrigida, a Japanese drag performer, has been endorsing cosmetics products for SABON and male salons such as Men's Brow. These drag queens are indeed celebrities and influencers, and involving them in marketing campaigns (in the form of influencer marketing or parasocial marketing), particularly those on social media platforms, can create potential benefits for businesses (Leung et al, 2022).

Today, many famous drag queens in Japan join Haus of Gaishoku, an international queer collective of performers, and appear in *Vogue Japan*, an influential fashion magazine. However, these activities and their influences are still limited compared with other celebrities. Audiences without knowledge or experience of such activities may only know about these drag-queen figures if they watch particular television programmes or follow social media sites (Feldman and Hakim, 2020). Fortunately, many people in Japan, especially the younger ones, have a positive attitude toward LGBTQ+ individuals, including drag queens (Fujita, 2018; Zhang, 2021). Thus, the power of parasocial relationships between celebrities and their followers can also be utilized here (Reinikainen et al, 2020). Education about and experiences of LGBTQ+ issues are the main reasons behind this positive approach (Zhang, 2021). The history of female impersonation may not contribute much to this experience since male kabuki performers are not considered LGBTQ+ characters (Zhang, 2016).

Despite some positive observations about the public's perceptions of drag celebrities (Fujita, 2018; Frankel and Ha, 2020; Zhang, 2021), there has been little examination of or distinguishing between the opinions of drag fans, anti-fans and non-fans. Canavan (2021), for example, found that some drag performers' fans appreciated their celebrities' authenticity, but Bishop et al (2014) revealed that some drag queens' anti-fans associated these figures with negatively valenced or aversive attributes. These pieces of information, although limited, suggest that drag queens' fans and anti-fans are thinking and feeling like other celebrities' lovers and haters (Kim et al, 2014; Chung and Cho, 2017). Meanwhile, non-fans' attitudes toward drag celebrities also need to be better investigated.

Celebrity images, celebrity relationships and consumer behaviours

Although the literature about drag-queen celebrities and their fans, anti-fans and non-fans is minimal, that involving ordinary celebrities can provide some helpful insights, particularly from a psychological standpoint. Specifically, the images of a celebrity perceived by consumers have essential impacts on their perceptions of the products and services associated with that celebrity and their intention to purchase or consume those products and services (van der Veen and Song, 2014). A similar psychological mechanism can also be observed for consumer-celebrity image congruence, which is the compatibility of a consumer's self-image and a celebrity's public image (Paul and Bhakar, 2018). Celebrity image, however, does not have a consistent structure. For example, Choi and Rifon (2007) proposed four dimensions of celebrity image: genuineness, competence, excitement and sociability. Alternatively, Mann et al (2023) suggested seven dimensions: social and ethical responsibility, life and style, professional capabilities, perspective towards celebrity's profession, orientation towards fans, attractive physique and public image.

From another perspective, the images of the peers (the fans and anti-fans) also have specific influences on consumers' perceptions and behaviours. In the field of body-image research, for example, it was observed that female college students compared their appearances with those of their peers, and appearance comparison can have an indirect impact on their eating behaviours (van den Berg et al, 2002). In research on fashions and trends, it was discovered that followers looked up to trendsetters to help decisions on the purchase and use of certain products, especially novel and brand items (Ramadan et al, 2018). Consumers' perceptions and behaviours, under peer influence, seem to reflect their attitudes toward social inclusion, a symbolic value that they may search for in their reference to consumer groups (Dyen and Sirieix, 2016).

In addition to celebrity and peer images, relationships among other people (celebrities vs fans, celebrities vs anti-fans, and fans vs anti-fans) may also affect consumers' perceptions and behaviours. As evidence, parents' relationships can influence children's current behaviours and future intimate expectations (Goldberg and Carlson, 2014). The impact can be extended to the school context, especially children's school engagement and performance (Mo and Singh, 2008). Performance can further be strengthened or weakened by the relationship between parents and teachers (Hughes and Kwok, 2005). Moreover, relationships among peers in the same context may affect the students' perceptions of the school environment and their behaviours (Forber-Pratt et al, 2014). People surrounding an individual, nonetheless, can be close or distant. Previous research has confirmed that the impacts of the closer peers are greater than the further ones (Xue and Silk, 2012), but proximity is a relative concept, and distant peers can quickly become close via social networking sites on the internet. Activities of celebrities, fans and anti-fans are apparent there (Kim and Kim, 2020). Then, the relationships among them may impact the perceptions and behaviours of non-fans.

Figure 6.1: Drag and other celebrity endorsers' impact on non-fan consumer intentions

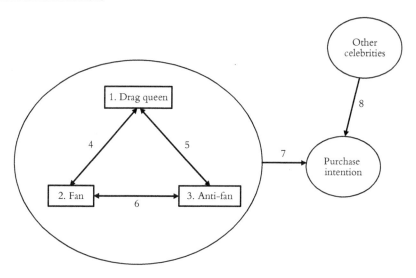

In summary (Figure 6.1), the non-fans, the ordinary-but-influenceable consumers, can have specific perceptions of the celebrities (empirical study's topic 1), the fans (topic 2) and the anti-fans (topic 3), and the relationships between the celebrities and the fans (topic 4), the celebrities and the anti-fans (topic 5) and the fans and the anti-fans (topic 6). All these perceptions may affect the consumers' intention to purchase the products endorsed by the celebrities (topic 7). However, in the drag queens' case, other celebrities may also participate in the endorsement process, so the influence of non-drag celebrities should also be considered (topic 8).

Method

Interview method and content

Given its exploratory nature, this study employed a qualitative approach with direct interviews as the data-collection method (Fujii, 2018). Two research questions (RQ) guided the interviews:

RQ1: How do non-fan consumers perceive drag celebrities, fans and anti-fans (part 1, topics 1–3), and the relationships among them (part 2, topics 4–6)?

RQ2: How do these perceptions affect the non-fan consumers' behavioural intentions toward the cosmetics products endorsed by the drag celebrities (topics 7–8)?

Eight topics were primarily emphasized during the interviews (Figure 6.1). The first group of interview topics (1 to 6) involved RQ1, while the second group (topics 7 and 8) was associated with RQ2. Interview topic 8 – the impact of non-drag celebrities on consumer purchase intention of the same or similar products – was included to have a comparative insight into drag celebrities' role.

Sample and sampling method

In this study, young consumers (Generation Z, born between the late 1990s and the early 2010s) were targeted as prospective participants. As explained earlier, non-fan consumers have few chances to meet drag celebrities in person, but they can receive information from and images of these celebrities via social media platforms, such as Instagram, Twitter and YouTube. Compared with the older generations, younger consumers have more opportunities to be exposed to these information sources (Goldring and Azab, 2021), making them suitable for this study.

Given this condition, Japanese students taking the consumer-behavior-related class and seminar at a public university with which the researcher was affiliated at the study time were purposefully approached (Palinkas et al, 2015). This sampling method aimed to generate a certain level of homogeneity in the respondents' answers to form an initial unified understanding of the research topic. Students who themselves were consumers and were studying consumer behaviour were relevant for this purpose.

The sampling and interviews took place in May 2022. All the students were informed about a study concerning cosmetic products, without mentioning the drag topic to avoid preconceived bias (Luse et al, 2018) and were asked to participate if they were interested. Eighteen students responded and gave their consent to be interviewed for about 30 minutes. The drag issue was introduced during the interview, and none of the students felt uncomfortable or awkward enough to drop out. One student, however, later identified themselves as a fan of drag queens, so their interview was consequently excluded. Of the remaining students, 16 were undergraduate, and one was a graduate. Similarly, 16 were female, and one was male (Table 6.1). The graduate student and the male student were kept in the sample to ensure a certain degree of heterogeneity (Palinkas et al, 2015). Nine of the 17 students did not know about drag queens before the interviews. This point further ascertained that, although the public's attitudes towards LGBTQ+ people, in general, have been improving in Japan in recent years (Fujita, 2018; Zhang, 2021), many people, including young and educated individuals, were still unaware of or had little knowledge about many specific issues of the community.

Since this study was theory-based, a sample of 17 participants was appropriate (Francis et al, 2010). However, no new information appeared in the last interview, so the point of data saturation was met (Saumure and

Table 6.1: Profiles of non-fan interview participants

Participant number	Biological sex	Student status	Cosmetics use history (from)	Prior knowledge of drag queens
1	Female	Undergraduate 3rd year	Middle school 3rd year	Yes
2	Female	Undergraduate 3rd year	High school 1st year	Yes
3	Female	Undergraduate 3rd year	University 1st year	No
4	Female	Undergraduate 3rd year	University 1st year	Yes
5	Female	Undergraduate 3rd year	High school 2nd year	No
7	Female	Undergraduate 3rd year	University 1st year	No
8	Female	Undergraduate 3rd year	High school 3rd year	No
9	Female	Undergraduate 3rd year	High school 1st year	Yes
10	Female	Undergraduate 3rd year	University 1st year	No
11	Female	Undergraduate 3rd year	University 1st year	Yes
12	Female	Undergraduate 3rd year	Middle school 2nd year	No
13	Female	Undergraduate 2nd year	High school 1st year	No
14	Female	Graduate 1st year	University 1st year	Yes
15	Female	Undergraduate 2nd year	Middle school 2nd year	Yes
16	Female	Undergraduate 2nd year	High school 2nd year	No
17	Female	Undergraduate 2nd year	High school 1st year	Yes
18	Male	Undergraduate 2nd year	High school only	No

Note: Participant 6 was excluded because they identified as a drag-queen fan during the interview.

Given, 2008). The interview process, therefore, stopped here. After the interviews, each participant was given a gift card for ¥500 (about $4).

Interview process and data analysis

The interviews began with the participants describing their history of using cosmetic products. The interviews then continued by introducing drag queens and their existence in the cosmetics world. While some participants knew about drag queens, others did not. In the latter cases, the participants were asked to search on a computer or smartphone for information involving these figures, notably pictures or videos. After ascertaining that all participants now had some knowledge about drag queens, the interviews proceeded with the topics mentioned in Figure 6.1. The interviews were semi-structured (Fujii, 2018). The sequence of the questions varied between the interviews, according to the information flow and the atmosphere.

All the interviews were held in Japanese to ensure their consistency. The interviews were recorded and transcribed simultaneously on Google

Pixel 6. The transcriptions were later transferred to Microsoft Word files. Next, the researcher and an assistant manually analysed the interview contents together following a deductive process (Elo and Kyngäs, 2008). Again, the interview points depicted in Figure 6.1 served as the coding scheme. The answers on each topic were highlighted using the comment function in Microsoft Word. After that, each topic's contents were further analysed to identify the most significant patterns to present in this chapter. An agreement between researcher and assistant was reached to ensure the reliability of the analysis (Kassarjian, 1977). Finally, the researcher translated the relevant quotes from Japanese to English. An independent researcher fluent in both languages helped to check and approve the translations to guarantee their appropriateness.

Findings

Research question 1, part 1: Non-fan consumers' perceptions of drag queens, fans and anti-fans

Topic 1: Perceptions of drag queens

The participants' perceptions of drag queens had two primary aspects: external and internal. Externally, drag queens wore bold and eye-catching make-up and dresses. They had excellent make-up skills and beautiful skin and looked extraordinary and glamorous. Internally, drag queens were seen to be people with a lot of courage and self-confidence. They had optimistic personalities, strong mentality and did not hesitate to do or express what they wanted. The perceptions of all participants, therefore, were positive.

> Drag queens are men, but they wear make-up like women; they wear fancy dresses, and their make-up is very flashy. I cannot do that kind of fancy make-up. However, other people must have negative opinions about what they [the drag queens] are like? Many people in my grandmother's generation probably wonder why men wear make-up. Still, I think it is lovely to be able to do what you like even though there are opinions like that. (Participant 4)

> I think it is incredible that you value your individuality. I respect that. I think it is good. I do not have any disgust because I think it is [their, the drag queens'] personality. It does not really matter what gender the person is. I think that is part of it. (Participant 12)

The participants showed total acceptance of drag queens, both their external features and internal personalities. They proudly set themselves apart from the older generation regarding their understanding of the LGBTQ+ community in general and drag queens in particular.

Topic 2: Perceptions of drag queens' fans

From the participants' perspective, fans of drag queens could be anybody, regardless of gender or sexuality. However, some participants thought these fans would be young or in the same generation as the drag queens. They believed the fans liked the unusual and bold make-up styles that drag queens wore. Overall, their perceptions were somewhat vague.

I think I am the kind of person who feels that way. It thinks it is interesting. [The fans have a] young image. (Participant 3)

Isn't it someone who dares to be that kind of passionate person? Also, it is fun to see such bright people, and I think those people are the fans. I guess it depends on the age of the person promoting the products [the drag queen]. If [the drag queens are] in their 30s, for example, I think people in their 30s will imitate [the drag queens'] make-up style because it is easy to fit. (Participant 17)

As the quotes demonstrate, images of drag queen fans were based mostly on their external attributes. The internal characteristics were missing.

Topic 3: Perceptions of drag queens' anti-fans

Most participants described anti-fans of drag queens as older people living in rural areas who did not encounter queer people or receive education about LGBTQ+ issues and probably were not using social media. The anti-fans were seen to dislike those who were different from the norms, such as men wearing make-up or LGBTQ+ individuals. In other words, they carried prejudices and stereotypes of drag queens.

Some participants thought the anti-fans disapproved of drag queens because they were unconfident and jealous. Some anti-fans felt happy in hating or opposing other people, especially those contradicting society at large and its standards.

Anti-fans are people with prejudice. They may think it is weird for men to wear make-up, or they do not have a good image of LGBTQ+ people. They may live in the countryside, so their prejudice may be substantial. They may have the same age as my mother [40 years old or above]. (Participant 8)

I think many people older than me have prejudices against LGBTQ+ people. So, I think that [anti-fans] are people in the older age group. (Participant 12)

So, the images of anti-fans were more explicit than those of the fans. Ideas of the external and internal elements were prominent, like those of the drag queens themselves.

Research question 1, part 2: Non-fan consumers' perceptions of drag queens', fans' and anti-fans' relationships
Topic 4: Perceptions of drag-fan relationships

According to the participants, the relationships between drag queens and their fans could primarily be described by the latter supporting the former by buying the products the drag queens endorsed, writing positive comments about them, promoting their images and following their social media. Some participants mentioned that the fans might want to meet the drag queens in person and make-up or dress like them.

> I think the most common thing is that if you can empathize with that person and understand their feelings, you may become a fan. You are in the same situation and have the same experience or something. I think some fans are watching with a supportive attitude, and many fans say that they like [the drag queens] simply because they like their style and way of thinking. After all, they want to meet them, and they like the products they recommend because they [the products] are excellent, and they like them [the drag queens]. (Participant 5)

> I think I will buy the ones I am introduced to if I am a fan. Or I will imitate the way [the drag queen] looks. I guess that is how it is [the relationship between a drag queen and a fan]. (Participant 10)

Overall, the impression of this relationship was active and cheerful, represented by the specific supportive actions (so, a conative image; Arroyo et al, 2023). This impression was formed based on the supportive nature of the association.

Topic 5: Perceptions of drag-anti-fan relationships

Unlike supportive fans, anti-fans tended to present their opposing attitudes towards drag queens primarily by posting negative comments on social media. Several participants thought that the drag queens should just ignore or endure these behaviours. Others expected drag queens to reply to the comments and defend themselves. In some instances, participants believed they should consult the police or other authority to prevent unpleasant incidents.

> I imagine that [the anti-fans would] write nasty things on SNS [social networking services]. With something you did not know about until

now [the relationships between drags and anti-fans], you may only see part of the issue or the wrong part, and you may have a negative image. I have seen [celebrities] say things back to anti-fans, but they do not do anything most of the time. (Participant 11)

Do you know the recent incident [a reality gameshow participant killed herself after being bullied online]? People may think that others do not know their names or faces, so they can write nasty things. Their negative comments may lead to suicide. I think it would be better to tighten the law or something. If you [a drag queen] can stand it [the negative comments], I think it would be good to be an influencer with a brave heart to fight. But if you cannot do it, you will appeal to them. (Participant 18)

In this case, some of the participants emphasized the conative or behavioural aspect of the impression they had of anti-fans (Arroyo et al, 2023). They seemed not to accept the unsupportive, and thus toxic, nature of the celebrity-anti-fan relationships and expected some real responses to prevent and stop this unhealthiness.

Topic 6: Perceptions of fan-anti-fan relationships

Most participants thought there could be fights or quarrels between drag queens' fans and anti-fans at some point in time. However, it was expected that these incidents would primarily happen on social media platforms.

Again, the participants' impression of this relationship involved the conative image element (Arroyo et al, 2023), but the impression was less vivid than the relationship between drag queens and anti-fans: 'Fans and antis do not seem to get too involved. If you force them, they will probably get into a fight. But if there is nothing, they will probably be in different worlds' (Participant 7); '[The interactions between fans and anti-fans may happen on] SNS or the comments section of YouTube' (Participant 14).

Research question 2: Impacts of non-fan consumers' perceptions on their intentions toward drag-endorsed cosmetics

Topic 7: Perceptions of the impact of drag queens

Some participants said that, since their make-up styles were not as bold and dramatic as those of drag figures, they would not buy drag-endorsed cosmetics. Other participants said they would consider buying a cosmetic product endorsed by a drag queen if that product (such as base make-up, foundation, eyeshadow, eyebrow make-up, skincare) matched their wants or needs. The match could be decided upon based on product quality and applicability, as well as, potentially, product–celebrity image congruence. In addition, several participants were willing to buy cosmetics promoted by drag queens because they trusted these figures and felt it appropriate to support them.

> I tend not to buy things I cannot use daily. I do not think I will buy them [the cosmetics with] fancy colours. (Participant 1)

> [I may buy] eye make-up. Or eyeliner. As for the image of a drag queen, the people I have seen put a lot of effort into eye make-up so the make-up does not fall off. So, it is convincing. (Participant 11)

> I will buy a product if the [drag queen] provides sufficient information, and I think it is good. It is not about what this person is wearing, but if they tell me the good points, I will buy it. (Participant 12)

These outcomes were confirmed by the participants' perceptions of drag queens, fans and anti-fans and their relationships mentioned in the previous topics. Specifically, since the impressions that drag queens created and promoted differed from those of the majority population, particularly these university students, the purchase of drag-endorsed cosmetics might be limited. The students' perceptions of drag queens' fans and anti-fans did not affect the participants' behavioural intentions: 'Perhaps I will not imitate [drag queens' make-up style]. Also, there are not [many chances] to see this kind of make-up' (Participant 3); 'I like to watch, but I do not want to do it myself' (Participant 7).

The relationships between drag queens, fans and anti-fans nonetheless might impact the participants. Some students admitted that their perceptions of drag queens and their intentions toward drag-endorsed products might be improved or strengthened if these relationships were positive, and worsened if they were negative. Other students explained that their attitudes (perceptions and behaviours) would not change regardless of these relationships. If they wanted to buy a product and/or support a drag queen, they would buy the product endorsed by that celebrity. It should be noted that the knowledge of relationships between drag-queens, fans and anti-fans was primarily based on what was seen on social media: 'The optimistic people take [the comments] positively, but the pessimistic people do not. Therefore, I do not see a lot of other people's comments' (Participant 9); 'I look at things [the drag queen] is advertising, normally' (Participant 15). These observations suggest that non-fans' perceptions and behaviours were closer to those of fans and that their perceptions and behaviours were further from these of the anti-fans.

Topic 8: Perceptions of the impact of non-drag celebrities

Except for Participant 18, who had only used colour-correcting cream for acne when they were in high school, the remaining students had different opinions about celebrity endorsement. Eight participants thought that non-drag celebrities might have more impact because their style was closer to the public. Four participants believed that drag celebrities' influences might be more substantial because their make-up techniques and effects were excellent and the detailed information they provided made them reliable. The final four saw no difference in the impact of the two types of celebrity.

My preference for this fancy make-up is not as much as regular products promoted by other idols. (Participant 16)

Maybe [I will buy a product promoted by] a drag queen. I think they are excellent. I guess that is why I am going to buy it. (Participant 9)

Regardless of the person [the endorser], I will decide [whether to buy based] on the product. (Participant 5)

Discussion

Previous research in Japan and other contexts revealed that images of drag queens were mostly positive, particularly among younger consumers (Fujita, 2018; Frankel and Ha, 2020; Zhang, 2021). The study here confirms this observation and extends it to the cosmetic products category. Drag queens, wearing bold, bright and flamboyant make-up, were ideal for endorsing such products (product-celebrity image congruence; Yoo and Jin, 2015). They also provided information, detail and advice about these products to a larger audience. However, not all items promoted by drag figures were suitable for ordinary consumers, probably due to their limited daily usability. So, the match between a product and consumers' needs was a prominent issue, in addition to that of the celebrity-consumer match (Paul and Bhakar, 2018).

Previous research also found that celebrity images significantly impacted consumers' attitudes (van den Berg et al, 2002). This chapter's study in Japan verified that this fact also applied to drag-queen celebrities. However, their power was limited compared with non-drag celebrities, even with a product category that fitted well with their images (cosmetics). By contrast, the inclusion of fans and anti-fans, as part of user imagery (images of the prototypical users of a product) and a component of brand associations (Parker, 2009), did not have much impact. It appears that peer images, although essential in evaluating body image and fashion trends (van den Berg et al, 2002; Ramadan et al, 2018), are not significant here. The non-fans are probably not as inclined to be included in specific consumer groups as the fans (Dyen and Sirieix, 2016).

Consumers' perceptions of the relationships between drag celebrities, fans and anti-fans did affect their attitudes. In particular, younger consumers, who were familiar with social networking services, were more prone to being affected by incidents among the stakeholders mentioned here (Goldring and Azab, 2021). Their awareness and knowledge of these occurrences might change their perceptions and behaviours. The effects of other people's relationships were not only apparent in the family and school environments (Forber-Pratt et al, 2014), they were also noticeable in the commercial context, particularly in Japan and in the field of cosmetic products.

Theoretical implications

The non-fan consumers of a celebrity-endorsed product are an essential part of the market (Gray, 2003). Although their attitudes toward the product and the endorser may differ from those of fans or anti-fans (Gamboa and Gonçalves, 2014; Delmar et al, 2018), they seem to be closer to the fans than the anti-fans, with positive and supportive approaches and potential behaviours. In many cases, the unconnectedness between the fans and anti-fans may not affect the non-fans, but, in specific circumstances, the unfriendliness and rivalry between them may impact non-fans. Meanwhile, non-involvement between a celebrity and their anti-fans (Chin, 2019; Kilvington and Price, 2019), may help to cool down potentially negative incidents and seems to be a suitable strategy in fan and anti-fan management.

The celebrity figures that are the focus of this study – the drag queens in Japan – have, to a degree, found acceptance in the general public, especially younger audiences. Nevertheless, the profiles of Japanese drag queen celebrities may take different forms than the literature has so far suggested (Choi and Rifon, 2007; Mann et al, 2023). Specifically, according to the young respondents interviewed in this study, their impressions of drag queens have two primary components. There are some external features concerning how the queens dress and make-up, and some internal attributes characterize the queens' personalities and mentality. Moreover, the non-fan participants also had some ideas about the relationships between the celebrities, the fans and the anti-fans. This seems to be the first time such a relationship was visualized. The perception of the relationships essentially reflected the conative element, while the fundamental elements of the image, the cognitive and affective ones (the thoughts and feelings) (Arroyo et al, 2023), were missing.

NON-FAN PERCEPTION AND BEHAVIOUR

Practical implications

After more than three decades (Tomohisa, 2008), more people in Japan now can recognize and accept drag queens. Famous drag queens can be endorsers of cosmetics – products that fit well with their external and internal characteristics (Yoo and Jin, 2015). Some cosmetics companies in Japan are engaging more drag queens to promote their products, especially items that a wider general public could use, in the same way that foreign businesses were already doing (Willson and McCartney, 2017; Hall and de Sousa Araújo, 2019). The drag queens' exceptional make-up designs, precision and skill, their authenticity and apparent honesty in information provision are strong points that could be utilized.

Since the drag-queen-fan population may only be a small number of (potential) consumers, the remaining market, in which the non-fans dominate (Gray, 2003) must also be adequately managed. Fortunately, the attitudes of many non-fans towards celebrities are similar to those of fans, so companies can confidently continue their celebrity-endorsement plans, including parasocial marketing tactics (Reinikainen et al, 2020). However, they must make vigorous attempts to control the relationships between celebrities, fans and anti-fans. Harmful incidents, especially on social networking sites, can spread to and affect other potential consumers. Celebrity crisis management (Colapinto and Benecchi, 2014) should therefore include fan and anti-fan control strategies to make these more meaningful and effective. Since the non-fans have more impressions with conative image elements, certain actions will appeal to these consumers and promote a sense of trust.

Conclusion

As celebrity figures, drag queens present positive and suitable images to serve as commercial endorsers of cosmetics products. Drag-queen fans tend to be younger members of the population, while anti-fans are older. Otherwise, according to the Japanese non-fans interviewed for this study, images of these two groups are relatively vague. In addition, the relationships between drag celebrities and their fans and anti-fans often occur across social networking platforms. The positiveness or negativeness of these relationships may affect a proportion of potential non-fan consumers, but not all of them. Moreover, the influence of drag-queen celebrities may be weaker than non-drag celebrities within the same product category.

These outcomes help to enrich the literature on drag queens and non-fan consumers in Japan. However, the study has some limits. First, the respondents were young consumers. The opinions of older consumers were not heard. Second, almost all respondents were female. The perceptions of male consumers were largely neglected. Third, the results were primarily grounded in non-fans' subjective perceptions. A comparison among the drag-queen celebrities, fans, anti-fans and non-fans belonging to different groups of age, occupation and location was missing. Fourth, only one product group was examined. The situations in other product categories remain unknown.

Future research can expand on the work of this chapter by including other participants, especially, in Japan, older, male and rural non-fan consumers. Researchers may target non-fan consumers of other products or in other countries to have more insights into this market force. In addition, they could adopt a quantitative method to establish the relative significance of drag and non-drag celebrities' impacts on consumers' attitudes. These outcomes would further enhance the knowledge about drag queens and non-fan consumers.

References

Arroyo, C.G., Barbieri, C., Knollenberg, W. and Kline, C. (2023) 'Can Craft Beverages Shape a Destination's Image? A cognitive intervention to measure *pisco*-related resources on conative image', *Tourism Management*, 95: 104677, doi.org/10.1016/j.tourman.2022.104677

Bishop, C.J., Kiss, M., Morrison, T.G., Rushe, D.M. and Specht, J. (2014) 'The Association Between Gay Men's Stereotypic Beliefs about Drag Queens and their Endorsement of Hypermasculinity', *Journal of Homosexuality*, 61(4): 554–567, doi.org/10.1080/00918369.2014.865464

Braunsberger, K. and Buckler, B. (2011) 'What Motivates Consumers to Participate in Boycotts: Lessons from the ongoing Canadian seafood boycott', *Journal of Business Research*, 64(1): 96–102, doi.org/10.1016/j.jbusres.2009.12.008

Brooks, S.K. (2021) 'FANatics: Systematic literature review of factors associated with celebrity worship, and suggested directions for future research', *Current Psychology*, 40: 864–886, doi.org/10.1007/s12144-018-9978-4

Campana, M., Duffy, K. and Micheli, M.R. (2022) '"We're All Born Naked and the Rest is Drag": Spectacularization of core stigma in RuPaul's Drag Race', *Journal of Management Studies*, 59(8): 1950–1986, doi.org/10.1111/joms.12848

Canavan, B. (2021) 'Post-Postmodern Consumer Authenticity, Shantay You Stay or Sashay Away? A netnography of RuPaul's Drag Race fans', *Marketing Theory*, 21(2): 251–276, doi.org/10.1177/1470593120985144

Carretta, R.F., Szymanski, D.M. and DeVore, E. (2019) 'Predictors of Disordered Eating and Acceptance of Cosmetic Surgery among Drag Queen Performers', *Body Image*, 30: 64–74, doi.org/10.1016/j.bodyim.2019.05.006

Chin, B. (2019), 'When Hated Characters Talk Back: Twitter, hate, and fan/celebrity interactions', in M.A. Click (ed) *Anti-Fandom: Dislike and Hate in the Digital Age*, New York: New York University Press, pp 291–314.

Choi, S.M. and Rifon, N.J. (2007) 'Who is the Celebrity in Advertising? Understanding dimensions of celebrity images', *The Journal of Popular Culture*, 40(2): 304–324, doi.org/10.1111/j.1540-5931.2007.00380.x

Chung, S. and Cho, H. (2017) 'Fostering Parasocial Relationships with Celebrities on Social Media: Implications for celebrity endorsement', *Psychology & Marketing*, 34(4): 481–495, doi.org/10.1002/mar.21001

Colapinto, C. and Benecchi, E. (2014) 'The Presentation of Celebrity Personas in Everyday Twittering: Managing online reputations throughout a communication crisis', *Media, Culture & Society*, 36(2): 219–233, doi.org/10.1177/0163443714526550

Delmar, J.L., Sánchez-Martín, M. and Velázquez, J.A.M. (2018) 'To be a Fan is to be Happier: Using the eudaimonic spectator questionnaire to measure eudaimonic motivations in Spanish fans', *Journal of Happiness Studies*, 19: 257–276, doi.org/10.1007/s10902-016-9819-9

Duffett, M. (2013) 'Introduction: Directions in music fan research: Undiscovered territories and hard problems', *Popular Music and Society*, 36(3): 299–304, doi.org/10.1080/03007766.2013.798538

Dyen, M. and Sirieix, L. (2016) 'How Does a Local Initiative Contribute to Social Inclusion and Promote Sustainable Food Practices? Focus on the example of social cooking workshops', *International Journal of Consumer Studies*, 40(6): 685–694, doi.org/10.1111/ijcs.12281

Ellis, J.R. (2022) 'A Fairy Tale Gone Wrong: Social media, recursive hate and the politicisation of Drag Queen Storytime', *The Journal of Criminal Law*, 86(2): 94–108, doi.org/10.1177/00220183221086455

Elo, S. and Kyngäs, H. (2008) 'The Qualitative Content Analysis Process', *Journal of Advanced Nursing*, 62(1): 107–115, doi.org/10.1111/j.1365-2648.2007.04569.x

Feldman, Z. and Hakim, J. (2020) 'From Paris is Burning to #dragrace: Social media and the celebrification of drag culture', *Celebrity Studies*, 11(4): 386–401, doi.org/10.1080/19392397.2020.1765080

Forber-Pratt, A.J., Aragon, S.R. and Espelage, D.L. (2014) 'The Influence of Gang Presence on Victimization in One Middle School Environment', *Psychology of Violence*, 4(1): 8–20, doi.org/10.1037/a0031835

Francis, J.J., Johnston, M., Robertson, C. et al (2010) 'What is an Adequate Sample Size? Operationalising data saturation for theory-based interview studies', *Psychology and Health*, 25(10): 1229–1245, doi.org/10.1080/08870440903194015

Frankel, S. and Ha, S. (2020) 'Something Seems Fishy: Mainstream consumer response to drag queen imagery', *Fashion and Textiles*, 7: 23, doi.org/10.1186/s40691-020-00211-y

Fujii, L.A. (2018) *Interviewing in Social Science Research: A Relational Approach*, New York: Routledge.

Fujita, A. (2018) 'Changing Perception of LGBT People through Performances: Theater and television in America and in Japan', *Journal of Urban Culture Research*, 17: 54–71, doi.org/10.14456/jucr.2018.10

Gamboa, A.M. and Gonçalves, H.M. (2014) 'Customer Loyalty through Social Networks: Lessons from Zara on Facebook', *Business Horizons*, 57(6): 709–717, doi.org/10.1016/j.bushor.2014.07.003

Goldberg, J.S. and Carlson, M.J. (2014) 'Parents' Relationship Quality and Children's Behavior in Stable Married and Cohabiting Families', *Journal of Marriage and Family*, 76(4): 762–777, doi.org/10.1111/jomf.12120

Goldring, D. and Azab, C. (2021) 'New Rules of Social Media Shopping: Personality differences of U.S. Gen Z versus Gen X market mavens', *Journal of Consumer Behaviour*, 20(4): 884–897, doi.org/10.1002/cb.1893

Gray, J. (2003) 'New Audiences, New Textualities: Anti-fans and non-fans', *International Journal of Cultural Studies*, 6(1): 64–81, doi.org/10.1177/1367877903006001004

Hall, D. and de Sousa Araújo, T. (2019) 'Digital Fashion Communication: The influence of Instagram-queer-makeup artists and their future developments on the industry', in N. Kalbaska, T. Sádaba, F. Cominelli and L. Cantoni (eds) *Fashion Communication in the Digital Age, FACTUM 2019*, Cham: Springer, pp 3–8.

Hill, A. (2015) 'Spectacle of Excess: The passion work of professional wrestlers, fans and anti-fans', *European Journal of Cultural Studies*, 18(2): 174–189, doi.org/10.1177/1367549414563300

Hughes, J. and Kwok, O.M. (2005) 'Influence of Student-Teacher and Parent-Teacher Relationships on Lower Achieving Readers' Engagement and Achievement in the Primary Grades', *Journal of Educational Psychology*, 99(1): 39–51, doi.org/10.1037/0022-0663.99.1.39

Kassarjian, H.H. (1977) 'Content Analysis in Consumer Research', *Journal of Consumer Research*, 4(1): 8–18, doi.org/10.1086/208674

Kilvington, D. and Price, J. (2019) 'Tackling Social Media Abuse? Critically assessing English football's response to online racism', *Communication & Sport*, 7(1): 64–79, doi.org/10.1177/2167479517745300

Kim, M. and Kim, J. (2020) 'How Does a Celebrity Make Fans Happy? Interaction between celebrities and fans in the social media context', *Computers in Human Behavior*, 111: 106419, doi.org/10.1016/j.chb.2020.106419

Kim, S.S., Lee, J. and Prideaux, B. (2014) 'Effect of Celebrity Endorsement on Tourists' Perception of Corporate Image, Corporate Credibility and Corporate Loyalty', *International Journal of Hospitality Management*, 37: 131–145, doi.org/10.1016/j.ijhm.2013.11.003

Leung, F.F., Gu, F.F. and Palmatier, R.W. (2022) 'Online Influencer Marketing', *Journal of the Academy of Marketing Science*, 50: 226–251, doi.org/10.1007/s11747-021-00829-4

Liew, H. (2019) 'Anti-fandom in the Xiaxue Empire: A celebrity blogger and her haters', *The Journal of Fandom Studies*, 7(3): 261–277, doi.org/10.1386/jfs_00004_1

Lunsing, W. (2002) 'What Masculinity? Transgender practices among Japanese "men"', in J.E. Roberson and N. Suzuki (eds) *Men and Masculinities in Contemporary Japan: Dislocating the Salaryman Doxa*, London: Routledge, pp 20–36.

Luse, A., Townsend, A.M. and Mennecke, B.E. (2018) 'The Blocking Effect of Preconceived Bias', *Decision Support Systems*, 108: 25–33, doi.org/10.1016/j.dss.2018.02.002

Mann, B.-J.S., Parmar, Y. and Ghuman, M.K. (2023) 'A New Scale to Capture the Multidimensionality of Celebrity Image', *Global Business Review*, 24(6): 1251–1275, doi.org/10.1177/0972150920919599

Mitsuhashi, J. [Hasegawa, K.] (2006) 'The Transgender World in Contemporary Japan: The male to female cross-dressers' community in Shinjuku', *Inter-Asia Cultural Studies*, 7(2): 202–227, doi.org/10.1080/14649370600673847

Moncrieff, M. and Lienard, P. (2017) 'A Natural History of the Drag Queen Phenomenon', *Evolutionary Psychology*, 15(2), np, doi.org/10.1177/1474704917707591

Mo, Y. and Singh, K. (2008) 'Parents' Relationships and Involvement: Effects on students' school engagement and performance', *RMLE Online*, 31(10): 1–11, doi.org/10.1080/19404476.2008.11462053

Mundel, J., Close, S. and Sasiela, N. (2022) 'Drag Dollars: Making room for queens in advertising', in N. Brennan and D. Gudelunas (eds) *Drag in the Global Digital Public Sphere: Queer Visibility, Online Discourse and Political Change*, London: Routledge, pp 89–112.

Palinkas, L.A., Horwitz, S.M., Green, C.A., Wisdom, J.P., Duan, N. and Hoagwood, K. (2015) 'Purposeful Sampling for Qualitative Data Collection and Analysis in Mixed Method Implementation Research', *Administration and Policy in Mental Health and Mental Health Services Research*, 42: 533–544, doi.org/10.1007/s10488-013-0528-y

Parker, B.T. (2009) 'A Comparison of Brand Personality and Brand User-Imagery Congruence', *Journal of Consumer Marketing*, 26(3): 175–184, doi.org/10.1108/07363760910954118

Paul, J. and Bhakar, S. (2018) 'Does Celebrity Image Congruence Influences Brand Attitude and Purchase Intention?', *Journal of Promotion Management*, 24(2): 153–177, doi.org/10.1080/10496491.2017.1360826

Petkova, G.T. (2019) *Female Deities, Dancers and Impersonators: From Mythology to Kabuki Theatre*, Sofia: Haini Publishing.

Plante, R.F. (2016) 'Putting on Makeup', in D.D. Waskul and P. Vannini (eds) *Popular Culture as Everyday Life*, New York: Routledge, pp 165–174.

Ramadan, Z., Farah, M.F. and Dukenjian, A. (2018) 'Typology of Social Media Followers: The case of luxury brands', *Marketing Intelligence & Planning*, 36(5): 558–571, doi.org/10.1108/MIP-01-2018-0039

Reinikainen, H., Munnukka, J., Maity, D. and Luoma-aho, V. (2020) '"You Really are a Great Big Sister": Parasocial relationships, credibility, and the moderating role of audience comments in influencer marketing', *Journal of Marketing Management*, 36(3–4): 279–298, doi.org/10.1080/0267257X.2019.1708781

Saumure, K. and Given, L.M. (2008) 'Data Saturation', in L.M. Given (ed) *The Sage Encyclopedia of Qualitative Research Methods*, Thousand Oaks, CA: Sage, pp 195–196.

Tomohisa, S. (2008) 'Drag Queens and their Bodies: Transferring the Transformative Performance from the United States to Japan [ドラァグ「クイーンとその身体:合衆国から日本への移転と変容をめぐって]', paper presented at the 42nd Japanese Society of Cultural Anthropology Annual Meeting, 31 May – 1 June 2008, Kyoto University, Kyoto, Japan.

van den Berg, P., Thompson, J.K., Obremski-Brandon, K. and Coovert, M. (2002) 'The Tripartite Influence Model of Body Image and Eating Disturbance: A covariance structure modeling investigation testing the mediational role of appearance comparison', *Journal of Psychosomatic Research*, 53(5): 1007–1020, doi.org/10.1016/S0022-3999(02)00499-3

van der Veen, R. and Song, H. (2014) 'Impact of the Perceived Image of Celebrity Endorsers on Tourists' Intentions to Visit', *Journal of Travel Research*, 53(2): 211–224, doi.org/10.1177/0047287513496473

Willson, J. and McCartney, N. (2017) 'A Look at "Fishy Drag" and Androgynous Fashion: Exploring the border spaces beyond gender-normative deviance for the straight, cisgendered woman', *Critical Studies in Fashion & Beauty*, 8(1): 99–122, doi.org/10.1386/csfb.8.1.99_1

Xue, M. and Silk, J.B. (2012) 'The Role of Tracking and Tolerance in Relationship among Friends', *Evolution and Human Behavior*, 33(1): 17–25, doi.org/10.1016/j.evolhumbehav.2011.04.004

Yoo, J.W. and Jin, Y.J. (2015) 'Reverse Transfer Effect of Celebrity-Product Congruence on the Celebrity's Perceived Credibility', *Journal of Promotion Management*, 21(6): 666–684, doi.org/10.1080/10496491.2015.1055046

Zhang, E. (2016) 'Memoirs of a GAY! Sha: Race and gender performance on RuPaul's Drag Race', *Studies in Costume & Performance*, 1(1): 59–75, doi.org/10.1386/scp.1.1.59_1

Zhang, T. (2021) 'Male Homosexuality in Japan from the Perspective of the Younger Generation: A case study of students at a National University', *Journal of LGBT Youth*, 18(4): 360–393, doi.org/10.1080/19361653.2019.1684415

PART III

Digitizing Drag

7

Cybernetic Drag: Embodiment, Technology and Digital Drag Performance in the US during the COVID-19 Pandemic

Shayne Zaslow

The COVID-19 pandemic in 2020 and 2021 upended every facet of life – communication, daily routines, leisure time, among countless other disruptions. While virtually every industry was impacted by the pandemic, nightlife and live performance were hit particularly hard. As an art form rooted in liveness, often at LGBTQ+ bars and clubs, it is unsurprising that drag performance was greatly impacted by pandemic restrictions. Drag artists in the US tend to be gig workers, often rendering them ineligible for traditional unemployment benefits. The closures of nightlife spaces and the inability to gather safely in person resulted in a sudden and total loss of income for drag artists. The effects of COVID-19 were felt by artists collectively (Buchholz et al, 2020; Warnecke, 2020; Jeannotte, 2021), but the precarity for drag performers (compared with theatre actors, for example, who often belong to actors' unions), and lack of fallback options made the imagined future for drag during the pandemic particularly bleak. It became imperative for drag to shift, creatively, to survive pandemic closures and distancing mandates.

Drag pivoted to increasingly diverse avenues, including a foray into the digital realm beginning in late March 2020. 'Digital drag' started with real-time performances on Instagram Live and ticketed live events via streaming platforms. Initially, digital drag was a true 'make it work' moment; drag artists were in crisis with no foreseeable income, so something had to be done immediately to provide desperately needed earnings. The simplest, quickest solution was attempting to mirror the 'analogue' live, real-time, in-person performance. Yet a perfect one-to-one replica of the analogue-live performance using digital media was not feasible.[1] Technical difficulties abounded, real-time interaction was largely lost, and much of the illusory magic of drag was stripped away in the harsh overhead lighting of performers' living rooms.

When social distancing restrictions lasted longer than initially anticipated, drag had to adapt, once again, to more sustainable solutions until in-person gatherings could safely resume. Digital drag thus became less about replicating the analogue-live, and instead began to mirror music videos: highly stylized recordings using technical effects to heighten or alter embodied performance elements. In other words, digital drag became a novel performance style all its own – one which necessarily interrogates the connections and tensions between embodied art, technology, and the very premise of liveness itself. While innovative, digital drag manifested the way it did in part due to the particularities and contours of the drag marketplace itself – performers had to navigate doing pandemic-era drag in fulfilling ways, but also in ways that would sufficiently align with marketplace norms such that they would be able to feasibly support themselves throughout the lockdown.

Drawing on five years of ethnographic research on local and digital drag communities, this chapter explores how the 'digital shift' transformed drag aesthetics, embodied performance, and community networks for working drag performers. The chapter argues that the digital shift allowed for an expansive reimagining of the drag art-world marketplace in terms of aesthetics and embodiment, the boundaries of drag's live aura, how working artists support themselves, and how local drag 'does' community.

Performance art and liveness

Existing works on performance studies and liveness (Phelan, 1993; Dixon, 2007; Frith, 2007; Auslander, 2008, 2012; Holt, 2010) seek to answer two central questions: how do we define performance art, and what does it mean for a performance to be 'live'? Loosely defined, 'performance' involves the body moving with intention through space – any physical, embodied art form, from dance to theatre acting to spoken word to drag, falls under the performance umbrella.

Performance largely hinges on corporeality. It is the site of the body as the vehicle through which the performance is done that attributes to its creative potential. The body is particularly important for performance art as political resistance and critique (Piper, 1981; Muñoz, 1999; Bowles, 2011), since it creates the boundaries of the art, while simultaneously informing the nuance of resistance. Drag allows performers to engage in embodied performance in ways beyond just challenging heteronormative gender constructs (Butler, 1990, 1993). Alternative drag performers – loosely understood as those whose aesthetic choices extend beyond the highly commodified femme drag showcased on platforms like *RuPaul's Drag Race* (RPDR) – may embody monstrous characters, using elements of horror and the macabre in their performances, in part as a response to the ways they themselves have been ridiculed, marginalized, and othered by heteronormative society (Reedy, 2021). For drag artists, the body is not only the site of marginalization, but also the site of transformation – importantly, beyond gender.[2]

In her 1993 text *Unmarked*, performance theorist Peggy Phelan (1993: 4) argues that it is 'representation without reproduction', or the real-time embodiment of the performance, which makes performance art a unique art form. It is not only the boundaries of the body that confine performance art, but so too does context. There is something distinct and significant about a performance happening in a shared physical space with audience members in real time: specifically, organic liveness alongside audience-artist interaction.

Technology and increasing usage of digital media necessitates categorical distinction between performances preserved via digitized media and those happening in real time (Auslander, 2008, 2012). Yet, even with the advent of digital technologies, live performance tends to hold a premium in terms of experience, which lies in its temporally rooted, embodied non-replicability for performer and audience alike. While performances can be recorded, the act and process of experiencing them, in real space and time with others, is highly sought after and presumed superior. Certainly, a studio recording of a song is categorically distinct from a live rendition (Frith, 2007; Holt, 2010), but what can we make of less clear-cut distinctions? What does it mean, for example, to say that something is 'pre-recorded live'? When considering digitized media, particularly livestreaming platforms, the notion that liveness must happen in the same physical space is challenged. The boundaries between digital liveness and analogue liveness are blurry. A 'pre-recorded live' album, or viewing an Instagram Live video after it airs, are examples that do not fit neatly into the analogue nor the digital. As the definition of liveness continues to shift with changes in technology and its usages, scholars studying performance and liveness are left asking what, if anything, is lost (or gained) in digital as opposed to analogue liveness, for performers and for the communities in which they are embedded?

Art, technology and community

Philip Auslander's work (2008, 2012) largely attempts to debunk the idea that liveness – or the 'original' version of replicated or recorded performances – is categorically superior and more authentic than non-live iterations. These claims mean even more in the digital age as boundaries of liveness continue to blur. Importantly, the analogue-live is not necessarily more authentic than its digital counterparts; particularly in the era of COVID-19, the social world had to move to a more heavily mediated, digital environment out of public health necessity. Live performances could not happen in an analogue context without significant concern for health and safety on the part of performers, audience members and backstage/venue staff.

Classic works interrogating the intersection of art and technology (Benjamin, 1935; Horkheimer and Adorno, 1944; Lazarsfeld and Merton, 1948) argue that mechanical replication of artworks diminish their 'aura', or their authenticity and uniqueness, particularly when reproduced and consumed through mass culture. In the internet age, similar concerns arise regarding the interfacing of art with the digital world; namely that technology (or broadly, modernity) dilutes genuine artistic endeavours, stripping the unique, organic humanity from art itself. Conversely, others offer a more optimistic outlook on the fusion of art with technology. These scholars argue that digital mediums create 'genuinely new, distinct, and avant-garde' styles of performance art (Dixon, 2007: 4). In other words, technology and the digital become tools to *enhance* rather than detract from performance art.

Donna Haraway's 'A Cyborg Manifesto' (1991) underscores a key component of digital innovation in her construction of the cyborg. Haraway's cyborg imaginary extends beyond the physical boundaries of the body, envisioning how the body itself can be fused with technology to create new ways of embodiment and making art in a digital age. Pairing the movement of the body with a digitized, projected backdrop, for example, creates an entirely different sensory experience for performers and audience members due to the direct interfacing of the body with technology. Often, artistic innovation lies in its very interaction with technology – it is the lights, the usage of medium, and aesthetics that create outside-the-box artworks.

Further, fusion of the body with technology through digital platforms offers a more expansive understanding of embodiment than is afforded by a less mediatized, analogue-live environment like a bar or club. While we might imagine the digital as being distinct, separate, and oppositional to the body, research shows that digital platforms revolutionize embodiment and can mobilize and empower community ties (Horak, 2014; Cavalcante, 2016, 2018; Miller, 2017). The digital's appeal lies in the ability for users to curate the self (and the body through digital manipulation) against a society that demonizes ways of being and moving through the world, particularly for marginalized individuals. Thus, the marginalized body continues to matter in the digital realm, as it is that very marginalization that necessitates the haven that the digital world can afford – though, the digital environment can (and in some cases, does) reproduce existing inequalities in the broader social world (Barker-Plummer, 2013; Wight, 2014). A digital utopia is not guaranteed, particularly for those already facing multifaceted marginalization.

The digital does not end with the individual, however, and for groups that seek solace and camaraderie online, digital communities can be powerful vectors of connection. Often, however, digital communities are presumed to be less authentic than their analogue equivalents. The fusion of the body with technology, like Haraway's cyborg construction that sits between reality and fantasy, challenges the idea that digital communities are somehow less 'real'. The analogue-live is not just assumed superior in terms of art – it is assumed superior for social life too. Concerns about loneliness and isolation during the COVID-19 lockdown restrictions often ignored how digital communication was strengthened, and that digital communities are not only real but deeply integral to socializing in a digital age. Even since physical spaces have reopened and in-person gatherings are permitted again, the ubiquity of hybrid communities remains in both digital and analogue social life, and in art worlds.

The digital drag shift raises central questions regarding the boundaries of embodied liveness. Do digital drag shows broadcast on Twitch, with pre-recorded music-video-style performances, constitute liveness if there is a host introducing the videos in real time? Does this iteration of liveness necessarily mean that drag performance loses its aura? And can its aura only be maintained in the analogue-live, or might we reimagine an aura that considers the digital? And further, what might a digital space mean in terms of inclusion and belonging, relative to analogue spaces?

Method

During the summer of 2021, I conducted semi-structured interviews with 38 drag performers across the United States and Canada. Respondents were recruited through Instagram through snowball sampling, and ranged in age from 23 to 54, with a mean age of 30 (median of 28). About one third of respondents were full-time drag performers, meaning that drag is their sole or primary income. On average, respondents had been doing drag for 6.5 years, with one performer having 34 years of drag performance under her belt. Of the respondents, 50 per cent identified as white, 16 per cent Black, 16 per cent Latinx (including Cuban Americans), 11 per cent multiracial and 3 per cent Asian. Most performers lived on either the east or west coast of the US, though not all in urban areas.

Interviews lasted 90 minutes, on average, and were largely conducted virtually via Zoom. All interviews were recorded with respondent permission and transcribed upon completion. Participants received $50 for their time at the conclusion of the interview through electronic cash payment. Respondents are referred to by their drag name throughout the discussion of findings, with respondents' permission. All respondents were also asked about pronoun preferences when discussing their drag personas.

Digital and analogue ethnographic observations supplemented the interview data. Throughout the project's duration, I attended over 100 drag shows, both analogue and digital, as a paying audience member. Almost all (95 per cent) of the shows included at least one local performer (that is, not a *Drag Race* or *Dragula* cast member). Most analogue shows attended were in Richmond, Virginia – a mid-size city in the south-east United States with a vibrant and small, but growing, local drag scene. Demographically, Richmond is about 48 per cent white, 47 per cent Black, with the remaining 5 per cent including Asian, Latinx and other races.

I took extra care, consideration and ethical precautions in collecting data for this project and spent a cumulative five years building trust within this community. Field notes were taken during and after analogue shows, with photographic/videographic data when possible. Digital observation notes included screenshots of performances when feasible. All data (interviews and ethnographic observations) relating to drag aesthetics were thematically coded in terms of performance style (and usage, if any, of digital tools) and stylistic choices.

Findings

Existing literature argues that, among the greatest benefits of liveness – and something that cannot be fully replicated digitally – is the artistic 'aura'. Digital drag raises important questions regarding what, exactly, constitutes drag's aura. Like the physical nightclub itself, much of drag's magic loses its lustre when the lights come on at last call. A recorded version of a live nightclub performance may capture basic mechanics of the performance – the song, how the artists looked/moved/acted, the spatial configuration and so on – but does comparatively little to capture anything intangible. The overwhelming cloud of perfume that follows a performer as they enter, the way the floor shakes when they drop into a split, the smell of cash as it rains upon them, and the scent of alcohol permeating the dancefloor's wooden floorboards are all things a video cannot, and will never be able to, capture. The interactions between performer and audience, and among audience members, in shared space and time is similarly undocumentable. Drag is not an art form designed for, nor accustomed to, recording. How, then, could drag adapt to COVID-19 social distancing restrictions that made the (safe) attendance of in-person shows at bars an impossibility, and still retain its aura?

I argue that digital media created a unique opportunity for drag as art to reimagine embodiedness and reconsider its reliance on (analogue) liveness. As digital drag moved away from attempting a one-to-one analogue-live replica, *cybernetic drag* – a dynamic fusion of embodied performance with digital tools – was born, in which performers leveraged technology to create innovative performances that transcend the analogue world. The digital loosened the rigidity of aesthetic and performance expectations, allowing all drag artists (especially 'alternative' performers) an opportunity for creative expansion. Further, attempts to preserve drag's analogue aura reveal that it is less tied to its artistic practices than to its community embeddedness. Thus, the digital offers novel ways of doing community by creating more diffuse networks and relying less on physical proximity, mitigating some of the inequalities and mechanisms of exclusion present in the analogue environment.

The early days of digital drag: from bars to Instagram

Digital drag first gained traction on Instagram through the Instagram Live feature that enables users to 'go live' with one another. Early in the pandemic, performers would advertise shows through social media as they had previously done through Instagram stories or grid posts, tweets and posts on Facebook. At showtime, hosts would 'go live' and performers would join as the host introduced them. Instagram Live splits the screen between users, with host on top and performer at the bottom. Often, show hosts held up handwritten signs with performers' virtual tipping information throughout the performance. Shows tended to move quickly and rarely lasted longer than an hour.

This early era of digital drag tried as well as possible to replicate an analogue-live drag show. Stylistically, performances tended to be lip-sync and dance numbers, reminiscent of what would be seen in a standard bar or club on any given night. Hosts also attempted to replicate the analogue-live with regard to pre- and post-performance banter between performer and host. Casting practices similarly mirrored analogue shows by sticking closely to the physical places and local scenes within which the host was enmeshed.

I watched the Instagram Live era last roughly through April 2020. While it most closely approximated analogue-live shows of any digital drag medium, it highlighted the ways in which many analogue components *cannot* be replicated digitally. Rather than loud music with a bass vibrating the room, performers danced around their living rooms to tinny recordings from phone or computer speakers. Instead of spotlights and disco balls, performers were limited to (often poor) overhead lighting within their homes. Perhaps the most striking difference, however, is the audience. While audiences tuned into Instagram Live shows, performers could not interact with them nor feel their presence during the show, leaving artists with the sense of performing in their living room for nobody – no cheers, no applause, and a significant decrease in money made from tips, earned virtually rather than hand to hand.

It is no coincidence that drag performers have jokingly referred to this period as the 'cursed era' of digital drag. Technical difficulties were almost guaranteed – Instagram Live was not designed with live artistic performance in mind. Of the Instagram Live shows I personally attended, none ran smoothly without at least one technical snafu. Whether a frozen performer or host, a delayed or lost internet connection, or sound difficulties, the Instagram Live era, while a valiant effort at maintaining analogue drag performance, left a lot to be desired for performer and audience alike. Perhaps the most redeemable factor of the Instagram Live era was, ironically, its actual liveness. Performer, host, and audience all gathering at the same moment, in real time, is unique to this era of digital drag, likely due, in part, to the plethora of technical difficulties this time inevitably entailed. While many of us were just learning Zoom and other tools that became pandemic communication staples, given how rapidly drag and other in-person activities needed to adapt to the digital, it makes sense why performers would turn to familiar technological tools such as Instagram: the learning curve was minimal, and it was as close to a one-to-one, analogue-to-digital conversion as seemed feasible at the time.

Preserving the liveness of drag performance online is not exclusive to local scenes. RPDR alumni watched their gigs rapidly evaporate with the same horror as local entertainers. In response, PEG Management (manager of many RPDR alumni) put together a Digital Drag Fest with the same sense of urgency that had spawned the Instagram Live era. Digital Drag Fest's advertising focused heavily on its liveness and inability to be replicated. Each 30-minute live performance aired only once, and no performances were recorded. This was part of its special appeal – an intimate digital event with limited ticket availability, allowing audiences to see their favourite TV drag queens live in their own living room. Performances aired on streaming platform StageIt, which permitted interaction between audience and performer in real time. In addition to notifications for virtual tips sent through StageIt's platform, audience members could type messages into a chat box that performers could read on air, in real time, which created unique interactive opportunities. For example, Alaska Thunderfuck, RPDR fan favourite, performed several request-only shows using StageIt's chat box.

In part, the efforts to preserve the live aura did, in fact, result in a unique experience, as Evan Lowenstein, founder and CEO of StageIt explained (Dunn, 2020): 'I think our users are in for a treat. … We have no interest in replacing physical live events, but hopefully our service can help turn people on … to a completely new experience.' There were components of Digital Drag Fest shows that could not be replicated in the analogue world, particularly for celebrity-level drag artists who audiences rarely, if ever, interact with one-on-one outside pricey meet-and-greets. Nonetheless, Digital Drag Fest included an upcharge for a limited number of pre-show digital meet-and-greet tickets, which entailed a chat between the performer and a small group of show attendees. Instagram Live shows were always free, with the expectation only of tips for performers and hosts.

Technical issues abounded for Digital Drag Fest performances, whether spotty internet at the performers' end resulting in lag, or poor sound quality.

While these technical issues are in part humanizing (it is easy to see RPDR alumni as larger-than-life mega-celebrities, and the mishaps and organic liveness that come along with these digital performances at their homes made their humanity more apparent), the performances themselves left quite a bit to be desired. Even the very best, tech-issue-free performances still had the feeling of watching a recorded club performance on YouTube. There is an intangible lustre notably missing.

These early iterations of digital drag underscore something important about drag's digital shift: the initial efforts to preserve analogue liveness as much as possible resulted in a relatively poor digital replica. The illusory magic of drag, the allure of the transformation, was largely lost in taking performances meant for analogue-live settings and transporting them into the digital medium. Largely, performers found this early era of digital drag wedded to liveness to be artistically unfulfilling. Instagram Live was highly limiting in terms of what performers could do that would be legible (enough) on, for example, half a phone screen. The nuance and details of extravagant looks were hardly visible on a small screen, never mind with poor lighting and a busy background. Most performances took place in performers' homes, rarely against a clean background that would allow their looks to stand out.

Situating liveness as necessary to preserve in the digital realm significantly limited drag's artistic potential in the digital world and revealed the tension between embodied analogue drag and digital drag. For digital drag to be sustainable and fulfilling, it had to pivot away from analogue liveness, which cannot be seamlessly replicated digitally, and instead reconsider how the digital might offer unique opportunities for drag performance: could artists instead work with technology to innovate and elevate pandemic-era drag performances?

The evolution of digital drag illustrates the innovative artistic practices that resulted from reframing technology as an asset rather than a burden. By abandoning replication of the analogue-live, drag in the pandemic era ventured down two different avenues that proved much more successful than Instagram Live, which entailed a rethinking and reimagining of the potentiality of the digital, and COVID-safe community practices.

Preserving the analogue-live aura: drive-ins and driveways

Drag artists adapted to pandemic challenges in new ways. While some turned to the internet, others opted for continuing in-person performing that took COVID precautions seriously while still preserving the analogue experience as much as possible. Many performers expressed that, for them, audience interaction was crucial to doing fulfilling drag – without a live audience, the allure of drag performance diminished considerably.

In Richmond, this took one of two forms: Driveway Drag, spearheaded by long-time Richmond drag performer Michelle Livigne, and Drive-in Drag, hosted at LGBTQ+ advocacy organization and thrift store Diversity Thrift. Among performers I talked to, all agreed that the analogue-live was special. Even in its COVID-cautious forms, many still found it preferable to digital liveness. Whether it was the audience, the performance style, or the camaraderie with other performers, the intangible aura of analogue drag remained important and something that many felt was worth maintaining during COVID however possible.

The transition from analogue-live in a club or bar to analogue-live outdoors had little impact on performance style. Performers could safely rely on tried-and-true numbers such that there was little difference between a driveway/drive-in number and a routine at an outdoor Pride festival. The minimal performance adaptation was not, however, the primary appeal for performers at these outdoor shows. Instead, it was about being in community with other performers and the attendees.

Richmond drag artist Chicki Parm had little interest in the digital medium – for her, fulfilling drag performance necessitates a live audience. When asked about her participation in virtual shows, she told me: 'Um … I just had no interest. At all. Like, it didn't feed my soul, the money was terrible, there was no point.' Chicki credits the outdoor shows, particularly Diversity Thrift's Drive-in Drag, as a beacon of light during a bleak time. 'I always have to shout out Diversity for their drive-in gig because that was like, my saving grace. That was the first time I really saw a lot of people again. So, like, every car felt like the most overwhelming reunion.' Other performers who also worked the Diversity drive-in shows shared similar sentiments. Grace Wetpants, who often hosts the shows, shared the following:

I mean, honestly, last summer [2020], the first two shows, I got out on stage and I saw all those people there, after months of seeing no one, and having no sense of community, and only having, like, my house party Zoom chats that I could be in with people. I was crying, like, as soon as I got up there. I started crying those first two shows, because it was just so overwhelming to feel like there still was a community, and that I could see these people from across the parking lot again. And the performers, we were all so incredibly touched, at the same time, to see everybody come out and support, even through that. It's been really cool to hear people tell us that … that it kind of got them through.

The driving force of the desire to preserve the analogue aura illustrates something crucial and unique about drag: it is as much about the art itself as it is about the context surrounding it. Drag comes to life as community-driven art through performance. Thus, the aura of the analogue is not about content, or art-for-art's-sake; it is instead about context – who, where, and how the performance is happening. Particularly in a drag scene like Richmond, which is small and consists of a core contingent of regular audience members, maintaining community matters just as much, if not more, than maintaining the actual production of art. Further, performers need not choose either digital performance or the analogue aura (many performers at least dabbled in both) to do community. The digital presented a unique opportunity to rethink both the aesthetics and the community component of drag. In doing drag digitally, community engagement may look different, but is, perhaps, no less present.

Digital drag 2.0: music videos and expanding networks

In April 2020, digital drag began shifting in form and style. Pioneered by the winner of *The Boulet Brothers' Dragula* Season 2 (2018), Biqtch Puddin', digital drag moved from glitchy Instagram Live to Twitch. Popular among gamers, Twitch allows users to stream gameplay and interact with other gamers in real time. Like Instagram Live, Twitch allows for an experience in which audience and performer (or gamer) gather in the same virtual space as the livestream happens in real time. Twitch offers more real-time interaction with the addition of a live chat used by both attendees and performers throughout the show. It also allows for a blending of live and pre-recorded content, which proved instrumental in dictating the future of digital drag.

In the earliest days of Biqtch Puddin's *Digital Drag Show*, Biqtch was live throughout the show (about 2 hours), introducing each performance as a pre-recorded video was shown with the performer's social media handle(s) and tipping information. Behind the scenes, moderators ensured minimal technological difficulties as videos streamed during the weekly shows. As digital drag evolved on Twitch, the style of hosting and degree of liveness also changed. Live hosts quickly fell by the wayside as fully pre-recorded shows began to gain popularity. Typically, a host would record introductions of each number prior to the performance airing. While these recordings were *played* live, and many performers on cast would attend these shows and interact with audiences throughout, nothing about the show itself was *actually live*.

Several noteworthy changes happened once digital drag found a more stable home on Twitch. First, the preservation of liveness above all else was no longer prioritized. Instead, digital drag moved towards music-video-style performances, marking a turn away from a battle *against* technology towards *embracing* technology to produce creatively innovative works. This shift spawned additional unique markers of the digital moment: first, a greater capacity for the number of performers per show (relative to the analogue-live) and, second, a more expansive, more level playing field that lessened the constraints of brick-and-mortar boundaries, fostering a more expansive, connected digital drag community.

The digital medium allowed for greater opportunities to integrate special effects into performances in ways not feasible in the analogue world. Thus, performances tended less to approximate the analogue-live, replacing reliance on liveness with the introduction of technological enhancements. Given the preference for special effects (such as fake blood and strobe lighting) among alternative drag performers, it is unsurprising that alternative artists tended to fare well and adapt quickly to the digital format. Given the intricate make-up techniques favoured by alternative drag artists, the digital also provided a novel showcase for their artworks beyond static photographs. Further, the digital created an opportunity to think beyond the inherent limits of analogue performance. From the number of performers cast to the kinds of performances that were feasible, digital drag allowed for an already-expansive art form to push boundaries even further.

Even among those with lukewarm feelings about digital drag, many performers (both those interviewed and other artists active in digital spaces) tended to speak favourably regarding the experimental opportunities that digital medium presented. Even early in the Twitch era, innovation abounded. Chicago drag king Dusty Bahls performed a fire-spinning digital number; Richmond performer Sweet Pickles dressed as a character from Disney's *Toy Story* and set toys on fire; Lucy Stoole, Chicago drag legend, created a cinematic masterpiece lip-syncing alone on a beach. In each of these instances, performers were able to incorporate elements into their numbers that would not be safe (fire) nor feasible (beaches don't exist in bars) in the analogue environment. Besides the opportunity to do things that were not analogue-friendly, digital drag offered different ways to conceptualize and execute a performance so it can be less like a single-shot, analogue-lite lip-sync and more like a music video or theatrical number. By using simple video editing (such as splicing frames together or altering playback speed), performers could embody several characters in one number, for example, without being restricted by the logistics of clothing reveals or quick changes as they would be at an analogue show. Chicago performer Degrassi Knoll created a silent-film-style performance in which they played all the characters, sometimes sharing the screen with different versions of themselves. Performers could also digitally collaborate to create group performances. For example, a group of drag kings, spanning coast to coast, collaborated for a 'Bohemian Rhapsody' number in which performers sometimes shared a screen, despite being thousands of miles apart physically. Group numbers and splicing music together to create a mix are nothing new for drag, but digital drag allowed for a kind of embodied, performance-based 'splicing' of both sound and body in ways not feasible in the analogue medium. It further created collaboration opportunities for artists who may not have ever had the chance to perform together in a solely analogue context.

Temporally, too, the digital proved to be expansive. Chicago drag performers Aunty Chan and Miss Toto curated a drag show based on Vines (6-second videos) – something that would not have been possible, nor compelling, as an analogue show. In the digital medium, the chaotic campiness of Vine itself, coupled with drag performers with a love for stupid humour, created a hilarious show with over ten performers that lasted under 30 minutes.

Beyond performance: cybernetic drag outside 'digital drag' shows

Drag artists did not limit themselves solely to performance-based digital endeavours. Poison Waters, Portland-based drag royalty and the most seasoned of my respondents, shared with me how digital tools transformed her opportunities to host events around the globe. While Poison is unique in her drag skill set ('My thing is, I'm not a … I don't dance, I don't sing in my real voice, I really don't get into the lip-sync thing. I'm a host. So, as a host, I like to guide events and guide the audience through what we're doing, and the whole experience.'), what isn't unique is how digital drag altered the embodied way she hosted in drag.

Virtual platforms, particularly for hosts, present a body that is only seen from the waist up. The right kind of lighting and digital effects create a glamorous (and forgiving) sparkle to the image of the performer projected on an attendee's screen at home. Creating a look for hosting in the digital medium often only requires construction from the waist up. From the waist down, the look – and arguably the body itself – ceases to matter. In the same way that cybernetic drag performances allow for a fundamental rethinking of the body in drag, digital 'live' hosting offers the same potential. The physical toll that drag takes on the body – swelling of feet and back ache from wearing heels, restricted breathing from a tightly laced corset, sore earlobes from heavy jewellery, head and neck aches that come after hours of wearing a heavy wig or headpiece – is also deeply impacted by this medium change. Indeed, upon returning to more regular in-person hosting gigs, Poison remarked that she and fellow performers had to (re)learn how to walk in heels.

Beyond aesthetic and corporeal impacts, the linchpin of drag's live aura – community – also matters in the digital medium. While more common in the age of mainstream exposure, gigs for local performers outside a couple of hours' driving distance tend to be infrequent. Poison Waters occupies a highly specific niche as an expert host of events as well as drag shows, having been booked to host events in cities around the country. Frequently, these tend to be events where she is not performing alongside other queens, but hosting, for example, drag bingo at an annual company event. Poison is quite well-travelled for a non-mainstream drag queen, but digital drag took her to distances she had never travelled in person:

So, for me, the pandemic taught me that I actually can do what I do without a living, breathing audience in front of me, which was a big surprise. I just … it didn't occur to me that I would ever be able to do that. And I could be just as effective and entertaining without having people in the room. And it also showed me that I can – that there's no limits to where I can go. I've literally hosted events in Ireland and in Australia and in India, and it's been fantastic because with, you know, social media – excuse me, virtual reality platforms – I can be anywhere!

More than most performers I talked to, Poison's outlook on digital drag was decidedly optimistic. For Poison to be able to do what she does without a physical audience in front of her illuminates how the digital allows for a restructuring and reimagining of doing community and social networks in a way that highlights the limitless potential of cybernetic drag. Poison explained that the virtual events she hosted during the height of the pandemic led to more virtual bookings, much in the same way as in-person gigs always had. Moreover, with more geographically diverse audiences attending virtual events, in real time, came more potential for geographically diverse bookings and more expansive social networks.

Increasingly diffuse social networks impacted digital drag performers too, not just hosts. Biqtch Puddin's *Digital Drag Show*, which remained among the largest and most well-attended weekly digital shows throughout most of its run (April 2020 through summer 2021), featured artists from across the globe. While casts tended to be mainly US-based, performers from Canada and the UK were not uncommon. Canada-based drag documentary duo Drag Coven offered up their YouTube channel (with nearly 90,000 subscribers) as a global living archive for digital drag performances. Performers could share their hard work – many performers spent hours creating digital numbers – with a wider audience that didn't hinge on receiving bookings.

Importantly, digital drag created a space in which performers who have historically been marginalized within drag scenes – AFAB and/ or BIPOC performers, kings, and those with less conventional drag aesthetics – were given more opportunities. Digital drag offers a generally more accessible marketplace. It is easier, for example, to control the presence of microaggressions – banning someone from a chat room or blocking them online is easier than removing or barring them from a brick-and-mortar space. There are downsides to the analogue that the digital also brought to light on a broader community level. As establishments whose revenue comes from alcohol sales, bars can be challenging places for people with substance-abuse issues, for example. The spaces tend to be poorly lit and cramped, presenting challenges for performers or attendees with visual impairments or mobility equipment. Bright lights and loud music can be overwhelming to the point of pain for neurodivergent people, and strobe lights can trigger seizures for folks with epilepsy or other seizure disorders. Moreover, the physicality of analogue performance can itself be challenging for performers with disabilities. The digital affords performance options that are less damaging to the body and less physically taxing. Many disabled artists can perform in-person gigs, but it often requires extensive exertion and subsequent recovery.

Non-binary Philadelphia-based performance artist Deej Nutz shared with me that digital drag was more accommodating to their needs as a disabled person. They shared the extent of the toll live performance takes on their body:

I have multiple sclerosis, so part of that is having a limited amount of energy for all the things. Everything from bathing, to dressing, to any appointments that might need to take place outside. Performing takes *a lot* out of me. So like, I'll be doing takes for virtual acts and I'll have to – I'll be done for the day because I can't move anymore and I'm just, like, on the floor: alright, I'm exhausted, I might take a nap here. And then that amount of energy is variable. You've probably heard of the spoon theory – I'll have ten spoons today and, say I'm practicing a routine: I've used all ten spoons and dipped into tomorrow. So now I have to recover. Every time I do a performance, especially if it's live, I now know that I have to have at least one to three days of, like, not doing anything to recover. So, doing virtual acts, I was able to participate in a lot more shows and I was able to kind of take my time with it and take breaks as needed. But I also learned just how much energy it takes to put anything together.

Many disabled performers know the risks and concessions they make to create art that is demanding on the body, particularly the disabled body. While those risks are often worth the fulfilment that comes from doing drag, pre-COVID and pre-digital drag, disabled performers often had to assume those risks or not perform at all. Digital drag creates a space in which the toll taken on disabled performers can be lessened since they can create more disability-friendly conditions (such as recording a performance in several sittings, using accessibility equipment they may have at home but may not be able to at a club, and being able to stay seated for some of the performance).

Community matters deeply to drag artists, as is evident for those who prioritized the preservation of analogue community gathering – however creative those gatherings had to be – over more frequent digital bookings.

Just as the digital offers a novel opportunity to unpack liveness, so too does it offer an opportunity to rethink community. Digital drag meant people could be booked anywhere and not be bound by location limitations, rendering local community networks less integral for bookings than in the analogue medium. The sheer number of digital performance opportunities meant that casts could be larger and more diverse, geographically and otherwise. Further, analogue community networks contain deeply entrenched dynamics and local politics; for example, venues may be selective about who they book due to concerns about revenue and drink sales. Certain performers may not get along, so the prospect of sharing a cramped dressing room may be uncomfortable. There is also no shortage of microaggressions perpetuated against marginalized members of LGBTQ+ communities by community members with more privilege – often, white cisgender gay men. Women, trans and non-binary folks, and BIPOC participants in drag scenes, have been vocal in online spaces about how some bars and clubs uphold community hierarchies and perpetuate exclusion. While the digital is by no means a utopia, its accessibility means that performers who may struggle securing local bookings, through no fault of their own, have ample opportunities both to curate their own digital shows and to be invited onto shows curated by others.

Discussion and conclusions

In 1985, when 'A Cyborg Manifesto' was originally published, Haraway said with confidence, 'We are all chimeras, theorized and fabricated hybrids of machine and organism; in short we are cyborgs' (p 150). Her statements are perhaps truer now, in the heavily media-saturated landscape of 2020, than ever. Yet she also argues that the relations between 'organism and machine' or human and technology, have been a border war, of sorts, in which the two are at odds. The cyborg represents a reworking of the tensions between the organic and the machine.

What I call *cybernetic drag* – a *fusion* of technology and drag, rather than a battle between the two that permeated early digital endeavours – illustrates a profound connection between Haraway's cyborg and Auslander's critiques of liveness, specifically the presumed superiority of analogue liveness. Haraway situates the cybernetic as part reality, part fiction. If 'reality', or realness, equates to authenticity, and we consider authenticity in the realm of liveness, Haraway's cyborg necessarily straddles a line between the live and the not-live and represents an innovative collaboration between the two.

Overall, the digital has offered more ways to conceptualize a drag show, from theme to casting to performance order to execution. Digital drag amounts to the creation of an art-cyborg: a creative entity transcending boundaries between technology and the material world, reality and fantasy, body and machine. Digital drag created space to imagine uncharted aesthetic choices and ways of doing embodied drag that are impossible within the confines of the analogue-live. The result is a fundamental rethinking of (live) drag with regard to the body. In part, drag's power lies in the ability to transform, to embody the improbable, impractical or impossible in everyday life. Cybernetic drag arguably creates even more possibilities for transformation.

Early digital drag, like the Instagram Live era, that prioritized replicating the analogue-live in the digital realm as much as possible illustrates the inherent tension that exists in trying to replicate the analogue through digital means. Ultimately, it results in an unsatisfying copy, underscoring the ways in which drag's analogue aura cannot be reproduced in the digital realm. However, once the grip on prioritizing liveness above all else loosened, a more harmonious relationship with technology emerged. In embracing technology rather than viewing it as a barrier to overcome, innovation abounded, with the emergence of more expansive ways of doing drag. The digital tools available to performers who embraced the new medium allowed for greater possibility for more fringe or alternative aesthetics. Cybernetic drag offers an opportunity to think beyond the corporeality of liveness – beyond the boundaries of the body and limitations of brick-and-mortar spaces. The digital affords performers a chance to go anywhere, be anyone, do anything with their drag, and do it in such a way that still engages audiences.

To be clear, there are things lost in the digital shift. The components that comprise drag's aura, however, are less about mechanics and performance aesthetics and much more about community – about *who* is doing what and *with whom*. Events like Drive-in Drag illustrate that, perhaps above all else, *community* is the aura worth preserving, and is the most pronounced, deeply felt loss in the digital realm. In this way, cybernetic drag presents a reimagining of antiquated ideas of artistic aura, propelling scholarly conversations on the topic into the digitized age. Cybernetic drag illustrates an aura that encompasses not just the art itself, but the community within and the contextual backdrop against which the art happens.

Community is not absent in the digital. Diffuse digital networks allow for a rethinking of community (and its connection to drag's aura) beyond locality. It is no coincidence that early digital drag shows often cast performers as if they were casting an analogue show, including mostly booking entertainers that lived near the host. Once the desire for one-to-one analogue replication lessened, however, so too did the importance of physical proximity. In fact, the digital created opportunities for more dialogue across physical borders, fostering a sense of collective community among drag artists across the country and the world.

Perhaps digital drag is the product of the pandemic and mainstreamed drag market aesthetics (Zaslow, 2022) – a fusion of these things that at once both subverts them (digital drag, aesthetically, defies much of mainstream drag's aesthetic rigidity) and fuses them into a new and different way of doing drag. In this newly imagined digital community, the microaggressions and barriers that often impact where, when and how marginalized performers engage the drag marketplace are easier to monitor and control and thus, mitigate. The digital allows for a more accessible environment that is more open to diverse performance styles *and* diverse identities. Digital drag was, in large part, born out of necessity for working artists to continue to support themselves financially. In this way, digital drag further expanded the marketplace itself – in the communities it reaches, in the styles of drag it creates space for, and in the performance opportunities it affords.

While the primary focus of scholars studying the art form has been drag's ability to reveal the contextuality and artifice of (presumed) natural, binary gender roles (Butler, 1990, 1993), digital drag highlights drag's far more expansive subversive potential. In all forms, drag performance is rooted in queer positionality: it is a commentary on and response to the reality of queer subjectivity in a cis-hetero-patriarchal society. The aesthetic possibilities afforded by the digital shift allow for more ways to tell queer stories through the art of drag.

Further, digital drag's rise to prominence in 2020, at a moment where survival was at the forefront of daily life, is significant insofar as it speaks to drag's power and importance for queer communities. Whether working artists struggling to financially survive the pandemic or queer communities collectively trying to survive the Trump administration, queer art prevails and matters deeply in these moments of crisis. For innovation, like digital drag, to be borne out of crisis speaks not just to the resilience of queer communities but the extent to which art is necessary for survival. At the height of the AIDS epidemic, it was moments of levity and charity, like drag benefit shows, that lifted spirits and carried queer communities through unimaginable loss and tragedy. Drag was also a way for those battling the virus to reckon with their own health and mortality (Davis, 2021). These moments – pandemics, political unrest, crises – are precisely the moments that drag is made for. As the US faces an increasing wave of legislation that seeks to ban drag performance across several states (ACLU, 2024), a deep understanding of drag as a powerful vector of community highlights exactly why these bans are so threatening. A more expansive definition of drag, which digital drag offers, is a direct challenge to those trying to silence and eradicate it. In this way, perhaps digital drag's affordances are more important than ever.

As the US has shifted its understanding of COVID-19 to be 'endemic' and thus analogue/in-person gatherings are once again the normalized and prioritized method of socializing, it remains to be seen just how profoundly the digital moment will impact local scenes. While digital drag has considerably waned in popularity, it has not died out. Chicago drag king

Lúc Ami was still streaming many of his shows on Twitch in 2022. Boston-based drag performer Majenta-with-a-J, host of *Full Spin: Visual Albums of Non-Stop Drag*, has resumed the in-person medium for the show, but all shows are recorded and broadcast for digital audiences. There are, in other words, ways that digital media can still be used in influential, innovative ways to reshape analogue performance. What sort of role this plays in the future of the drag marketplace culture – in terms of aesthetics, performance spaces, and community dynamics – remains to be seen, but digital drag has shown the incredible power that drag has to adapt and change, and the central role it continues to play in queer communities, especially through moments of crisis.

Notes

[1]   Difficulties were not limited to artistic industries; converting school classrooms from in-person to digital learning, for example, resulted in socialization problems and learning loss (Mervosh, 2022).

[2]   Drag is often read as a *gendered* transformation, in part due to Butler's (1990, 1993) usage of the art form to unpack gender performativity. However, drag's transformative potential is not limited to gender alone, with even more expansive possibilities now afforded by digital media.

References

ACLU (2024) 'Mapping Attacks on LGBTQ Rights in U.S. State Legislatures', [online] Available from: aclu.org/legislative-attacks-on-lgbtq-rights?impact=speech [Accessed 12 June 2024].

Auslander, P. (2008) *Liveness: Performance in a Mediatized Culture* (2nd edn), Abingdon: Routledge.

Auslander, P. (2012) 'Digital Liveness: A historico-philosophical perspective', *PAJ: A Journal of Performance Art*, 34(3): 3–11.

Barker-Plummer, B. (2013) 'Fixing Gwen: News and the mediation of (trans) gender challenges', *Feminist Media Studies*, 13(4): 710–724.

Benjamin, W. (1935 [2008]) *Art in the Age of Mechanical Reproduction*, London: Penguin.

Bowles, J.P. (2011). *Piper: Race, Gender, and Embodiment*. Durham: Duke University Press.

Buchholz, L., Fine, G.A., and Wohl, H. (2020) 'Art Markets in Crisis: How personal bonds and market subcultures mediate the effects of COVID-19', *American Journal of Cultural Sociology*, 8: 462–476.

Butler, J. (1990) *Gender Trouble*, New York: Routledge.

Butler, J. (1993) *Bodies That Matter: On the Discursive Limits of 'Sex'*, New York: Routledge.

Cavalcante, A. (2016) '"I Did it All Online:" Transgender identity and the management of everyday life', *Critical Studies in Media Communication*, 33(1): 109–122.

Cavalcante, A. (2018) *Struggling for Ordinary: Media and Transgender Belonging in Everyday Life*, New York: New York University Press.

Davis, M.B. (2021) 'Glamour, Drag, and Heath: HIV/AIDS in the art of three drag queens', *TSQ: Transgender Studies Quarterly*, 8(1): 113–120.

Dixon, S. (2007) *Digital Performance: A History of New Media in Theater, Dance, Performance Art, and Installation*, Boston: MIT Press.

Dunn, B. (2020) 'Digital Drag Fest – Catch your favourite RuPaul DQ's from the comfort of your own home', *The Buzz*, [online] Available from: thebuzzmag.ca/2020/04/digital-drag-fest-catch-your-favourite-rupaul-dqs-from-the-comfort-of-your-home [Accessed 12 June 2024].

Frith, S. (2007) 'Live Music Matters', *Scottish Music Review*, 1(1): 1–17.

Haraway, D. (1991) 'A Cyborg Manifesto: Science, technology, and socialist-feminism in the late twentieth century', in *Simians, Cyborgs and Women: The Reinvention of Nature*, New York: Routledge, pp 149–181.

Holt, F. (2010) 'The Economy of Live Music in the Digital Age', *European Journal of Cultural Studies*, 13(2): 243–261.

Horak, L. (2014) 'Trans on YouTube: Intimacy, Visibility, Temporality', *Transgender Studies Quarterly*, 1(4): 572–585.

Horkheimer, M. and Adorno, T.W. (1944 [1994]) 'The Culture Industry: Enlightenment as mass deception', in *Dialectic of Enlightenment*, pp 94–136.

Jeannotte, M.S. (2021) 'When the Gigs are Gone: Valuing arts, culture, and media in the COVID-19 Pandemic', *Social Sciences & Humanities Open*, 3: 1–7.

Lazarsfeld, P. and Merton, R.K. (1948 [1957]) 'Mass Communication, Popular Taste and Organized Social Action', in B. Rosenberg and D.M. White (eds) *Mass Culture: The Popular Art in America,* Glencoe: Free Press, pp 457–473.

Mervosh, S. (2022) 'Pandemic Learning Loss: The role remote education played', The New York Times, [online] 28 November, Available from: nytimes.com/2022/11/28/briefing/pandemic-learning-loss.html [Accessed 12 June 2024].

Miller, B. (2017) 'YouTube as Educator: A content analysis of issues, themes, and the educational value of transgender-created online videos', *Social Media + Society*, April–June 2017: 1–12.

Muñoz, J.E. (1999) *Disidentifications: Queers of Color and the Performance of Politics*, Minneapolis: University of Minnesota Press.

Phelan, P. (1993) *Unmarked: The Politics of Performance*, New York: Routledge.

Piper, A. (1981) 'Ideology, Confrontation and Political Self-Awareness', *High Performance*, 4(1).

Reedy, A. (2021) The Monster as Queer Opportunity: Monstrous (Re) Construction, Embodiment, and Approbation on *The Boulet Brothers' Dragula* [Master's thesis], Northern Illinois University.

Warnecke, L. (2020) 'Art and Performance during the Time of COVID-19 Lockdown', *Agenda*, 34(3): 145–147.

Wight, J. (2014) 'Queer Sweet Home: Disorientation, tyranny, and silence in digital space', *Cultural Studies, Critical Methodologies*, 14(2): 128–137.

Zaslow, S. (2022) 'Mainstream Novelty: Examining the shifting visibility of drag performance', *Sexualities*, 27(1–2): 330–355.

8

Drag Social Media Influencers as Opinion Leaders: Their Role in Promoting Drag Entertainment in India

Khyati Jagani

Consumer attention to and consumption of drag entertainment shows has increased recently. From a once-hidden, quiet, private, leisure or protest activity, drag has now become a recognized entertainment phenomenon (Barnett and Johnson, 2013; Berbary and Johnson, 2017). Drag performance demonstrates the diverse ways to practise and experience gender. Rupp and Taylor (2003) discuss it as a political and social movement. Drag also challenges conventional notions of gender and sexuality (Taylor et al, 2004). Through their performance, the drag artist breaks the illusion of 'typical' appearances of gender to accentuate the performative nature of gender and sexuality. Within the drag performance, masculinity, femininity and queerness circulate freely. Previous literature has argued that drag is a transgressive practice that destabilizes gender by focusing on the social constructions of femininity, masculinity, heterosexuality and homosexuality (Taylor et al, 2004).

Drag is a form of art without any boundaries of gender or social or ideological restrictions. Drag queens and kings represent the drag culture and community through femininity, beauty, performance, style and fashion (Barnett and Johnson, 2013; Baxter et al, 2022). In developing countries such as India, drag culture is nascent, but it is slowly but surely moving towards recognition, acceptance and involvement in the mainstream. India has a thriving drag scene with celebrities and social media influencers (SMIs). Drag SMIs include Gentleman Gaga (Sanket Sawant), an actor, model and stylist; Hiten Noonwal, a designer, model and professor of fashion design;

and Empress Xara (Adam Pasha), winner of an international super queen competition, among others (Dragvanti, 2023). However, drag shows in India are limited, primarily taking place in cities and in upper-class society.

Indian drag queens have performed alongside international drag queens at nightclubs and hotels, but Indian drag stands apart and reflects the influence of Bollywood, showcasing its own culture, heritage and dignity (Sandhu, 2019). Besides social issues of recognition and acceptance, Indian drag also experiences the challenge of being compared with Western drag performers. Indian drag SMIs play a crucial role in improving such scenarios (Bakshi, 2004). They create relevant and authentic content for their audience and their unmatched style helps to build a positive perception of Indian drag culture.

Social media influencers in general first appeared in the early 2000s and have since progressed from the work being a home-based hobby to a lucrative full-time career. SMIs are now capitalizing on their popularity to develop their careers in mainstream media, such as the film and TV industries (Abidin, 2019). In terms of marketing, SMIs are segmented based on the number of followers and classified as micro-, meso- and macro-influencers (Hatton, 2018; Porteous, 2018). SMIs create posts with information and testimonials about a particular product, for example, resulting in increased information value and product knowledge. They are also seen to transfer their attractiveness and aesthetic value to that product (Schouten, et al, 2019). Influencers are independent third-party endorsers who have developed a network by sharing their experiences and lives through pictures, location check-ins and stories (De Veirman et al, 2017).

Previous literature has discussed drag from the perspective of gender (Egner and Maloney, 2015), the gendered life experience (Berbary and Johnson, 2017), identity (Fox, 2008), ideology and culture (Gonzalez and Cavazos, 2016) and performance, desire and transphobia (Litwiller, 2020). Little research has examined drag from an SMI perspective. Another gap is in the hierarchy of effects (HOE) theory: it discusses the impact of advertising on consumers' decision-making processes and covers a series of stages for advertisers to follow to achieve purchase behaviour. HOE discusses persuasion as a one-sided interaction, where there is no mechanism for consumers to respond or provide feedback to the advertising message. However, SMI followers can comment on and share their perspectives on the posts of the drag SMIs. O'Keefe, (2016) found that two-sided persuasion is more credible. Yao (2021) supports this argument in digital marketing and suggests that two-sided promotions are more effective than one-sided communication.

This chapter investigates how drag SMIs persuade potential consumers and promote drag entertainment shows. Armstrong et al (2016) define persuasion as 'all influences that lead people to action'. The chapter aims to identify the process that drag SMIs use to persuade their followers to consume entertainment shows by engaging the followers with their content. It applies

HOE to study the process of persuasion followed by drag SMIs to promote drag entertainment shows through their content on social media. The context of the study is the promotion by drag SMIs of drag entertainment shows that happen offline in clubs and events in India.

Literature review

For over a decade, social media has provided a platform for content creators to talk about their lives, share their opinions and express their feelings to a large audience without any barriers (Morris and Anderson, 2015). Since the early 2000s, researchers have defined SMIs in varied contexts. Freberg et al (2011: 90) described SMIs as a 'new type of independent third-party endorsers who shape audience attitudes through blogs, tweets, and other social media applications'. Dhanesh and Duthler (2019) define an SMI in the public relations context as 'a person who, through personal branding, builds and maintains relationships with multiple followers on social media and can inform, entertain, and potentially influence followers' thoughts, attitudes, and behaviors'.

Developing oneself as a successful SMI depends on an individual's ability to create an online identity that would appeal to social media users and brands who are seeking influencers for promotional activities (Khamis et al, 2016). The key to consumer persuasion is the influencer's relationship with their followers (Abidin and Thompson, 2012). Research on SMIs has also noted other strategies to create relationships with their followers, such as online discussions and offline, in-person meetings (Abidin and Thompson, 2012; Abidin, 2015). Regardless, credibility and authenticity are essential (Abidin and Ots, 2015).

Drag

Drag performers have often been mistakenly described simply as cross-dressers or female/male impersonators in earlier literature (Barnett and Johnson, 2013). Drag queens are often also identified as transsexual and transgender, although not many drag performers would identify themselves in this way (Barnett and Johnson, 2013).

In everyday parlance, the drag moniker means 'making oneself appear to be someone of another gender', but the drag look might be generically gendered, based on another person specifically (celebrity), or designed to emulate a social role (Newton, 1972). One common misconstruction comprises cross-gender presentation in which, according to the misconception, a biological male must dress and appear feminine to engage in drag. While many drag queens assume a feminine aesthetic, it is not always the case. Bio-queens, for example, perform their biological sex roles with exaggerated or heightened gender appearances. Some literature has argued that drag queens are 'people who create their authentic genders' (Rupp and Taylor, 2003: 44). The 'performer' element points to drag's theatrical and performance elements: on stage or off stage, drag takes on a persona of a theatrical nature and assumes its attitude and aesthetics (Barnett and Johnson, 2013). Until recently, drag performances only took place in leisure spaces, such as restaurants, bars, Pride parades, parties, political rallies and fund-raising events (Barnett and Johnson, 2013).

From a gender-identity perspective, Butler (1990: 43) argues that gender identity is a form of cultural fiction; it is 'a repeated stylization of the body, a set of repeated acts within a highly rigid regulatory frame that congeal over time to produce the appearance of substance, a natural sort of being'. Drag is a parody of normative and fixed conceptualizations of gender. According to Butler (1991: 42), drag 'constitutes the mundane way gender gets appropriated, worn, theatricalized, and done ... implying that gendering is an impersonation and approximation'. Previous literature on drag has argued that gender is a philosophical category, not 'what one is, but more fundamentally, is what one does' (West and Zimmerman, 1987: 140). By embellishing the feminine, drag queens display the fictional element of dichotomous processes of gendering. By stylizing themselves, drag artists disrupt regulatory notions of the 'self' and reveal the limitations of identity (Bakshi, 2004). Drag offers the opportunity to advocate the right for gender equality through the medium of performance and art (Levitt et al, 2018). While blurring the lines of gender, drag raises critical societal issues around gender discrimination and marginalization (Berkowitz and Belgrave, 2010; Mann, 2011).

History of drag in India

Drag queen artists have been active in India since the early 2000s (Kumar, 2023), but these performances were only at private parties and in digital spaces. In 2017, drag shows began to get the spotlight at an event organized by the Kitty Su nightclub at the Lalit Hotel, New Delhi called 'Drag New Year'. With such a high-profile hotel chain organizing a drag event, drag shows became more accessible to a wider audience (Sandhu, 2019). Drag shows are still, however, at a nascent stage in India.

Meanwhile, men performing in female roles has a long history in India. It is also well accepted and practised in several Indian classical dance forms, such as Kathakali and Kuchipudi, along with indigenous theatre (Putcha, 2013; Sandhu, 2019). Indian drag is similar to yet different from Western drag in more ways than one. Drag artists in India follow many of the styles of their Western counterparts in terms of drag names, make-up, terminology and lip-syncs. However, in the Indian drag performance, hints of Indian culture and history are reflected. From wearing the Indian saree and salwar kameez to performing Bollywood music and dancing styles, using folk dance and acting in TV soap operas, Indian drag performers set themselves apart (Sandhu, 2019; Khubchandani, 2020).

Drag social media influencers

Drag events and performances have gained acceptance and popularity through the globally renowned TV show *RuPaul's Drag Race*, a primary catalyst for bringing visibility to and proliferation of drag performances. *Drag Race* became a platform that questioned audiences' perceptions of drag (LeMaster, 2015). Now, as drag performance as an art form has become a part of popular culture, it has a presence on social media such as Instagram. The appearance of drag performers on social media has created awareness for those who may otherwise be unaware of them (Baxter et al, 2022). Alongside this, global brands such as MAC, Lush, Ikea and Absolut have begun to collaborate with drag performers to promote their brands in advertisement and social media marketing (Baxter et al, 2022). Drag queens have also been on the covers of various international editions of the global fashion magazine *Vogue*. This attention generates further opportunities for drag performers to reach more online and offline events and followers (Baxter et al, 2022). Drag events bring together audiences from different sexualities and genders, and due to their enormous reach, social media enables drag SMIs to promote drag events and shows (Ong and Goh, 2018) to a wide variety of audiences. Drag SMIs may interact with their followers offline during (and perhaps before and after) their performances and online through social media posts, messages and comments.

Hierarchy of effects model

The hierarchy of effects (HOE) model has been discussed extensively in literature on advertising (see also Preston and Thorson, 1984). In the model, the audience responds to the advertised message methodically. The HOE describes consumer stages for establishing an attitude towards a brand and purchase intention. The literature has extensively tested different versions of the model (Barry, 2002; Smith et al, 2008). All reveal a systematic process divided into sequential stages. Lavdige and Steiner (1961) discuss awareness, knowledge, liking, preference, conviction and purchase in their model. The HOE predicts a sequence that follows the process of cognition (awareness, knowledge) followed by affect (liking, preference, conviction) followed by behaviour (purchase) (Smith et al, 2008). The HOE model is adopted in the present study to understand how a message delivered by an influencer impacts and influences a follower's decision to consume drag events and shows. Drawing from the theory of HOE with reference to the body of knowledge on drag culture, this chapter asks how drag SMIs promote shows and persuade followers through their content.

Method

As a qualitative exploratory study (Creswell and Clark, 2007), the study implemented two critical methods for collecting data. The first phase was netnography. The second phase involved in-depth interviews with drag SMIs and their followers from India. The purpose of conducting in-depth interviews was to identify themes around which to answer research questions (Creswell and Clark, 2007).

Part 1

The first part of the study conducted a netnography of drag SMIs profiles for ten months, from January 2022 to October 2022 (Kozinets and Nocker, 2018; Kozinets, 2019). Nine SMIs were selected, based on the number of followers, frequency of posts, comments per post and engagement rate. In terms of number of followers, the study included both micro- (under 10,000 followers) and meso- (10,000 to 1 million followers) influencers (Pozharliev et al, 2022). Regarding the frequency of posts, it was ensured that the influencers posted at least once a week, with a minimum of ten comments per post and an engagement rate (showing how active followers are) of at least 1 per cent (Influencer Marketing Hub, 2023). The netnography focused on collecting data on the interactions between drag influencers and their followers. Kozinets (2019: 69) defines netnography as a 'particular kind of online ethnography whose use is commonplace in marketing, consumer research, tourism, and many other academic business and communication research field'. Netnography seeks to 'affirm the pre-eminence of the construction of meaning and its understanding, providing a cultural approach to study the social interaction that transpires through interactive media' (Kozinets and Nocker, 2018). The objective of conducting netnography was to identify the process followed by drag SMIs for promoting their shows and to observe the follower engagement generated by the posts. Table 8.1 lists the drag influencers selected for netnography, along with the number of posts, number of followers and their area of specialization, as of July 2023.

All posts and interactions between the drag influencer and their followers were extracted and analysed. Posts with texts, videos and images were extracted and analysed. The data were analysed using the thematic analysis method. Content written by the influencer in the post and the comments on the posts were analysed separately. For this study, each post and each comment was considered a unique data point. Table 8.2 presents a summary of the netnographic data collected.

Table 8.1: Drag influencers in India selected for netnography

Drag influencer	Number of posts on Instagram	Number of followers on Instagram	Drag artist's specialty / expertise
Hiten Noonwal	2,000	7,949	Professor, model, fashion designer, performance artist, TedX speaker
Sanket Savant (Gentleman Gaga)	249	34,800	Fashion stylist, drag queen, performing artist
Patruni Chidananda Sastry (Suffocated Art Specimen)	4,605	11,400	Dancer, singer, actor, TEDx speaker, CEO (Dragvanti)
Suruj Rajkhowa (Glorious Luna)	1,082	18,100	Make-up, style, image making, editorial, activist
Alex Mathew (Maya The Drag Queen)	601	26,900	Artist, TEDx speaker, actor
Siddhant Khodlekere (The Lady Bai)	212	5,124	Drag queen, performer
Prateek Sachdeva (Betta Naan Stop)	576	7,879	Drag queen, dancing, lip-syncing queen, actor, model
Kiran Kore	1,796	203,000	Folk dancer, make-up artist
Sushant Divgikr (Rani Kohenur)	1,437	2.1 million	Performer

Table 8.2: Netnographic data on drag influencers and followers (January–October 2022)

Data source	Number of data points
Image-based posts	925
Videos	854
Comments	37,759

Part 2

The second part of the study involved interviews with nine drag SMIs. All of these were Indian or of Indian origin. They were all meso- or micro-influencers on social media. Following this were semi-structured in-depth interviews with 20 social media users who follow at least one drag meso-, micro- or mega (over 1 million followers)-influencer. Table 8.3 summarizes the social media profiles of the drag influencer interviewees. (The number of followers on Instagram is as of July 2023.)

The semi-structured interviews produced insights into how a drag SMI persuades their followers by exploring characteristics unique to drag and

Table 8.3: Drag social media influencers interviewed

Interviewee	Drag name	Number of Instagram followers	Instagram handle	Specialty/expertise
Adam Pasha	Empress Xara	101,000	@adampashaofficial	Indian queen and super model
Priyanshu	Jolene Queen Sloan	58,400	@jolenequeensloan	Premier Punjabi queen
Ashish	Cumsin Haseena	8,400	@thechopranextdoor	HR executive and founder of Beunic India
Sanket Savant	Gentleman Gaga	34,800	@gentleman_gaga	Fashion stylist, drag queen, performing artist
Zeeshan Ali	Zeesh	11,200	@zeeessshh	Make-up artist, designer, stylist, photographer, model, performance artist
Marcus Oliviera	Hashbrownie	7,225	@infinityshades_ofmine	Make-up artist and consultant, performing artist
Hiten Noonwal	Hiten Noonwal	7,949	@hiten.noonwal	Professor, model, fashion designer, performance artist, TedX speaker
Kiran Kore	Kiran Kore	203,000	@kirankoreofficial	Folk Dancer, Make-up artist
Pavan Kumar	Pavan	10,300	@pavank_artist	Eye Make-up Tutorial, Product Reviewer, Dancer

how this feeds into promotion of drag events. The author recorded the interviews with permission from all the respondents. Each interview lasted for an average of an hour. The in-depth interviews and netnography data post-transcription were analysed through inductive research and interpretive procedures (Miles et al, 2014).

Data analysis

The data from the netnography and in-depth interviews were analysed separately using thematic analysis (Braun and Clark, 2006). According to Braun and Clark (2006), there are six steps for conducting thematic analysis: data familiarity, generating initial codes, identifying themes, reviewing themes, defining and naming themes and, finally, producing the report. For this study, the data was analysed in three phases. The first phase conducted the netnographic data using thematic analysis. The second phase conducted a thematic analysis of data from in-depth interviews with influencers and followers – the latter with the aim of observing responses and reactions to drag SMI posts. The third stage merged the thematic analysis of netnography and interview results using a side-by-side comparison method. Findings from in-depth interviews identified the process, and results from the netnography confirmed the process. The objective of the side-by-side comparison was to verify the process followed by the drag SMIs to promote drag entertainment shows. The analysis generated five stages for promoting drag events, as shown in the following section.

Results and discussion

This discussion presents the essential findings into how drag SMIs persuade followers and promote drag events. The main themes identified through interviews and netnography relate to the process and stages adopted by drag SMIs, as represented in Figure 8.1.

Interviews with drag SMIs revealed numerous touchpoints and moments of truth from which to engage and interact with followers. Drag SMIs opine that they are not just promoting drag events and shows; they are building a community of like-minded members having the same passion for the art of drag as they have. All the while, they support each other by promoting their shows and those of other artists. In this regard, one drag interviewee explained: 'On my social media, I have made a community of members. Thus, as a community, everyone supports each other by sharing promotions of other artists' upcoming shows.' Drag SMIs also mention that their content educates their followers and other visitors by providing information about

Figure 8.1: Drag influencer promotion process

what drag stands for, reducing misconceptions about drag, and demystifying drag culture. Another drag influencer disclosed:

I share a lot of my posts and my friends' posts which talk about different types of drag, like comic drag, tribunal drag, etc., so, just bringing out different aspects of drag. Drag is not just about dressing up as a woman and performing; it is much more. It can be expressing your femininity; it can be about expressing another form. Through my content, I try to normalize and talk about the fact that drag is not just dancing and singing; it is about expressing themselves and their gender.

Adopting and extending the HOE model, the study found a five-stage promotion process of drag events and shows by drag SMIs: attention and curiosity, desire and conviction, participation, event activation, and nurturing and prospecting.

Attention and curiosity

Interviews with drag SMIs found that they create interactive challenges to draw attention. The challenges could be asking the followers to test certain things or the drag SMI challenging themselves to try something difficult. In this context, one influencer stated that they created an image-creating challenge and fashioned unique images to explain what a drag stands for to their followers. In this regard, another drag SMI revealed: 'Drag faces a lot of hatred and challenges from society and rejection. So, through my handle, I created a 31-day image-creating challenge and created 31 different looks for August. I talk about different aspects and issues through my 31 looks.' The challenges also stimulate attention from existing followers regarding drag performances, which would help generate curiosity among the followers. In this regard, one of the followers interviewed said: 'The drag influencer I follow creates fascinating trivia and occasions on their social media handle, like asking the followers most thought-provoking questions and fun activities like ramp-walks.' These challenges, trivia and other activities attract attention and curiosity about the drag influencer, an initial touchpoint for their followers. For example, to attract attention, build interest and promote engagement, a drag SMI might post a video of them performing a song and, in the comments section, ask their followers about their favourite music. Drag influencer Pavan Kumar (@pavank_artist) put up a short video in which they performed a semi-classical dance: 'So soothing if you hear this song! Let me know your favourite song which makes you dance.'

Drag influencers also promote their performances by sharing the event posters provided to them by the organizers. However, drag influencers take it upon themselves to attract a larger crowd for the show. They sometimes post a small video as a story or reel showcasing the upcoming performance, which helps create curiosity among their audience regarding that act. As one drag influencer mentioned: 'I post teaser performance videos showcasing my performance before every event; in some, I dress up, and in some, I shoot in my regular clothes to make them guess my final look. The teaser video creates curiosity and makes the audience desire to see the whole act.' This further works as a moment of truth for consumers to decide whether to consume that particular act.

Desire and conviction

Drag performers are famous for their idiosyncratic acts and unique styles, often combining cultural context, complicated choreography and historical significance. They express themselves through their performances, often creating a satire of specific social practices and asking the most critical questions on gender and identity. In this context, one drag performer stated:

> I am a classical dance performer, and people do not understand it, so, before my performance, I create a short performance video about my upcoming show and post it on Instagram, explaining its history and meaning. So, they can come and enjoy the show instead of coming and seeing it with a question mark on their face. So, I build a background before the show.

Through a pre-performance explanation post, this drag performer gets the opportunity to create desire and conviction in the minds of their followers to attend the drag event and be part of it. Followers of drag SMIs find the pre-performance explanation videos helpful and appealing. It also allows them to experience the background of the drag performance and 'put a face' to the actual event they will be a part of. A follower mentioned: 'I appreciate the drag influencer explaining the significance and meaning of their performance because it clarified many aspects for me along with some misconceptions.' Similarly, a drag influencer might perform a small part of their upcoming show to introduce the meaning and significance of the act in the show. Drag influencer Kiran Kore (@kirankore) posted a video in full costume and make-up, but the mini-performance was not on a stage. After performing a small part of the song, they would stop and explain the meaning of the song and the reason they chose it. In this regard, Kiran Kore also posted a 'What do you think?' video, in which they performed a free-style dance to a popular song, in casual clothes.

Participation

Following a pre-performance explanation post, influencers might create an event walk-through for their followers. The objective is to engage the followers with the upcoming event by taking them through what will happen during and around the event, including after-show parties. They also share information about the event's key attendees and other performers. A drag SMI said: 'I post videos about what will happen in the event, who will be there, who else will perform, and other post-performance activities.' The event walk-through with the influencer gives the followers a glimpse of the event, creating another touchpoint to generate follower engagement. A follower stated: 'When the event walk-through by the drag influencer was at the final point, I decided that I needed to attend the show.'

Drag influencers also engage with their followers by creating either an Instagram story or a live video showcasing the entire selection of dresses, make-up, hair, shoes and other accessories, often asking for the reviews and feedback of their followers in choosing the right look for the performance. This level of follower participation through event in-preparation content generates a sense of involvement in the decision-making process of the drag SMI. In this regard, a drag SMI stated

A few days before all my performances, when I am selecting my make-up, dress and hair, I create different event in-prep videos to get reviews from my followers, as many of them will be present in my final show during the drag event. So, it helps me connect with them beforehand.

Along with getting reviews, drag influencers also conduct crowd tests and polls for votes on their outfits and accessories. Followers of drag SMIs found the event in-prep videos highly interactive, making them feel a part of it all. In this regard, a follower said: 'I look forward to the event in-prep videos by the drag artist, as they are too much fun and make me feel like I have a relationship with the influencer, which is why they ask for my opinion.' Glorious_luna posted their event in preparation video with the caption, 'Look Reveal! Have done hair and make-up + styling. What do you think?'

Event activation

Event activation is on the day of the performance. A drag SMI shares a short live video during the show. It gives followers a glimpse into the actual event, the music, the audience and the show's energy. One drag SMI explained: 'I create a live video showing my followers a snip-it about the performance, ongoing performance, the crowd, and how much fun everyone is having.' The influencers share this with followers who could experience the live performance in person. The objective is to display how much fun people participating were having, and all the fun those not attending were missing out on. In this context, a follower mentioned: 'I had seen a few live videos of the Drag influencer's performance. They seemed so awesome that I decided to book my tickets the next time they performed in my city.' Drag influencer Sanket Savant (@gentelmangaga) shared a live video of their performance, with some of the audience shots captioned as, 'Serving some Kooth Vibes'.

Nurturing and prospecting

The promotion does not end with the drag event. The day after the show, influencers create post-performance content and share it on social media. This content typically includes videos of the event, including the crowd sharing how much fun they had during the show; photos that the influencer took with their followers; photos of them with other drag performers; and images and videos from the after party. The objective of the post-performance video is to nurture the audience that came to the show and to prospect a potential audience by creating a feeling of missing out and thoughts of 'next time' among those that did not come to the show. In this regard, one drag SMI stated: 'I post a small video of what happened in last night's show and put a small video about my performance, share some photos that I look with my audience, and also give information about my upcoming events.' By sharing information about future events, drag influencers invite their followers to participate in the next such exciting event. This stage of the process creates a circular loop and connects with stage one, creating attention and interest in the next drag event. One drag influencer explained: 'All my acts are different from each other; I never repeat the same act, and all my performances tell a new story.' In this regard, a follower admitted: 'The last event by the drag I follow seemed wonderful. I wish I had participated in it.' As a part of their social media promotion, Sanket Savant (@gentlemangaga) created a post about their performance from the day before, captioned, 'About Last Night'.

Discussion

This chapter's findings adopt the HOE model's communication process and identify stages followed by drag SMIs to promote drag entertainment shows. The first stage of the process, attention and curiosity, aims to capture interest in the shows and set this communication apart from the other regular content posted by the drag SMIs. In the HOE model, awareness is the first stage of persuasion (Smith et al, 2008). In this context, however, the followers are already aware of the drag artists and have decided to follow them on social media. So, the process starts with attracting attention and forming curiosity in the followers' minds, whether they are consumers of drag shows or merely following a drag performer on social media.

Desire and conviction is the second stage of promotion. Research by Barry (2002), similar to this chapter, discusses conviction as a stage of consumer persuasion of the advertised message. Through a pre-performance explanation post, the drag performer has the opportunity to create desire and conviction in the minds of their followers to attend the drag event and be a part of it. Followers of drag SMIs find the pre-performance explanation videos helpful and appealing. It also allows them to understand the background to the drag performance and familiarity with the event they will be a part of.

The next stage is to generate participation by interacting with the follower. Here, the influencers might post an in-preparation video showing options for dresses and make-up for the upcoming event and asking their followers to share their opinions and vote on favourites. Developed in an offline advertising context, the HOE model (Smith et al, 2008) does not consider two-way communication, but, with social media, drag SMIs can engage and interact with their followers through their content and invite participation from them.

Event activation is the purchase and consumption stage. It occurs when the drag show is in action. Literature on the HOE model defines this stage as a purchase (Lavdige and Steiner, 1961) and as the stage of intention in the process of consumer response models (Yoo et al, 2004), but drag SMI does not stop here. Drag artists create content even during their performances, and share small glimpses of what is happening at the event. This then assists in prospecting the new target consumers for purchase and nurturing the present consumers to participate again. While the HOE model (Lavdige and Steiner, 1961) does not discuss nurturing, the consumer decision-making model, also known as the Engel-Blackwell-Miniard model (Engel et al, 1968), discusses consumer post-purchase behaviour in terms of repeat purchases and post-purchase evaluation. However, previous literature does not discuss the prospecting of potential consumers resulting from the fear of missing out.

Conclusion

An evolving culture in India, drag is slowly but surely getting the attention of the masses. Once a niche community, drag culture, drag entertainment shows and drag SMIs are rapidly establishing a presence in the mainstream space, both online and offline. Drag queens who are active on social media have much credit to take for this change. They reach many followers through their social media handles, primarily on Instagram and YouTube. A literature review on drag culture identified two significant research gaps. First, research on Indian drag is conducted from a cultural point of view and not a marketing perspective (Sandhu, 2019). Second, the impact and role of a drag queen as a social media influencer has not been studied. Therefore, this chapter explores the stages followed by drag SMIs promoting drag entertainment shows. To the author's knowledge, this is the first study to do so. The study identified popular drag SMIs on Instagram and conducted netnography and interviews with drag SMIs and their followers. It demonstrates how a drag SMI creates follower engagement, forms persuasion and promotes drag shows, adopting the HOE model. The results indicate a five-stage process drag influencers follow to promote drag events, by gaining attention and curiosity, desire and conviction, participation, event activation, and nurturing and prospecting.

Theoretical and managerial implications

The research findings suggest that organizers and brands should consider engaging drag SMIs to promote drag shows as they can persuade and attract followers to those shows. Furthermore, drag events provide a unique opportunity for brands to interact with their consumers while collaborating with drag SMIs to promote their brands on social media. Brands across the spectrum have begun to collaborate with drag SMIs for promotion, but such sponsorship tends to happen only during Pride month. The findings in this chapter suggest the strength and robust process of drag SMI promotion. A brand could benefit from such collaboration and break through the clutter that influencer marketing has fallen into by using the same normative influencers, which provides no exceptional visibility to social media users. This chapter has observed that drag SMIs, through social media, share their struggles and stories and represent the entire community, building a relationship with their followers and increasing their trust in them. In addition, with their bold, larger-than-life presence, drag influencers appear more striking and attention-grabbing than any typical influencer.

This chapter not only superimposes the HOE model but, in the given context, also extends the HOE model. The six stages of the model present awareness and knowledge as the cognitive stage; liking, preference and conviction as the effective stage; and purchase as the behavioural stage. This chapter studies drag queens as social media influencers promoting drag shows. Given that study context, unlike the HOE model, the process will not start with awareness and knowledge because online social media users are already aware of drag events since they are already following the drag SMIs. So, the process would begin with the drag SMI drawing attention to and building curiosity about future drag shows. Given the nature of these shows and the two-way communication opportunity provided by social media, the drag SMI creates active engagement and drives followers' participation, generating preference for the event. It will finally lead to event activation, the final purchase per the HOE model. While the HOE model ends at the purchase, which is the behaviour stage, the present model adds the final stage of nurturing and prospecting, as the repeat purchase and new sales conversion for future shows will occur at this stage and close the entire promotion loop.

Limitations and directions for future research

One limitation of this study is the lack of accompanying academic research that looks at drag not just from the perspective of culture and gender identity but also from the viewpoint of social media influence. There is a vast amount of literature on influencer marketing, but there are no studies on drag performers as SMIs interacting with their followers and affecting their decision-making. Future research could further explore drag performers from the lens of SMI and explore the consumer behaviour process impacted by influencer marketing.

Another limitation of the research in this chapter is the sample size. First, the context of the study is that of a developing country (India) in which only a small number of drag performers have made it to the level of SMI regarding the number of followers and engagement rate. Second, among the drag SMIs approached, only nine agreed to be interviewed for the study. Future research could attain a more comprehensive sample size by including drag influencers from other developing countries and conducting a cross-country study. Lastly, there is a limitation in that the persuasion process is from the perspective of theory generation, and there is a need for theory testing and generalization. Future studies could conduct quantitative research to test the model.

References

Abidin, C. (2015) 'Communicative Intimacies: Influencers and perceived interconnectedness', *Ada: A Journal of Gender, New Media, and Technology*, 8: 1–16.

Abidin, C. (2019) 'Yes Homo: Gay influencers, homonormativity, and queerbaiting on YouTube', *Journal of Media & Cultural Studies*, 33(5): 614–629.

Abidin, C. and Ots, M. (2015) 'The Influencer's Dilemma: The shaping of new brand professions between credibility and commerce', AEJMC 2015 Annual Conference, San Fransisco.

Abidin, C. and Thompson, E.C. (2012) 'Buymylife.com: Cyber-femininities and commercial intimacy in blog shops', *Women's Studies International Forum*, 35(6): 467–477.

Armstrong, J.S., Du, R., Green, K.C. and Graefe, A. (2016) 'Predictive Validity of Evidence-Based Persuasion Principles: An application of the intext method', *European Journal of Marketing*, 50(1/2).

Bakshi, S. (2004) 'A Comparative Analysis of Hijras and Drag Queens', *Journal of Homosexuality*, 46(3–4): 211–223.

Barnett, J.T. and Johnson, C.W. (2013) 'We Are All Royalty: Narrative comparisons of a drag queen and king', *Journal of Leisure Research*, 45(5): 677–694.

Barry, T. (2002) 'In Defence of the Hierarchy of Effects', *Journal of Advertising Research*, 42(3): 44–47.

Baxter, D., Jones, S. and Leer, C. (2022) 'Audience Diversity and Well-being at UK Drag Events', *Event Management*, 26: 127–140.

Berbary, L.A. and Johnson, C.W. (2017) 'En/Activist Drag: Kings reflect on queerness, queens, and questionable masculinities', *Leisure Sciences*, 39(4): 305–318.

Berkowitz, D. and Belgrave, L.L. (2010) 'She Works Hard for the Money: Drag Queens and the management of their contradictory status of celebrity and marginality', *Journal of Contemporary Ethnography*, 39(2): 159–186.

Braun, V. and Clark, V. (2006) 'Using Thematic Analysis in Psychology', *Qualitative Research in Psychology*, 3(2): 77–101.

Butler, J. (1990) Gender Trouble: Feminism and the Subversion of Identity, New York: Routledge.

Butler, J. (1991) 'Imitation and Gender Insubordination', in D. Fuss (ed) *Inside/Out: Lesbian Theories/Gay Theories*, New York: Routledge, pp 13–31.

Creswell, J.W. and Clark, V.L. (2007) 'Designing and Conducting Mixed Methods Research', Thousand Oaks, CA: Sage.

De Veirman, M., Cauberghe, V. and Hudders, L. (2017) 'Marketing Through Instagram Influencers: The impact of the number of followers and product divergence on Brand attitude', *International Journal of Advertising*, 36(5): 798–828.

Dhanesh, G.S. and Duthler, G. (2019) 'Relationship Management through Social Media Influencers: Effects of followers' awareness of paid endorsement', *Public Relations Review*, 45(3): 101765.

Dragvanti (2023) Drag Directory, Dragvanti, [online] Available from: dragvanti.com/dragdirectory [Accessed 28 July 2023].

Egner, J. and Maloney, P. (2015) 'It Has No Color, It Has No Gender, It's Gender-Bending: Gender and sexuality fluidity and subversiveness in drag performance', *Journal of Homosexuality*, 63(7), 875–903.

Engel, J.F., Kollat, D.T. and Blackwell, R.D. (1968) Consumer Behavior, New York: Holt, Rinehart and Winston.

Fox, R. (2008) 'Sober Drag Queens, Digital Forests, and Bloated Lesbians', *Qualitative Inquiry*, 14(7): 1245–1263.

Freberg, K., Graham, K., McGaughey, K. and Freberg, L. (2011) 'Who are the Social Media Influencers? A study of public perceptions of personality', *Public Relations Review*, 37(1): 90–92.

Gonzalez, J.C. and Cavazos, K.C. (2016) 'Serving Fishy Realness: Representations of gender equity on RuPaul's Drag Race', *Journal of Media & Cultural Studies*, 30(6), 659–669.

Hatton, G. (2018) 'Micro-influencers vs. Macro influencers', *Social Media Today*, [online] 21 July, Available from: socialmediatoday.com/news/micro-influencers-vs-macro-influencers/516896 [Accessed 28 July 2023].

Influencer Marketing Hub (2023) 'Instagram Influencer Sponsored Post Money Calculator', *InfluencerMarketingHub*, [online] Available from: influencermarketinghub.com/instagram-money-calculator/#toc-1 [Accessed 28 June 2023].

Khamis, S., Ang, L. and Welling, R. (2016) 'Self-Branding, Micro-Celebrity, and the Rise of Social Media Influencers', *Celebrity Studies*, 8(2): 191–208.

Khubchandani, K. (2020) Ishtyle: Accenting Gay Indian Nightlife, Ann Arbor, MI: University of Michigan Press.

Kozinets, R.V. (2019) 'YouTube Utopianism: Social media profanation and the clicktivism of capitalist critique', *Journal of Business Research*, 98: 65–81.

Kozinets, R.V. and Nocker, M. (2018) 'Netnography: Online ethnography for a digital age of organization research', in A. Bryman and D.A. Buchanan (eds) *Unconventional Methodology in Organization and Management Research*, Oxford: Oxford University Press, pp 127–146.

Kumar, S. (2023) 'Activism and Therapy', in, A. Alman, J. Gillespie and V. Kolmannskog (eds) *Queering Gestalt Therapy: An Anthology on Gender, Sex and Relationship Diversity in Psychotherapy*, Abingdon: Routledge.

Lavdige, R.J. and Steiner, G.A. (1961) 'A Model for Predictive Measurements of Advertising Effectiveness', *Journal of Marketing*, 26(2): 156–169.

LeMaster, B. (2015) 'Discontents of Being and Becoming Fabulous on RuPaul's Drag U: Queer criticism in neoliberal times', *Women's Studies in Communication*, 38(2): 167–186.

Levitt, H.M., Surace, F.I., Wheeler, E.E. et al (2018) 'Drag Gender: Experiences of gender for gay and queer men who perform drag', *Sex Roles*, 78(5–6): 367–384.

Litwiller, F. (2020) 'Normative Drag Culture and the Making of Precarity', *Leisure Studies*, 39(4), 600–612.

Mann, S.L. (2011) 'Drag Queens' use of Language and the Performance of Blurred Gendered and Racial Identities', *Journal of Homosexuality*, 58: 793–811.

Miles, M.B., Huberman, A.M. and Saldana, J. (2014) Qualitative Data Analysis: A Methods Sourcebook, Thousand Oaks, CA: Sage.

Morris, M. and Anderson, E. (2015). 'Charlie is So Cool Like: Authenticity, popularity and inclusive masculinity on YouTube', *Sociology*, 49(6): 1200–1217.

Newton, E. (1972) Mother Camp: Female Impersonators in America, Chicago: University of Chicago Press.

O'Keefe, D. (2016) 'Persuasion: Theory and Research' (3rd edn), Thousand Oaks, CA: Sage.

Ong, F. and Goh, S. (2018) 'Pink is the New Gray: Events as agents of social change', *Event Management*, 22(6): 965–979.

Porteous, J. (2018) 'Micro-influencers vs. Macro-influencers, What's Best for Your Business?, *Social Bakers*, [online] 10 July, Available from: socialbakers. com/blog/micro-influencers-vs-macro-influencers [Accessed 20 June 2023].

Pozharliev, R., Rossi, D. and Matteo, D.A. (2022) 'Consumers' Self-Reported and Brain Responses to Advertising Post on Instagram: The effect of number of followers and argument quality', *European Journal of Marketing*, 56(3): 922–948.

Preston, I.L. and Thorson, E. (1984) 'The Expanded Association Model: Keeping the hierarchy concept alive', *Journal of Advertising Research*, 24: 59–65.

Putcha, R.S. (2013) 'Between History and Historiography: The origins of classical Kuchipidu dance', *Dance Research Journal*, 45(3): 91–110.

Rupp, L.J. and Taylor, V. (2003) Drag Queens at the 801 Cabaret, Chicago: University of Chicago Press.

Sandhu, A. (2019) 'India's Digital Drag Aunties', *Dress*, 45(1): 55–73.

Schouten, A.P., Janssen, L. and Verspaget, M. (2019) 'Celebrity vs. Influencer Endorsements in Advertising: The role of identification, credibility, and product-endorser fit', *International Journal of Advertising*, 39(2): 258–281.

Smith, R.E., Chen, J. and Yang, X. (2008) 'The Impact of Advertising Creativity on the Hierarchy of Effects', *Journal of Advertising*, 37(4): 47–61.

Taylor, V., Rupp, L.J. and Gamson, J. (2004) 'Performing Protest: Drag shows as tactical repertoires of the gay and lesbian movement', *Research in Social Movements, Conflict, and Change*, 25: 105–137.

West, C. and Zimmerman, D.H. (1987) 'Doing Gender', *Gender and Society*, 1: 125–151.

Yao, Q. (2021) 'Informing, Implying or Directing? Testing the effects of message sidedness, conclusiveness and their interaction in national and local Google ads campaigns', *Journal of Research in Interactive Marketing*, 15(2): 623–640.

Yoo, C.Y., Kim, K. and Stout, P.A. (2004) 'Assessing the Effects of Animation in Online Banner Advertising', *Journal of Interactive Advertising*, 4(2): 49–60.

9

Conclusion: Studying Drag Marketplace Cultures – Critical Reflections and Future Directions

Mario Campana, Rohan Venkatraman, Katherine Duffy,
Mikko Laamanen and Maria Rita Micheli

In their seminal piece in the *Journal of Consumer Research*, Arnould and Thompson (2005) discuss marketplace cultures as a key research programme within marketing and consumer research. Marketplace cultures look at the 'ways in which consumers forge feelings of social solidarity and create distinctive, fragmentary, self-selected, and sometimes transient cultural worlds through the pursuit of common consumption interests' (p 873). Inspired by the tradition of sociological and cultural work on the power and marketplaces, from McCracken (1986) to modern work in the consumer culture theory canon, the chapters in this collection have explored how consumers, marketplaces and drag artists have forged a cultural world based on deviance, solidarity, commodification and dissent. The chapters that make up this collection, and the authors who have contributed to them, explore these intersections in ways that coalesce (and are thus organized) around three main substantive areas that inform contemporary drag marketplace cultures: politicizing drag identities, marketizing drag and digitizing drag.

In this concluding chapter to the book, our primary goal is to offer directions for future research into drag marketplace cultures, and we do so by taking a macro-level critical reading of the conversations that the various chapters have with each other. As we assembled this book, it became clear that the authors of each chapter not only spoke to one or more of the key substantive areas just mentioned, but also to one or more of three larger, more abstract themes embedded into contemporary drag marketplace cultures (henceforth marketplace themes) – artisanship (Chapters 2, 4, 6, 7 and 8), stigma (Chapters 2, 3 and 5) and commodification (Chapters 2, 3,

4 and 7). In turn, the themes of artisanship, stigma and commodification were further used to problematize a key issue that is germane to the question of why drag is an interesting marketplace culture – the issue of legitimacy. Drag has historically been a subcultural enterprise, a creative expression of queerness that seeks to defy normativity (see, for example, McCormack and Wignall, 2022), but, in its myriad interactions with the contemporary (often mainstream) marketplace, as explored in the chapters that comprise this book, we see a constant problematizing of the nature of drag, of drag artists and of the dominating nature of marketplace cultures.

In the sections that follow, we first explore the three emergent theoretical narratives of artisanship, stigma and commodification, highlighting theoretical confluences between the arguments and perspectives presented within this book. We then offer a critical reflection on the interplay between marketplaces, drag and legitimacy that orchestrate much of today's drag marketplace culture. Finally, we offer directions for future research.

Emergent theoretical narratives of drag marketplaces

Artisanship

A common narrative across the chapters in this book is the artistic and individual nature of drag, a theme that highlights both what makes drag a fascinating addition to the conversations around marketplace cultures and the challenges in explicating what studying drag adds to broader conversations. Indeed, if an art form is so individualized, where lies the space for theoretical abstraction?

The various chapters in this book draw, either directly or indirectly, on the notion of artisanship, and the role of drag artists as artisans, in bridging the relationship between drag performers and the marketplace. Emerging from sociological work on creativity and creative practice (Gerosa, 2022; Mulholland et al, 2022), artisanship is often understood as knowing how to work with certain materials and transforming them through an appropriate technique, thus using one's knowledge and skills to yield a desired result (Ostrom, 1980). While the notion of the artisan is not a modern one – Marx (1867) refers to the artisan as one part of the petty bourgeoisie – there has been a renewed focus on the role of the artisan within a modern marketplace (Bell et al, 2019; Gerosa, 2022, 2024).

This renewed focus on artisans is reflected in this book in two ways – a focus on the interplay between the artisan and the nature of the craft, and the artisan as a person brand – highlighting two potential avenues through which drag artists relate to the marketplace.

The interplay between artisan and craft speaks to existing work on craft that frames the individual artisan as a creative entrepreneur, and that the consumption of the craft is as much therefore as a consumption of the artisan

(Costin, 1998; Bell et al, 2019). Shayne Zaslow (Chapter 7) speaks to this through their work on digital drag, highlighting how the production and consumption of drag as a contemporary art form expands through digital intermediation. Zaslow highlights the role of the drag artist as a key part of this expansionary trend when they discuss the creation of the art-cyborg as a fusion of technology and drag, defining it as a 'creative entity transcending boundaries between technology and the material world, reality and fantasy, body and machine' (Chapter 7). In this, they reinforce and expand the interdependencies between identity and materiality that emblematize the expressive nature of craft and the shaping role of the individual (Rancière, 1983; Bell et al, 2019; Maguire, 2019).

Zaslow's implicit recognition of the shaping role of the artisan segues neatly into a pair of chapters (6 and 8) that, when read in conjunction, serve to highlight the mutually constitutive roles of artisans and marketplaces, where the artist serves as a vehicle for marketplace communications, and the market affirms and legitimizes the drag artist as a 'valid' intermediary. Bình Nghiêm-Phú (Chapter 6) and Khyati Jagani (Chapter 8) both seek to understand how drag artists act as influencers (Kobilke, 2023), but they diverge in their approach and findings. In Jagani's work, drag artists are framed in the role of social media influencers, designating them as both marketplace intermediaries that seek to expand the drag market and, importantly, person-brands that connect artisanal meanings to a broad audience. In Chapter 8, on the role of drag performers in India as marketplace intermediaries, Jagani finds that drag artists leverage their strong links to art and community – two notions pertinent to India – as a means of seeking legitimacy in a marketplace that is ostensibly hostile to queer identities (Yadav and Kirk, 2018). Here they seek to move beyond subcultural legitimacy and seek legitimacy from and through the marketplace as they market their art and, concurrently, themselves. Conversely, in Chapter 6, Nghiêm-Phú examines how other marketplace actors – specifically non-fan consumers – contribute to the marketplace legitimacy of drag artists. By examining how fans and non-fans of drag differ in their response to products marketed by drag artists in their role as influencers, Nghiêm-Phú's work shows how contestations between market actors (fans and non-fan consumers) can cement drag artists as legitimate intermediaries, albeit less glamorously than perhaps the drag artists would hope for. Through this, he revisits tensions between legitimacy, stigma and commodification, and highlights how even the artisanship and expertise of drag artists may be flattened as they become marketized.

This pair of chapters (6 and 8), when read in conjunction, ask an important question – are there contexts in which the artisan nature of drag artists can be an asset? This question is a conceptual jumping-off point for Both, Razal and Venkatraman (Chapter 4), who focus on how large marketplace actors, such as brands, seek out the artisanal authenticity and subcultural legitimacy of drag artists as they look to move those meanings onto their brands, à la McCracken (1986). The artistry and, indeed, the inherent queerness and eye-catching nature of the drag artists are leveraged by brands who seek to use the charisma and expertise of the drag artists to frame their brand as subculturally relevant. Rather than the artists seeking legitimacy, they are legitimized through their marketization (Mundel et al, 2023). Similarly, in Chapter 2, Luigi Squillante highlights how, while *RuPaul's Drag Race* (RPDR) has valorized a narrow spectrum of drag as legitimate, a consequence of that flattening has been the simultaneous broadening of the appeal of drag to otherwise hostile audiences. The person-brands of the queens from RPDR no longer just represent the individual queens but carry larger socio-political charges that brands aim to capitalize on (Fournier and Eckhardt, 2019).

There are inherent tensions to the artisanal nature of drag becoming integrated into questions of legitimacy. For example, researchers (both within and outside this book) have shown how the mainstreaming of drag has resulted in the coalescing of specific aesthetic categories as legitimate (McCormack and Wignall, 2022; Zaslow, 2022). These tensions speak to a duality between normative marketplaces and the historical stigmatization of drag – a theme explored in the next section.

Stigma

Stigma is an attribute of an individual that is deeply discrediting (Goffman, 1963). Consumer culture research has extended the conceptualization of stigma from an attribute discrediting people to attributes discrediting brands, consumption practices, organizations, industries, markets and more. LGBTQ+ stigma is one of the most enduring. Goffman (1963) classifies it as a tribal stigma, which is among the most resilient and difficult to eliminate (Campana et al, 2022). For Goffman, stigma is an attribute that is not redeemable and tarnishes the individual's social standing. The social evaluation of the individual remains negative, and the individual is considered as having a secondary or lesser place within society. Research on consumers and marketplaces has considered LGBTQ+ stigma in a similar way. If someone identifies as LGBTQ+, then, automatically, they are associated with discredited attributes and identities and occupy a lower rung on the social ladder. While this has been true historically, more recent literature on stigma has found that stigma is 'fragmented' (Eichert and Luedicke, 2022) and 'diffracted' (Bettany et al, 2022). Different individuals within the LGBTQ+ spectrum might experience stigma differently, also depending on the context. For example, white gay married couples can be normalized in many everyday societies to the extent that they do not experience stigma in daily interactions. However, other gay people who do not conform to societal expectations (such as polyamorous couples) may experience stigma (Eichert and Luedicke, 2022). Furthermore, stigma is also diffracted (Bettany et al, 2022). Stigma is experienced in very different ways by different identities at the intersection of race, ethnicity, religion and social class backgrounds. As such, the stigma experienced by a transgender woman of colour is very different from the stigma experienced by a white gay man (Bettany et al, 2022).

Drag queens' experiences of stigma have also been fragmented and diffracted, as the chapters in this book discuss, either implicitly or explicitly. Drag queens, and drag in general, have traditionally carried a double stigma (Newton, 1979; McCormack and Wignall, 2022; Venkatraman et al, 2024), whereby they have been stigmatized by mainstream society as defying the norms around gender and sexuality, while at the same time being ostracized and discriminated against within the LGBTQ+ community because they are 'men who dress up like women' (Newton, 1979). In the last 15 years, however, drag has received a renewed interest, attention and overall allure (Venkatraman et al, 2024). As Squillante points out in Chapter 2, drag has managed to reach this stage thanks to *Drag Race*, which has allowed a marketization of drag by complying with contemporary neoliberal norms. Overall, RPDR has empowered drag queens within society, providing them with a global platform that they have never experienced before. Being visible, being represented and being treated as superstars – while at the same time being humanized as people struggling with, for example, drug addiction, or showcased as fragile people who are outcast by their families – has supported a normalization of their stigma (Campana et al, 2022; Venkatraman et al, 2024). This has allowed drag queens to achieve subcultural legitimacy (Kates, 2004). Drag queens are now celebrated by the LGBTQ+ community and they are seen as fitting into wider societal standards.

However, the subcultural legitimacy and normalization of stigma are not equal for all members of the drag community. As Pia Seimetz and Jan-Hendrik Bucher discuss in Chapter 5, only a specific type of drag artist has been able to take advantage of this enhanced visibility, legitimacy and normalization of stigma. Drag has been traditionally split between more normative gender performances – where a man typically dresses like a diva of the 1980s and lip-synchs on their songs – and the genderfuck club kids that have been experimenting more explicitly with moving beyond gender norms (McCormack and Wignall, 2022). Usually, artists within the latter category experience even more stigma than mainstream drag, as Seimetz and Bucher discuss by analysing the case of Tunten in Berlin. These identities have less of a platform compared with mainstream drag, and this stigma has not improved – has worsened, even – with the advent of *Drag Race*. As the drag queens from the show received more and more attention, other drag artists started to imitate their style. This commodified style of drag is what consumers around the world now expect to see when they go to a drag show. This has reduced the performance opportunities of other styles of drag, such as Tunten, which subverts social norms more explicitly and is less commercially accessible.

The homogenization of drag styles has caused a lot of friction within the community. In practice, while the normalization of stigma allows for subcultural legitimacy, it also allows for the flattening of the multiplicity of drag performances to a unified standard, which excludes and further stigmatizes non-mainstream drag identities like Tunten. This is the cause of what we term 'exploitative legitimacy'. Exploitative legitimacy, in contrast to the subcultural legitimacy of drag artists, happens when a group is legitimated by taking advantage of a power dynamic *to the detriment of another social group*. In this case, mainstream drag is legitimated because RPDR promotes this style of drag to the detriment of the styles and identities of drag that do not conform to this.

Throughout this book, the chapters (3 and 5 in particular), observe a tension between empowering and flattening and between subcultural and exploitative legitimacy. For instance, Paul Haynes (Chapter 3) suggests how flattening drag performances, or exploitative legitimacy, could produce ways of reproducing mainstream toxic masculinity power structures, where drag becomes a form of cultural appropriation, disempowering drag performers and the individuals they represent. On the contrary, Seimetz and Bucher in Chapter 5 argue that these dynamics are not necessarily in opposition but can work together. Thus, we suggest that exploitative legitimacy can help construct subcultural legitimacy. Mainstream drag can create platforms where marginalized forms of drag can have exposure, are empowered and partake in the neoliberal and capitalist market logic. While subcultural legitimacy is a theme that has been explored within marketing and consumer research literature (for example Kates, 2004), the tension between subcultural and exploitative legitimacy has yet to be fully unpacked. As such, we suggest that further research is needed to fully examine this dynamic and explore how the interplay of subcultural and exploitative legitimacy can potentially work together to destigmatize and normalize LGBTQ+ identities.

The discussion between stigma and legitimacy also brings us to rethink the relationship between these two constructs when it comes to drag, LGBTQ+ individuals and broader consumer culture. Our framework as presented here is based on a synthesis of the book's chapters and questions whether we can disentangle the notion of stigma from the notion of legitimacy. Organization studies already question the link between stigma and legitimacy (Hampel and Tracey, 2019; Helms et al, 2019). Specifically, Helms et al (2019) argue that legitimation and stigma are two different constructs, which can be linked. LGBTQ+ individuals are legitimate but still stigmatized. For instance, while same-sex marriage is now legitimate in many countries, same-sex couples may still experience stigma based on the more or less accepting community in which they live. Some service-providers still discriminate against same-sex couples, denying services based on religious beliefs. On the other hand, Hampel and Tracey (2019) argue that stigma and legitimacy are two opposites of the same continuum, so you cannot have legitimacy if people remain stigmatized. When a person, an organization, a brand or a consumption practice is destigmatized, then it becomes legitimate (Hampel and Tracey, 2019). Similarly, research in consumer culture has explored destigmatization as a process through which consumers, consumption practices (Sandikci and Ger, 2010), brands and markets (Humphreys, 2010a) become legitimate. However, this distinction has not really been unpacked fully.

This book allows us to start a conversation in consumer research as to the meaning of stigma and the meaning of legitimacy. While drag queens are stigmatized, they are not searching for elimination of the stigma or of being destigmatized. They search for the stigma to be normalized. Stigma is what makes drag queens who they are. They have been performing in response to the societal stigma they have experienced. However, the chapters highlight that they do all search for some form of legitimation, which could be subcultural, marketized or exploitative. Stigma, then, becomes something that does not need to be hidden or avoided (Campana et al, 2022) but something that can lead drag queens to some form of legitimation. This question of the commodification of drag – tied intimately to its marketization and normalization – is a theme we explore next.

Commodification

Moving on from 'the golden age of drag in the zeitgeist' (Brennan and Gudelunas, 2017: 1) provides our critical jumping-off point in terms of commodification. The 2022 image of the *RuPaul's Drag Race All-Star* Season 7 cast ringing the opening bell at the NASDAQ stock market in New York both highlights the contractually obligated stars fulfilling their duties and points starkly to the critical juncture of the continued commodification of drag. Across the chapters in this book, underlying tensions permeate in considering the role that RPDR has played in bringing inclusivity and visibility of drag to mainstream audiences. This points to Feldman and Hakim's (2020: 386) acknowledgement of the growth of 'highly polished, brand-conscious celebrity drag entrepreneurs'. This process of commodification has turned subcultures into products, images and stereotypes to be commercialized. In Chapter 3, Haynes documents this marketization of drag, as evidenced by shows such as RPDR, its centrality to Pride month, and focuses on the engagement metrics of drag performers alongside the continued growth of live shows and events as creating challenges in tandem with opportunities.

As drag has become a global, digitally enabled undertaking (as highlighted by Zaslow in Chapter 7), Squillante (Chapter 2) uses a market values perspective to examine how, through the creation and reproduction of neoliberal subjects, the system of values propagated by shows such as RPDR resonates with what has currently become seen as common sense within neoliberal societies, providing a fundamental prerequisite of congruence between queer and mainstream. While stressing that the cultural integration driven by the show appears inextricably connected to 'queer homologation and normativization' (Chapter 2), through the format of the show, the drag performers are both staged and edited while simultaneously being marketed to their audiences (Hodes and Sandoval, 2018). Within the parameters of RPDR, drag is categorized into meaningful, codified categories that can be built into strategies for winning and commercial success (Brennan and Gudelunas, 2017).

In considering the commercial implications and successes of drag culture, the aura and charisma of RPDR reflects self-commodification practices through the curation of personal brands, social media engagement and continued objectification (see Chapter 4). This speaks to Feldman and Hakim's (2020) earlier media studies work that emphasizes the 'celebrification' of drag culture and questions the ethics of this – specifically the ways it supports homonormative narratives of the 'good queer' while simultaneously delimiting the visibility of queer bodies and politics that are deemed acceptable in the mainstream. McCormack and Wignall's (2022) sociological perspective contrasts the once-marginal position of drag queens with this celebrity status (Newton, 1979; Rupp et al, 2010; Zhang, 2016). In Chapter 4, Both, Razal and Venkatraman contend that, while mainstreaming has resulted in drag becoming a 'vehicle for enterprise as opposed to a means through which dominant power structures might be mocked, queried or dismantled' (Feldman and Hakim, 2020: 388), these arguments ignore the subversive potential of mainstream drag, and how radical queer forms of drag extend beyond mainstream venues. They argue that the lack of broader subversion in mainstream drag is about the 'type' of drag that has been mainstreamed as much as the deradicalization that occurs through this process of mainstreaming.

Haynes' (Chapter 3) perspective acknowledges this tension whereby, as drag has evolved to be a more inclusive mode of performance and expression, as evidenced by the diversity of stories that underpin contemporary drag culture, it becomes clear that attempts to capture an essence of drag and draw it into mainstream entertainment face resistance from the performers and performances it aims to co-opt. Through this framing, an unresolved tension emerges in the potentially exploitative nature of marketizing drag culture versus the drive to seize entrepreneurial opportunities.

Considering drag as a form of creative labour or the development of a cultural brand (Campana and Duffy, 2021) emphasizes the inherent production codes, deadlines, tools and knowledge at work in the craft of drag. Both Razal and Venkatraman (Chapter 4) highlight the artistry of competitors and how it compromises their valorization. In the central focus of their chapter, they emphasize drag as an artisanal practice, which encapsulates its unique position within the marketplace in a way that moves beyond gender parody or subversion (Butler, 1990, Coles, 2007). Through this lens, the authors view drag as a non-material cultural artefact and drag performers as artisans, while drawing attention to the ways in which their networks of symbols, rituals and language become more and more normalized in the marketplace as they are adopted and then reproduced by brands and wider consumers. For example, within the RPDR parameters, the life stories and self-making practices of contestants are packaged as a product of commercialization, and the entrepreneurial opportunities are emphasized. Employing this lens of cultural artisanship allows us to examine the commodification process and provides an opportunity to develop a dialogue about consumption practices informed by normalized views of gender and beauty. The contradiction remains, however, in that mainstream commercialization and commodification of drag may lead to the continued reinforcement of gender norms as the practices become dislocated from their queer cultural context. Within this contradiction, it becomes even more important to examine the self-commodification of drag's personal brands and social media promotion and the resulting objectification.

Legitimization of drag marketplace cultures

Artisanship, stigma and commodification emerge in this book as marketplace themes that speak to the broadening of drag from a hidden subculture to a modern marketplace icon. The chapters in this book have also implicitly or explicitly oriented themselves around a question that speaks to the continued transformation of the normativity of drag and the question of whether drag as a marketplace culture is legitimate or not. Based on these insights, we develop a framework of legitimation of drag marketplace culture, based on artisanship, stigma and commodification (see Figure 9.1).

Legitimacy here is the perception or assumption that the actions of an entity are desirable, proper or appropriate within some socially constructed system of norms, values, beliefs and definitions (Suchman, 1995: 574). From a consumer research perspective, there has been a vast array of studies addressing the market practices of legitimation from consumer approaches to stigma (for example Humphreys, 2010a, 2010b; Humphreys and Latour, 2013; Scaraboto and Fischer, 2013; Dolbec and Fischer, 2015; Huff et al, 2021; Valor et al, 2021; Dolbec et al, 2022; Mimoun et al, 2022), associated barriers to identity construction (Sandikci and Ger, 2010) and the dynamics in managing both the mainstream marketplace and marginalized

Figure 9.1: Framework of legitimation of drag marketplace culture

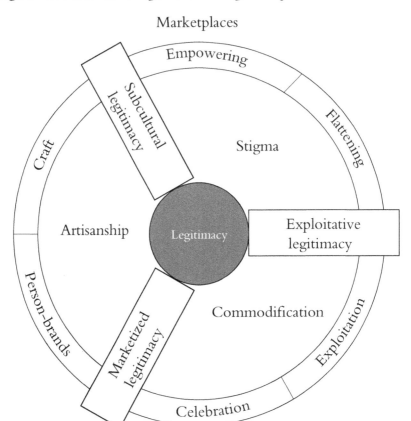

consumer identities (Coskuner-Balli, 2013; Coskuner-Balli and Thompson, 2013). Humphreys (2010b) discusses that there are different types of legitimacy: normative, which is 'the degree to which an organization adheres to the norms and values in the social environment'; regulative – 'the degree to which an organization adheres to explicit regulative processes', and cultural-cognitive – the degree to which an organization is known and understood by social actors. To be legitimated, market actors (organizations, brand, consumers) need to achieve all three types of legitimacy (Humphreys, 2010b).

On the one hand, the chapters in this book suggest that drag marketplace culture needs to build on normative, regulative and cultural-cognitive legitimacy (Humphreys, 2010b) to operate. On the other, we propose that drag marketplace cultures need to include other types of legitimacy, which are necessary for the drag marketplace culture to be legitimate. Specifically, the legitimation of drag marketplace culture (the core of Figure 9.1) is built at the intersection and continual navigation of the other three types of legitimacy – subcultural, marketized and exploitative (the three blades within the framework in Figure 9.1). These three types of legitimacy are pushed and sustained by the three marketplace themes that emerged in the chapters – artisanship, stigma and commodification (the inner circle in Figure 9.1). In turn, these marketplace themes showcase competing forces in drag performances (the outer circle). For instance, within artisanship, drag performers are constantly split between focusing their craft and building a personal brand – a recognized and acclaimed persona within the marketplace. These competing forces sustain specific types of legitimacy.

Subcultural legitimacy refers to both the perceived authenticity, validity and acceptance of a subculture within a larger society, and the perceived authenticity, validity and acceptance of practices, consumers, brands and other market actors within a subculture (Kates, 2004). This book highlights how subcultural legitimacy can be constructed through the *artisanship* that drag queens practise, specifically through the craft that drag queens put into constructing their performances (for example the lip-sync, the make-up, the body transformation) as well as through their *stigma*, which becomes an empowerment tool. Stigma makes drag performers unique and relates them to the other members of the subculture, such as other LGBTQ+ individuals.

Exploitative legitimacy refers to the acknowledgment of drag as legitimate, but with the understanding that, at the same time, this legitimacy is based on exploiting or taking advantage of certain conditions that put people in a power-imbalance situation. Exploitative legitimacy is reached through flattening the experience of the *stigma* of marginalized drag identities, by, for instance, adhering to the mainstream norms of doing drag (as on RPDR) and through the *commodification* and exploitation of drag.

Finally, *marketized legitimacy* refers to the concept that an entity or system gains legitimacy by effectively operating within market dynamics and meeting the expectations and preferences of its actors. In this context, legitimacy is derived from the entity's ability to satisfy the demands of the market and its participants. This marketized legitimacy is built both on the artisanship that goes into the construction of a personal brand of drag performers and the marketization of drag as a consumable art form, which is part of its commodification.

We view the continued friction between these types of legitimacy as the theoretical spine of our discussion. In tracing across the chapters, we see manifestations of empirical instances of these legitimacies at play and opportunities for reflection on the dynamism of legitimation processes in considering wider drag culture in relation to the marketplace. Our framework opens multiple directions for future research, within the marketplace culture of drag and beyond.

Future research

Drag culture continues to expand and mutate in the multitude of spaces that we have grappled with across the chapters in this book – in artisanship, cultural practices, marketplaces and political and technological capabilities. As such, based on the contribution of this book, there is a multiplicity of avenues that research in marketing, consumer research and beyond can undertake.

First, it is important to move away from the narrow representation of marketplace queer culture and embrace the diversity of queer experiences. These chapters demonstrate the inadequacy of mainstream platforms like *RuPaul's Drag Race* in capturing the richness of these experiences. Such limited representation raises questions about the experiences of individuals in non-mainstream platforms, which are currently under-represented in marketing and consumer research. While this book attempts to extend beyond the monolithic representation of queer culture by delving into contexts such as drag in Japan and India and Tunten in Germany, future studies should explore alternative narratives, contexts and identities within the queer community. This will allow for a better understanding of the diversity and complexity of queer experiences that may be overlooked by the dominant discourse perpetuated by mainstream drag shows.

This consideration raises another question regarding the impact of commodification and marketization on the authenticity of drag. The chapters highlight the power of drag in providing visibility to stigmatized identities due to its authenticity. However, the commodification of drag through capitalist logic may have negative impacts on that authenticity. Therefore, further research is needed to explore how the commercialization of drag affects its authenticity. This research should examine the tension between market success and the preservation of the subversive, authentic roots of drag culture. Furthermore, as drag has gained recognition as a form of progressive expression, it is worth questioning the extent of this progressiveness. It is important to conduct research that critically analyses the performative aspects of drag's progressive image to explore whether drag's progressiveness is only superficial or genuinely contributes to societal change.

The capitalist logic within the drag marketplace is also linked to instances of rainbow capitalism and rainbow washing – the appropriation and commercialization of LGBTQ+ symbols from mainstream brands and organizations for marketing purposes. Drag queens opening the New York stock exchange is a sign of how pervasive rainbow capitalism is in current times, which questions drag authenticity and its political impact. Furthermore, it is unclear to what extent these instances of rainbow capitalism are an effective way to represent drag and normalize stigma (Campana, et al 2022) or whether they are ways to exploit drag without contributing to the political inclusion of drag within society. Hence, on the one hand, future research should delve into how commodifying LGBTQ+ identities for profit affects the core values of drag and whether it fosters genuine inclusivity or reinforces stereotypes; on the other hand, building on Holt's (2004) idea of brands as cultural resources, research could investigate the therapeutic aspects of mainstream brands and drag, such as RPDR. How do drag brands serve as a cultural resource for individuals, especially those within the LGBTQ+ community? Understanding the impact of drag can contribute valuable insights into its role beyond mere entertainment.

The increasing commercialization and commodification of drag culture have raised concerns about the potential exploitation of drag performers as workers. By conducting audience studies, researchers can better understand whether this trend represents a mere commodification and repurposing of drag, or a shift in long-standing binary perceptions due to the normalization of queered advertising and branding. To fully comprehend drag culture, including its performers, audiences and the surrounding social contexts, future research should explore issues such as precarity, exploitation and labour within both mainstream and subculture contexts. Additionally, future research should also consider how heterosexual and LGBTQ+ audiences consume drag, and how this intersects with factors such as class, race and gender.

Commodification and marketization of the drag marketplace also raise questions about spaces where these practices happen. Clubs, bars and theatres have been the spaces where drag has traditionally been performed, but the potential of digital media in reshaping analogue performance, as highlighted by Zaslow (Chapter 7), calls for in-depth exploration. Future research should investigate the transformative power of digital spaces within the drag culture, understanding how they contribute to the subversion of norms and the expansion of the drag narrative.

In conclusion, this book opens up several new avenues for future exploration around the concept of legitimacy. One area that requires further investigation is the different types of legitimacy, including exploitative legitimacy, a mechanism that we have identified through our analysis of the chapters. While existing literature, particularly in psychology, has examined the legitimation of exploitation in relation to worker performance in the field (Kim et al, 2020), it remains unclear how exploitation becomes a form of legitimacy within the drag marketplace culture. Additionally, research is yet to explore the relationships between subcultural legitimacy, marketized legitimacy and exploitative legitimacy, as well as normative, regulative and cultural-cognitive legitimacy (Humphreys, 2010a). Research should delve into how these processes unfold within the drag culture, impacting its acceptance and recognition both within and outside the LGBTQ+ community.

References

Arnould, E.J. and Thompson, C.J. (2005) 'Consumer Culture Theory (CCT): Twenty years of research', Journal of Consumer Research, 31(4): 868–882.

Bell, E., Mangia, G., Taylor, S. and Toraldo, M.L. (2019) 'Introduction: Understanding Contemporary Craft Work', in: E. Bell, G. Mangia, S. Taylor and M.L. Toraldo (eds), The Organization of Craft Work: Identities, Meanings, and Materiality, New York: Routledge, pp 1–20.

Bettany, S., Coffin, J., Eichert, C. and Rowe, D. (2022) 'Stigmas that Matter: Diffracting marketing stigma theoretics', Marketing Theory, 22(4): 501–518, doi.org/10.1177/14705931221087711

Brennan, N. and Gudelunas, D. (eds) (2017) RuPaul's Drag Race and the Shifting Visibility of Drag Culture: The Boundaries of Reality TV, Cham/Basingstoke: Palgrave Macmillan.

Butler, J. (1990) Gender Trouble: Feminism and the Subversion of Identity, New York: Routledge.

Campana, M., and Duffy, K. (2021) 'RuPaul's Drag Race: Between cultural branding and consumer culture', in C. Crookston (ed) The Cultural Impact of RuPaul's Drag Race, Chicago: Intellect.

Campana, M., Duffy, K. and Micheli, M.R. (2022) '"We're all Born Naked and the Rest is Drag": Spectacularization of core stigma in RuPaul's Drag Race', Journal of Management Studies, 59(8): 1950–1986.

Coles, C. (2007) 'The Question of Power and Authority in Gender Performance: Judith Butler's drag strategy', Esharp: Electronic Social Sciences, Humanities, and Arts Review for Postgraduates, 9: 1–8, api.semanticscholar.org/CorpusID:54092893

Coskuner-Balli, G. (2013) 'Market Practices of Legitimization: Insights from consumer culture theory', Marketing Theory, 13(2): 193–211.

Coskuner-Balli, G. and Thompson, C.J. (2013) 'The Status Costs of Subordinate Cultural Capital: At-home fathers' collective pursuit of cultural legitimacy through capitalizing consumption practices', Journal of Consumer Research, 40(1): 19–41.

Costin, C.L. (1998) 'Introduction: Craft and Social Identity', Archaeological Papers of the American Anthropological Association, 8(1): 3–16.

Dolbec, P.-Y. and Fischer, E. (2015) 'Refashioning a Field? Connected consumers and institutional dynamics in markets', Journal of Consumer Research, 41(6): 1447–1468.

Dolbec, P.-Y., Castilhos, R.B., Fonseca, M.J. and Trez, G. (2022) 'How Established Organizations Combine Logics to Reconfigure Resources and Adapt to Marketization: A case study of Brazilian religious schools', Journal of Marketing Research, 59(1): 118–135.

Eichert, C.A. and Luedicke, M.K. (2022) 'Almost Equal: Consumption under fragmented stigma', Journal of Consumer Research, 49(3): 409–429.

Feldman, Z. and Hakim, J. (2020) 'From Paris is Burning to #dragrace: Social media and the celebrification of drag culture', Celebrity Studies, 11(4): 386–401.

Fournier, S. and Eckhardt, G.M. (2019) 'Putting the Person Back in Person-Brands: Understanding and managing the two-bodied brand', Journal of Marketing Research, 56(4): 602–619.

Gerosa, A. (2022) 'The Hidden Roots of the Creative Economy: A critical history of the concept along the twentieth century', International Journal of Cultural Policy, 28(2): 131–144.

Gerosa, A. (2024) The Hipster Economy: Taste and Authenticity in Late Modern Capitalism, London: UCL Press.

Goffman, E. (1963) *Stigma: Notes on the Management of Spoiled Identity*, New York: Simon & Schuster.

Hampel, C. and Tracey, P. (2019) 'Introducing a Spectrum of Moral Evaluation: Integrating organizational stigmatization and moral legitimacy', Journal of Management Inquiry, 28(1): 11–15.

Helms, W.S., Patterson, K.D.W. and Hudson, B.A. (2019) 'Let's Not "Taint" Stigma Research with Legitimacy, Please', Journal of Management Inquiry, 28(1): 5–10.

Hodes, C. and Sandoval, J. (2018) 'RuPaul's Drag Race: A study in the commodification of white ruling-class femininity and the etiolation of drag', Studies in Costume & Performance, 3(2): 149–166.

Holt, D. (2004) *How Brands Become Icons*, Boston, MA: Harvard Business School Press.

Huff, A.D., Humphreys, A. and Wilner, S.J.S. (2021) 'The Politicization of Objects: Meaning and materiality in the U.S. cannabis market', Journal of Consumer Research, 48(1): 22–50.

Humphreys, A. (2010a) 'Megamarketing: The creation of markets as a social process', Journal of Marketing, 74(2): 1–19.

Humphreys, A. (2010b) 'Semiotic Structure and the Legitimation of Consumption Practices: The case of casino gambling', Journal of Consumer Research, 37(3): 490–510.

Humphreys, A. and Latour, K.A. (2013) 'Framing the Game: Assessing the impact of cultural representations on consumer perceptions of legitimacy', Journal of Consumer Research, 40(4): 773–795.

Kates, S.M. (2004) 'The Dynamics of Brand Legitimacy: An interpretive study in the gay men's community', Journal of Consumer Research, 31(2): 455–464.

Kim, J.Y., Campbell, T.H., Shepherd, S. and Kay, A.C. (2020) 'Understanding Contemporary Forms of Exploitation: Attributions of passion serve to legitimize the poor treatment of workers', Journal of Personality and Social Psychology, 118(1): 121–148.

Kobilke, L. (2023) 'All Those Glamazons We Subscribe to: Mapping a network of key influencers spreading the art of drag on YouTube', in N. Brennan and D. Gudelunas (eds) Drag in the Global Digital Public Sphere: Queer Visibility, Online Discourse and Political Change, Abingdon: Routledge, pp 65–88.

Maguire, J.S. (2019). 'Wine, the Authenticity Taste Regime, and Rendering Craft', in E. Bell, G. Mangia, S. Taylor and M.L. Toraldo (eds) The Organization of Craft Work: Identities, Meanings, and Materiality, New York: Routledge, pp 60–78.

Marx, K. (1867/2004) Capital, A Critique of Political Economy, Volume I, London: Penguin.

McCormack, M. and Wignall, L. (2022) 'Drag Performers' Perspectives on the Mainstreaming of British Drag: Towards a sociology of contemporary drag', Sociology, 56(1): 3–20.

McCracken, G. (1986) 'Culture and Consumption: A theoretical account of the structure and movement of the cultural meaning of consumer goods', Journal of Consumer Research, 13(1): 71–84.

Mimoun, L., Trujillo-Torres, L. and Sobande, F. (2022) 'Social Emotions and the Legitimation of the Fertility Technology Market', Journal of Consumer Research, 48(6): 1073–1095.

Mulholland, J., Massi, M. and Ricci, A. (2022) 'Introduction to the Artisan Brand', in J. Mulholland, M. Massi and A. Ricci (eds) The Artisan Brand, Cheltenham: Edward Elgar, pp 1–12.

Mundel, J., Close, S. and Sasiela, N. (2023) 'Drag Dollars: Making room for queens in advertising', in N. Brennan and D. Gudelunas (eds) Drag in the Global Digital Public Sphere: Queer Visibility, Online Discourse and Political Change, Abingdon: Routledge, pp 89–112.

Newton, E. (1979) Mother Camp: Female Impersonators in America, Chicago: University of Chicago Press.

Ostrom, V. (1980) 'Artisanship and Artifact', Public Administration Review, 40(4): 309–317.

Rancière, J. (1983) 'The Myth of the Artisan Critical Reflections on a Category of Social History', International Labor and Working-Class History, 24: 1–16.

Rupp, L.J., Taylor, V. and Shapiro, E.I. (2010) 'Drag Queens and Drag Kings: The difference gender makes', Sexualities, 13(3): 275–294, doi. org/10.1177/1363460709352725

Sandikci, Ö. and Ger, G. (2010) 'Veiling in Style: How does a stigmatized practice become fashionable?', Journal of Consumer Research, 37(1): 15–36.

Scaraboto, D. and Fischer, E. (2013) 'Frustrated Fatshionistas: An institutional theory perspective on consumer quests for greater choice in mainstream markets', Journal of Consumer Research, 39(6): 1234–1257.

Suchman, M.C. (1995) 'Managing Legitimacy: Strategic and institutional approaches', The Academy of Management Review, 20(3): 571–610.

Valor, C., Lloveras, J. and Papaoikonomou, E. (2021) 'The Role of Emotion Discourse and Pathic Stigma in the Delegitimization of Consumer Practices', Journal of Consumer Research, 47(5): 636–653.

Venkatraman, R., Ozanne, J.L. and Coslor, E. (2024) 'Stigma Resistance through Body-in-Practice: Embodying pride through creative mastery', Journal of Consumer Research, doi.org/10.1093/jcr/ucae015

Yadav, V. and Kirk, J.A. (2018) 'State Homophobia? India's shifting UN positions on LGBTQ issues', Globalizations, 15(5): 670–684.

Zaslow, S. (2022) 'Mainstream Novelty: Examining the shifting visibility of drag performance', Sexualities, 27(1–2): 330–355.

Zhang, E. (2016) 'Memoirs of a GAY! Sha: Race and gender performance on RuPaul's Drag Race', Studies in Costume & Performance, 1(1): 59–75.

PART IV

Epilogue

10

Kinky Boots: Reflections on Making and Marketing Tubular Sex

Pauline Maclaran

Shiny scarlet snakeskin thigh-length boots with heels so high they rival the Eiffel Tower ... sashaying across the stage ... hot stuff ... two and a half feet of tubular sex. ... But the moment the fragile heel snaps, artist and audience stumble back down to earth, the bubble burst, and rudely reminded this is just a man in women's shoes!

The above vignette captures the theme at the heart of the film *Kinky Boots* (2005), a British comedy drama that was my first immersion in the world of drag queens and one that inspires my reflections for this epilogue. Indeed, despite being described as 'breezy, forgettable fluff' by one critic (Johnston, 2005), *Kinky Boots* has become a highly successful global phenomenon since it was made into a stage musical with an award-winning score by Cindi Lauper. Debuting at the Adolfo Theatre, Chicago in 2012, the dazzling musical has gone on to capture hearts around the world, completing several US and UK tours, as well as performing in many other international venues, including Korea, Japan, Finland and Australia. 'Filled with glitter and glam and a whole lot of sole, *Kinky Boots* is a reminder to celebrate your life triumphantly', according to its website,[1] and the 63 performances scheduled for 2024 in the US testify to its enduring appeal. But this is not the marketing story I want to elaborate on right now, so let's return to the original film that spawned such success, and the intended subject of my present commentary.

Loosely based on a true tale of marketing acumen, the film's narrative revolves around the intersection of drag and marketplace culture. It is a heartwarming story of inclusion and gaining acceptance. Much of the film's comic effect comes from the juxtaposition of two contrasting central characters, Charlie Price (played by Australian actor and film-maker, Joel Edgerton), a shy, deferential English businessman, and Lola (played by multi-award-winning British actor, Chiwitel Ejiofor), a feisty, fabulous drag queen. The plot focuses on their unlikely relationship as they work together to save Charlie's business enterprise.

Kinky Boots is a marketing story par excellence. Charlie inherits the ailing family business, a shoe factory in Northampton, on the death of his father. Realizing the dire state of company accounts, Charlie visits London in a desperate search for funding to avoid laying off his workers. That evening, as he leaves a bar, he confronts drunken youths who are harassing Lola. In the scrap that follows, Lola accidentally knocks Charlie out with her boot and he awakens sometime later in her dressing room where she is tending to him. During this encounter backstage, Charlie notes the difficulties Lola experiences as she squeezes into female-sized boots and notes, especially, the fragility of the heels. Back at his factory in Northampton, Charlie watches the endlessly dull production line of traditional men's dress shoes, all uniformly the same, stacking up with nowhere to go. There is no longer a viable market for them as there was in his father's day. Inspired by an employee's suggestion of the need to find a niche market, a light bulb flashes in his head as he thinks of Lola, her colleagues and their broken heels. His new target market will be high-heeled boots for drag artists – feminine footwear that can withstand the weight of a man. He seeks Lola's advice to this end and subsequently employs her as his design consultant. The film's narrative continues with various trials and tribulations for both Charlie and Lola before bringing the innovative range of boots to market. Lola faces stigmatization by shop-floor workers in the factory before she wins their acceptance. Charlie breaks up with his fiancée, later falling in love with the marketing-savvy employee with whom he bonds during the development of their niche market. Ultimately, its Lola and her drag queens who emerge as the heroines to save the day (and the factory) when they showcase the sexy boot collection in a Milan fashion house with a sensational drag performance on the catwalk.

So, what does this film have to teach us about drag and how can the chapters in this book shed further light on one of my favourite films? First, most certainly, there are the performance aspects of drag, writ large in the shape of the wonderfully extravagant boots that replace the men's dress shoes on Charlie's production line and with which he targets his new niche market. As the chapters in this present volume so clearly illustrate, drag is first and foremost about entertainment: an excessive, highly-stylized art form that creates a spectacular effect in its performances. In this respect,

Lola's flamboyant drag appearances must surely rate as iconic. Her stage performance singing 'Whatever Lola Wants (Lola Gets)' is one of the best renditions I have ever heard of this song that dates back to the 1950s, made famous by legendary jazz singers Sarah Vaughan and Ella Fitzgerald. Stunning a bemused Charlie and his marketing assistant who are in the audience to check out their intended market, Lola proudly parades her wares on stage, her sonorous singing soaring through the theatre. Her Dolly-Parton-style blonde wig cascades curls around her broad shoulders encased in a shimmering turquoise outfit that exudes allure and enchantment.

Perhaps the most memorable performance by Lola, however – the one that inspired the title of this epilogue – is when Charlie presents her with his initial boot prototype for drag queens. Looking aghast at the boot in his outstretched arms, Lola savagely regales Charlie for the dull design and, worst of all, the sensible heels that are almost completely flat. Like an avenging tiger seizing its prey, she snarls and bares her teeth, rolling her Rs in emphasis as she speaks:

> Burgundy. Please, God, tell me I have not inspired something burgundy. Red. Red. *Red. Red*, Charlie boy. Rule 1: *Red* is the colour of sex! Burgundy is the colour of hot-water bottles! *Red* is the colour of sex and fear and danger. …You are making sex now. Two and a half feet of irresistible tubular sex!

As we can see (check out the video on YouTube![2]), Lola's dramatically delivered speech encapsulates the sheer excess and exaggeration that go into drag performances, the carnivalesque aspects transporting us to a world apart, a world far from the mundanities of everyday life.

And this brings us neatly to the next point that this volume has clarified for me. Drag is not about appropriating womanhood to mock or have a negative impact on women. Rather, it has its own identity paradigm and this is a key thread that the chapters together bring out. This identity is a subversive one that questions and queers as Judith Butler (1991) highlights through her theorizing. The heteronormative matrix explains how culture validates certain masculinities and femininities that provide norms against which other gender identities are evaluated and often marginalized or shunned because they do not meet these norms. For Butler, gender is something we do rather than have and is continually being reinforced through discursive practices that remain unquestioned in our daily lives. As such, resignifying moments can occur when there is a disruption of the ongoing iteration of these norms. Accordingly, Butler singles out the drag queen as having this disruptive potential because her gender parody resists existing power structures and normative cultural expectations, exposing gender as a cultural code that can be imitated. Ultimately drag results in 'a parodic performance of both genders' (Vallorani, 2016), a parodic performance materialized so wonderfully in the resplendent kinky boots that Lola helps Charlie design.

Yet, as this volume illustrates so well, drag's disruptive potential is not straightforward and, while drag in its mass-marketed form, such as in *RuPaul's Drag Race*, may subvert gender ideology, it does so by potentially reinforcing another ideology, one that underpins the neoliberal subject position. This means that, in order to gain acceptance from the mainstream, the glamorous drag queens on *Drag Race* exhibit the now obligatory '*Apprentice*-style' overconfidence and individualism that emphasizes their capacity to succeed in the competitive marketplace. In turn this leads to a homologation of a particular form of drag that silences its more politicized aspects and does not reflect the true diversity of drag. Moreover, even RuPaul himself has been criticized for privileging cisgender male queens and not being sufficiently inclusive. This is especially so given his response to a journalist asking whether he would allow a biological woman to compete:

> Drag loses its sense of danger and its sense of irony once it's not men doing it because at its core it's a social statement and a big f-you to male-dominated culture. So for men to do it, it's really punk rock, because it's a real rejection of masculinity. (RuPaul, quoted in Aitkenhead, 2018)

Such a prescriptive statement raised alarm bells for many drag artists, not least transgender individuals. Arguing that trans women (and others) also have a right to explore their femininity, Al-Kadhi (2018) critiques RuPaul for his limited notions of who is allowed to be involved in the parodying and exploration of their gender through drag. The chapters in this present collection have really brought this criticism home to me.

On reflection, then, it's fair to say that *Kinky Boots* also contributes to such homologation, not only through its depiction of Lola and her colleagues as glamorous drag queens, but also through the commercial success they achieve, culminating in the drag queen extravaganza on the Milan catwalk, a success that marks them out as the heroines of the film. And there can be no doubt that these same themes have ensured the film's global success as a musical. Yet, I understand now that such portrayals of drag to be limited in scope and even ultimately impeding drag's disruptive potential. In other words, my eyes have been opened to the diversity of drag! For example, the Berlin drag subculture of Tunten deliberately eschews the type of mainstream inclusion that RuPaul symbolizes in order to retain its radical nature. In contrast to the exaggerated style of glamorous drag queens, who may imitate icons like Marilyn Monroe, Cher and Lady Gaga, Tunten, despite their bold make-up, often seem more like ordinary people. The most significant differentiating factor, however, is that Tunten drag performances convey strong political messages and the artists use make-up and costumes to underline these. By remaining marginalized, not only from mainstream drag but also the LGBTQ+ community more widely, Tunten seek to retain their powers of radical critique.

None of the potential diversity and politicization of drag is portrayed in *Kinky Boots*, although, given that the film is now 25 years old, perhaps we can forgive it on the grounds that it was at the vanguard of mainstream drag. Together with the global film and musical success that it inspired, it has certainly helped bring more widespread understanding and appreciation of drag artists. But we must recognize its limitations in terms of the dialectical dance between the mainstreaming and critical potential of drag – that is certainly what this present volume has emphasized to me.

Nor does *Kinky Boots* explore in any depth the many nuances of stigma resistance that can be expressed through creative embodied practices such as drag (Venkatraman et al, 2024). Certainly, the film attempts to deal with the theme of stigmatization when Lola faces down her main opponent in the factory, Don, a macho shop-floor worker who turns others against her through his relentless mockery. The moment of reckoning happens in the local pub where Lola and Don engage in an arm-wrestling contest. The match becomes tense, with each competitor demonstrating their prowess before Don realizes the strength of Lola's grip is about to defeat him. The tension mounts as his colleagues cluster around the table, about to witness Don's humiliation. Ultimately, Lola allows Don win to avoid shaming him, thereby allowing his masculine pride to remain intact. Her generous act of kindness towards the man who has so cruelly teased her wins him over and gains his respect, ensuring he mobilizes the workforce to make the boots for their new niche market. Lola's denial of her strength, however, also entails her collusion in preserving the heteronormative matrix by reinforcing notions of femininity as belonging to the weaker sex.

Similarly, the centring of Charlie's narrative in the film (his love story, his factory being saved and so forth), as well as the reduction of Lola to just a glamorous drag queen, mean that heteronormativity prevails and the more traumatic and stigmatized aspects of queer life are not explored (Zandvliet, 2021). Indeed, the fact that Lola's sexual identity remains ambiguous throughout the film – we are never sure whether she is sexually attracted to Charlie, Lauren, both or neither – has been highlighted by critiques. Consequently, according to some, her gender-bending consists mainly of her flamboyant sartorial choices, limiting her powers to subvert gender norms, and offering reassurance rather than provocation to viewers (Holden, 2006). For others, however, this conservative take is misjudged. Wang (2014), for example, argues that Lola's ambiguity means a straight audience cannot easily dismiss her as not applying to them. This makes her a more powerful figure in their view. A good illustration of this is when Lola responds to a factory worker who asks her why she wears women's clothing if she doesn't want to seduce men: 'Ask any woman what she likes in a man. Compassion, tenderness, sensitivity. Traditionally the female virtues. Perhaps what women secretly desire is a man who is fundamentally a woman.'

Taking the wind out of her interrogator's sails, Lola's disconcerting words leave him and his colleagues in a reflective mood. At the same time too, the film's audience are forced to rethink assumptions that drag queens are necessarily gay. In addition, Lola appears to identify not only as a drag queen, but also as a transvestite, a double identification, according to Wang (2014), that compounds the ambiguity still further, the former being most often associated (but not always) with gay men and the latter with straight men. Together, all of these factors force the film's audience to rethink their assumptions about drag queens and, more broadly, to query gender norms. As Wang (2014: 59) so eloquently puts it: 'The value of *Kinky Boots* lies in its deliberate exportation of the pedagogical device of drag from the gay community to the film's heterosexual audience, using its sexually ambiguous drag queen as the cultural intermediary.'

I have deliberately brought my commentary round to end on this positive note about *Kinky Boots* because I have such a soft spot for the film. I can, of course, see its many weaknesses as discussed in the light of this new and fascinating collection of works on drag that open up so many veins of future scholarship in the area. But, speaking for myself, first I would like to see a sequel to *Kinky Boots,* one developing the complexities noted around Lola and placing her central to the narrative. Her tale has yet to be told. And the theme music to *Kinky Boots 2*? I guess it has to be 'Lola' by The Kinks (1970), one of the greatest songs of all time. An iconic song befitting an iconic drag queen.

Notes

1 kinkybootsthemusical.com
2 'Kinky Boots | 'Burgundy' (HD) - Joel Edgerton, Chiwetel Ejiofor, Nick Frost | MIRAMAX', youtube.com/watch?v=RcnnkK7_qWI

References

Aitkenhead, D. (2018) 'RuPaul: "Drag is a big f-you to male-dominated culture"', The Guardian, [online] 3 March, Available from: theguardian.com/tv-and-radio/2018/mar/03/rupaul-drag-race-big-f-you-to-male-dominated-culture [Accessed 16 April 2024].
Al-Khadi, A. (2018) 'No, RuPaul, the Drag Queen World does Not Only Belong to Men: Everyone can explore femininity', The Independent, [online] 4 March, Available from: independent.co.uk/voices/rupaul-drag-race-transgender-guardian-interview-gender-identity-patriarchy-a8239041.html [Accessed 16 April 2024].

Butler, J. (1991) *Gender Trouble: Feminism and the Subversion of Identity*, New York: Routledge.

Holden, S. (2006) 'With 'Kinky Boots,' a Drag Queen Saves the Day', The New York Times, 14 April.

Johnston, T. (2005) 'Kinky Boots', Time Out, [online] 4 October, Available from: timeout.com/movies/kinky-boots-1 [Accessed 18 June 2024].

Vallorani, N. (2016) 'On the Bridge: Of carnivalesque, homosexuality, inbetween spaces and border Crossing', *De Genere*, 2: 59–74.

Venkatraman, R., Ozanne, J.L. and Coslor, E. (2024) 'Stigma Resistance through Body-in-Practice: Embodying pride through creative mastery,' *Journal of Consumer Research*, doi.org/10.1093/jcr/ucae015.

Wang, G. (2014) 'Kinky Boots: How to talk about sex without talking about sex', The Morningside Review, [online] 1 May, Available from journals. library.columbia.edu/index.php/TMR/article/view/5436 [Accessed 16 April 2024].

Zandvliet, S. (2021) Into the Spotlight: A Comparison of Queer Representation in Kinky Boots and Everybody's Talking About Jamie [thesis], Utrecht University.

11

Reflections on the Business, Consumption and Performance of Contemporary Drag

Mark McCormack

This book is motivated by a distinctive question: how should business and consumer research understand the new marketplace of drag? It is an important question, and the chapters provide engaging and insightful responses to it. The question also invites a host of supplementary questions, research projects and hopefully fertile debates.

Underlying the question is the recognition of the broad trend of the past 20 years that has seen the steady rise of drag and a wider engagement from mainstream culture. Whereas drag was once a marginalized subculture within already stigmatized LGBT+ cultures (Newton, 1979), drag has become mainstream and is vibrant both in less marginalized LGBT+ spaces and in arts and performance cultures across North America and the UK. Heteronormativity persists, however, and there remain huge inequalities in the demographics of drag performers who can benefit from this mainstreaming (McCormack and Measham, 2024), yet drag is present in heterosexual bars and nightclubs, museums and theatres primarily through a touring economy of national and international drag performers (LeBlanc, 2021; Baxter et al, 2023).

As a gay man, my engagement and consumption of drag has run the gamut of experiences that are possibly typical of gay men of my generation. In no particular order, they include Lily Savage and Dame Edna Everage as 'themselves' on TV; gender-bending and cross-dressing in films for comedic effect, from the *Carry On* films to *Mrs Doubtfire*; movies where drag was centre stage, such as *The Adventures of Priscilla, Queen of the Desert*, *The Birdcage* and *Hedwig and the Angry Inch*; and seeing Tina C, Pam Ann and many drag performers in London in my late teens and early 20s. I was sadly born slightly too late to see *Hinge and Bracket* on the TV, or Lily Savage at the Royal Vauxhall Tavern, but old enough to watch *RuPaul's Drag Race* (RPDR) from the beginning, including its Season 1 filter.

There is much complexity and fascinating debate to be had regarding these experiences. Was Dame Edna a drag queen? Is Pam Ann? Should straight actors play drag queens in films like *Priscilla,* and should a drag performer have starred in *The Birdcage*? Laamanen et al explore these nuanced debates in the introductory chapter to this book, with fresh and insightful perspectives that successfully incorporate recognition of the changing drag scene and both the challenges and advances brought about by RPDR.

When I interviewed Christopher Green for my first drag project (McCormack and Wignall, 2022), he was explicit and passionate that Tina C (his creation) was not a drag queen but a character in a form of performance that could make serious points in a creative and humorous manner. As part of a broader discussion about the interconnections between drag, theatre, community and culture, he said:

> I think everything I do is character comedy or it is theatre. It exists as part of a societal positioning but mainly as a theatrical strategy. And I think I'm really interested in – as a performer, as a theatre major – in different theatrical strategies. And a man dressing as a woman is a theatrical tool, just like playing the piano is a theatrical tool or you know a satirical song is. And I think it's a very powerful one but it doesn't say very much about me or my life.

I don't rehearse all the questions and debates here, not least because there is a wealth of research on these question from cultural studies and sociology (Baker, 1994; Brennan and Gudelunas, 2017; Crookston, 2021), as well as in this book. Rather, unlike any other research I have conducted, I can pinpoint the moment from my own experience where the idea for my next research project crystallized in my mind.

It was December 2016, and it was a freezing cold Sunday evening in Newcastle, in the upper north-east of England. I was going with some friends to see a touring performance of US drag performers, titled *Comedy Christmas Extravaganza.* It included RPDR performers Shangela, William and Alaska, as well as Lady Bunny. We had bought meet-and-greet tickets (where you enter the venue earlier, 'meet' the performers and take photos with them) because this was the first touring show of its kind to reach Newcastle, and I was particularly keen to see Lady Bunny, of whom I had long been a fan but had never seen perform because she hadn't toured the UK for many years.

It was that night when I realized just how significantly drag cultures had changed in the UK. Newcastle is a major city in the UK. It is not really known for its LGBT+ scene, but houses the only sizable queer scene in the north-east of England. The gig was held at the O2 Academy, which has a capacity of 2,000. The first surprise of the night was when we arrived and saw the entry queue circling around the building. What must have been over 100 people had arrived more than an hour early, and while the queue included many gay and bisexual men, the age range was wider than might be expected, and there were also many ostensibly heterosexual couples and teenagers with parents. The event was not just at capacity, but people were queuing long in advance to see their favourite US drag performers. Even though many of the crowd were university students, it was a stark contrast from my university years just over ten years earlier.

The second surprise – and the moment I knew there were social trends that needed studying – was just before the drag performer Alaska was about to take to the stage. The gig was occurring less than six months after Alaska was crowned winner of *RPDR All Stars 2*, one of the most highly rated seasons of the *Drag Race* franchise. My group was fairly close to the stage (and the downstairs area was standing only) and we had noticed that there were increasing numbers of teenage girls gathering near the front. Unexpected, though, was the level of screaming, applause and appreciation when Alaska appeared on stage – a reception closer to what Justin Bieber or One Direction were receiving at the time, not what we were used to witnessing for drag performers.

It was clear that Alaska had achieved a level of fame and celebrity that was distinct from drag acts who had broken into the mainstream from previous generations (see also Mercer et al, 2020). This may seem unsurprising now – Alaska runs not just a successful podcast, *Race Chaser*, but a podcast network, Moguls of Media – at the time, however, it was remarkable. That Lady Bunny's set included lip-syncing while eating take-out chicken nuggets and, separately, performing 'Tomorrow' with explicit lyrics and a dildo in hand, to people of all ages including 16 and 17 year-olds happily chaperoned by their parents, is also emblematic of one of the quirks that happens when LGBT-located drag performance and the mainstream intersect.

In the spirit of the questions of this book, how would consumer research conceptualize these moments? And what broader disciplinary and theoretical questions can drag performance and its mainstreaming serve as a case study to answer?

The importance of multiple disciplines

At the time of writing, in spring 2024, it is not long since I attended the Royal Festival Hall in London's Southbank Centre to see RuPaul talk about his new memoir, *The House of Hidden Meanings*. Recognizing that RuPaul is one of the most influential drag performers ever (regardless of how one evaluates that influence), I was excited to see him perform (out of drag or in boy drag, depending on your terminology). But, being a sociologist, having conducted research with queer performers, and merely existing online, I also knew that RuPaul is a polarizing figure. My own research has found drag performers deeply critical of him and RPDR (McCormack and Measham, 2022), and books have been dedicated to exploring, understanding and, fundamentally, critiquing the influence of RPDR (for example Brennan and Gudelunas, 2017; Crookston, 2021).

I was somewhat apprehensive, intellectually at least, about the reception of the event. Would London welcome RuPaul? How diverse would the audience be, or would it be mainly white and heterosexual? Would the event be … enjoyable? I found my concerns, although tentative and slight, to be unfounded. The audience was diverse – though perhaps not as diverse as the city of London – and it was rapturous in its applause when RuPaul first entered the stage, giving a prolonged standing ovation. Throughout the event, the audience laughed and applauded in the right places and did not interrupt or heckle in the sections that may have been more likely to be critiqued online. Likewise, the Q&A section had no controversial or difficult questions. Perhaps the grandiosity of the Royal Festival Hall provided some protection in this regard, but, fundamentally, the diverse audience was there to see RuPaul, hear him, and be present in front of a major celebrity.

My point here is to speak to the limits of critiques of representation, diversity and inequality related to RPDR when they are the only intellectual engagement with drag. Such critiques can downplay the emotional and cultural significance of the visibility and celebration of drag. The people going to see RuPaul were excited, eager participants and RuPaul clearly meant a great deal to a good proportion of them. This is not to argue against academic critiques of RuPaul or RPDR – I have made them myself regarding the impact on queer cultures and nightlife in the UK (McCormack and Measham, 2024) – but it is to recognize that they cannot be the only intellectual framing or engagement with RuPaul, RPDR and drag more generally. Multidisciplinarity is one such guard against an intellectual approach that is too narrow or focuses on specific aspects rather than the totality of the phenomenon of contemporary drag.

This book poses vital questions – and offers some initial answers – to what a consumer-research approach to drag looks like. As Laamanen et al make clear in 'Introduction: What are Marketplace Cultures of Drag?' (Chapter 1), consumer research can provide distinctive and important insights into how drag is consumed as a product and brand; how it is a system of consumption, as 'an iconic maker and maker of a marketplace'; and how to understand the operation and challenges of the drag marketplace. A consumer-research approach is also apposite given how closely celebrity and commodification have been central to the success of RPDR. This popularity and mainstreaming is facilitated by a 'celebrification' of popular culture, where celebrity is a commodity that is actively constructed and produced by the media and the 'celebrity industry' (Rojek, 2001). Part of the success of the RPDR franchise is its use of the reality TV format (Gamson, 2013), and its ability to harness social media through memes and self-branding (Mercer and Sarson, 2020).

This does, however, lead to marked inequality in income and the broader rewards of drag performance, dependent on this ability to develop such fame and, indeed, appear on a version of RPDR. There are significant questions as to whether the mainstreaming of drag exploits performers and drag culture more broadly (Vesey, 2017; Feldman and Hakim, 2020). Many contestants on RPDR have taken on significant debt to ensure that their 'looks' are at a high enough quality to compete at the so-called 'Olympics of drag' – with no guarantee that the investment will be recouped as this is dependent on being embraced by the fan base and maintaining a successful drag brand (Campana and Duffy, 2021; LeBlanc, 2021).

This book explores these issues and more in the opening part, 'Politicizing Drag Identities'. Luigi Squillante (Chapter 2) uses a Foucauldian analysis to consider how RPDR operates in a neoliberal framework and considers how 'marketable specialness' is the unique selling point in the 21st-century marketplace where *some* sexual diversity is required, rather than being uniquely queer. Of course, a consumer-research approach must not disregard or ignore the foundational research in cultural studies and sociology that documented and explained the cultural significance of drag as a form of queer performance in a context of marginalization and oppression (e.g. Newton, 1979; Rupp and Taylor, 2003). These issues have not vanished, even as many progressive trends related to gay sexuality have occurred. In the United States in particular, drag finds itself in the crosshairs of the culture war.

Indeed, contemporary writing about drag cannot ignore how it has become part of the culture war, particularly in the US – where the reactionary critique manufactures fear about drag performers reading children's books to children (in the presence of their parents), often called *Drag Queen Story Time* (Davis and Kettrey, 2022). In the US, this comes from the far right, yet the critique of this manifestation and context of drag is another example where radical feminism finds itself arguing alongside far-right conservatives (see Rubin, 1993). The radical feminist position contends that drag is an appropriation of womanhood akin to blackface. Powerfully using Deleuze and Guattari, Paul Haynes (Chapter 3) shows that this comparison is not valid and that drag has created its own 'identity paradigm' that is more inclusive. The literality of the radical feminist critique does not align with the polyvocality, irony and playfulness of contemporary drag.

I would add here that one important component is the empirical reality of how drag is practised. Speaking with older members of the drag community, I have heard stories of how some drag performers were overtly misogynistic and, in this context, their drag may be problematic in the ways that 'womanface' would suggest. Yet this was never the only or (arguably) dominant form of drag, and the contemporary drag scene recognizes gender diversity. Many of the performers I have interviewed speak explicitly about the importance of celebrating womanhood and femininity and rejecting misogyny (McCormack and Wignall, 2022). Ideology and theory are important, but they must be in conversation with empirical reality. This, along with the sophisticated arguments by Haynes, is a useful understanding of how drag celebrates women and mocks damaging gender norms.

Consumer research, digital transformation and drag cultures

This book is about understanding drag from a consumer-research perspective and developing a set of empirical and conceptual apparatus to further undertake such research in the future. It succeeds in this endeavour, and I particularly enjoyed the chapters that really lay out these concepts and document what is happening in drag cultures related to consumption, marketing and business.

Many puns and innuendos have been used in writing about drag performance, as befits an art form that revels in such forms of humour. There is a certain charm to Both, Razal and Venkatraman's opening chapter in the part 'Marketizing Drag' (Chapter 4) with a pun about craft ('crafty queens'). The contextualization of drag within subculture, craft and artisanship – and how these connect with community – is noteworthy, particularly in the context of how drag performers connect these elements with branding and making money. An insightful component of Chapter 4 is consideration of how drag performers connect the marketplace with the queer community – this has most often been theorized through cultural appropriation, but the focus on how queer individuals (drag performers) leverage their own culture and experience in a marketplace is insightful and offers a counter-perspective.

The discussion in Chapter 5 by Seimetz and Bucher on different types of legitimacy and distinct drag cultures is valuable, and the longitudinal component in documenting the tensions and resolutions is powerful. I have previously highlighted that some critiques of RPDR and the mainstreaming of drag seem to unintentionally homogenize drag cultures (McCormack and Wignall, 2022). The reality is that multiple, diverse drag cultures continue to exist and, even if they are highly unequal in terms of visibility and financial reward (significant issues to be sure), the vibrancy of sub- and countercultural drag persists (Ghaziani, 2024). To read a case of how these tensions and challenges have been engaged with and to some extent resolved was fascinating and potentially a useful road map for other places where this tension will surely arrive in the future.

I also found the exploration of non-fan consumers of online drag performers in Japan to be really interesting. This chapter, by Binh Nghiêm-Phú (Chapter 6), provides unique insight into the remarkable success of drag performers' entrance into the beauty market, and the development of make-up brands for drag performers. The success and limitations of drag performers in marketing and selling beauty products is fascinating, and a topic that likely would not have been considered outside consumer research.

The focus on the digital is also a welcome addition in this book. The expansion of 'Instagram queens' is well-known, and often a topic of debate on RPDR, where social media stars are considered to be less-effective performers than those who have 'put in the hours' in queer venues. Shayne Zaslow's chapter (Chapter 7) draws on an impressive ethnography to consider the complexity of the digital shift, and how it impacts on 'liveness', both within queer venues and online. The notion of 'cybernetic drag' is certainly intriguing and can be used as a concept to foster further research on the impacts of this in the future.

Chapter 8 by Khyati Jagani, on how drag social media influencers work to be successful, developing a stage model of this work, again applies relevant theories and methods to develop a model that considers a hierarchy of effects and the impact of advertising and purchase behaviour. Demonstrating the originality of this chapter and book more generally, it is still somewhat disconcerting – in a good way – to read a chapter on drag that is focused on the effectiveness or otherwise of advertising to influence consumer behaviours.

Highlighting how ripe drag is for further research from a business and consumer-research perspective, there are many areas that are not fully covered in this book. I would, for example, be fascinated to read an academic study on the scope, success and business model of drag podcasts that have become a staple of much mainstream drag. Drag brunches are increasingly popular (Siddons, 2019), and are emblematic of the heterosexualization of some drag performances – more consideration of the economics of drag brunches would be of great interest. Likewise, in my research, I have always been deeply aware of the work and labour of drag, with many performers discussing the complexity of working as a freelancer, paying taxes, making clothes and so on. Further consideration of this would also be a valuable endeavour in this area. I'm sure readers will have identified other gaps in the book, and if this spurs them to undertake their own studies in the area, it has achieved one of its aims.

The precarity of queer venues and reconfiguring business support

The history of drag tells us that queer venues and cultures are vital for drag to flourish as a form of queer art, activism and representation (Baker, 1994; Edward and Farrier 2021). All the queer drag performers who have become stars in mainstream culture have a history of performing in and being part of LGBT+ scenes and cultures – from Lily Savage at the Royal Vauxhall Tavern in London to RuPaul at the Pyramid Club in New York. Even as some drag has gone mainstream, broader drag cultures remain diverse, subcultural, political and vital outlets of expression for queer people (Ghaziani, 2024).

Yet, the recent history of LGBT+ cultures and venues has been focused on debates about whether, when and how the LGBT+ scene is 'dying', declining or being co-opted by straight cultures (see Ghaziani, 2014, 2024 for critical explorations of this issue). Queer performance has often been appropriated or exploited without due recognition and is particularly evident in nightlife trends, from New York disco and ballroom culture to Detroit house and Ibiza Balearic raves (Buckland, 2012). The impact of COVID-19 and associated closures of venues and broader changes in how people engage with nightlife further exacerbated the challenges for the venues and cultures that form the ecosystems of drag culture (an issue I discuss in detail elsewhere – see Campkin, 2023; McCormack and Measham, 2024).

The feeling that RPDR UK was produced for straight audiences fed into a broader concern about the lack of support for queer nightlife from production companies and cultural institutions like the BBC. One venue owner told me how he regularly had television crews requesting interviews, consultations or the possibility of filming on his premises. He said:

> I have production companies on my case all the time. 'We want to do a documentary, we want to do a treatment.' ... They don't want to pay me. ... All these production companies ask for X, Y and Z access and they all immediately say they've got no budget, and I say, 'You're all getting paid.' It's a constant battle where people think this is free. And I'm not just talking about profits, I'm talking improving the space and improving rates of pay.

In addition to this, there is the reality of how mainstream businesses and media, including the producers of the various *Drag Race* franchises, essentially extract from the queer ecosystem the drag performers with the potential to provide the most financial success.

One of the core difficulties for queer nightlife is to develop a sustainable financial and cultural footing while maintaining the ethos, practices and values that make it queer. This balancing act has become particularly challenging in a context where broader society engages and co-opts various elements of queer culture, such as the increasing mainstream engagement with drag performance.

In research on building a sustainable queer nightlife in London, I called for businesses to reconfigure how to support queer venues and the broader ecosystems of drag and queer nightlife (McCormack and Measham, 2022). While there are people working hard to do this, there is a lack of ethos around corporate social responsibility – instead, it is seen as sufficient for companies to book individual break-out drag stars to perform at an event. This may not amount to rainbow-washing, but it is certainly a form of value-extraction from a community that needs business support. Coming from a research-strategy perspective in UK higher education, there is space for business academics and consumer research to consider how research, impact and knowledge-exchange activity can be part of reconfiguring what business support of drag, queer venues and nightlife might look like in a sustainable manner.

At the time of writing, I have, in the space of two weeks, seen three living legends of drag perform. In addition to RuPaul at the Southbank Centre, I saw Dave Lynn in a small gay pub in Brighton and Coco Peru at the King's Head Theatre in Islington (a queer venue in north London). The different contexts of each performance and performer, although broadly speaking the same generation of drag, is a stark illustration of the different contexts of drag and the ecosystems in which they exist. All three of these artists have had drag careers spanning more than 30 years, won awards, appeared in television and on film, have regularly performed at key LGBT+ venues and are recognized as key figures in drag history.

Coco Peru gave – as always – a compelling solo show that included powerful soliloquies and captivating songs that spoke meaningfully to the importance of drag, queer community and learning between generations. The scripted show took place in a sizable London theatre venue that showcases LGBT and queer artists and art; and the venue collected donations in a bucket at the end of the show, because its ongoing sustainability in central north London is not ensured. Dave Lynn performed a two-hour set in the Bedford Tavern, a gay venue and self-styled 'backstreet boozer' in Brighton, with a small stage and mostly local audience. It featured live singing and audience interaction and was in many ways the exemplar of live drag in a 'local' queer venue. These performances also challenge dominant (perhaps heteronormative) notions of success. While there was undoubtedly some thrill to seeing RuPaul in the flesh – and, indeed, to see a celebrity drag queen sell out a major London venue – it was without question the least fulfilling of the performances as an audience member.

The notion of creating less-rewarding art to create greater success is hardly original or groundbreaking. I close on the comparison, not because of that point but to recognize the markedly different *contexts* in which performers are working – and to connect the backstreet boozer in a meaningful way with the Royal Festival Hall. I welcome consumer research and business studies interest in drag – and this book showcases the contributions to knowledge that are possible – and I urge academics in this emerging area to consider not just the mainstreaming and the success but also the grassroots performance, the art and cultural value and the challenges faced by many drag performers in the 21st century.

References

Baker, R. (1994) Drag: A History of Female Impersonation in the Performing Arts, New York: New York University Press.

Baxter, D., Leer, C. and Graham, A. (2023) 'Dragging up the Night: Exploring the changing dynamic of audiences at drag events in the UK', Journal of Policy Research in Tourism, Leisure and Events, 15(2): 125–139.

Brennan, N. and Gudelunas, D. (eds) (2017) RuPaul's Drag Race and the Shifting Visibility of Drag Culture: The Boundaries of Reality TV, Cham/ Basingstoke: Palgrave Macmillan.

Buckland, F. (2012) Impossible Dance: Club Culture and Queer World-Making, Middletown, CT: Wesleyan University Press.

Campana, M. and Duffy, K. (2021) 'RuPaul's Drag Race: Between cultural branding and consumer culture', in C. Crookston (ed) The Cultural Impact of RuPaul's Drag Race: Why Are We All Gagging?, Bristol/ Chicago: Intellect, pp 108–130.

Campkin, B. (2023) Queer Premises: LGBTQ+ Venues in London Since the 1980s, London: Bloomsbury.

Crookston, C. (ed) (2021) The Cultural Impact of RuPaul's Drag Race, Chicago: Intellect.

Davis, A.J. and Kettrey, H.H. (2022) 'Clear and Omnipresent Danger: Digital age culture wars and reactions to drag queen story hour across diverse subreddit communities', Social Currents, 9(1): 25–44.

Edward, M. and Farrier, S. (eds) (2021) Drag Histories, Herstories & Hairstories: Drag in a Changing Scene, Volume 2, London: Bloomsbury.

Feldman, Z. and Hakim, J. (2020) 'From Paris is Burning to #dragrace: Social media and the celebrification of drag culture', Celebrity Studies, 11(4): 386–401.

Gamson, J. (2013). 'Reality queens', Contexts, 12(2): 52–54.

Ghaziani, A. (2014) There Goes the Gayborhood?, Princeton: Princeton University Press.

Ghaziani, A. (2024) Long Live Queer Nightlife: How the Closing of Gay Bars Sparked a Revolution, Princeton: Princeton University Press.

LeBlanc R. (2021) 'RuPaul's Franchise: Moving toward a political economy of drag queening', in C. Crookston (ed) The Cultural Impact of RuPaul's Drag Race, Chicago: Intellect.

McCormack, M. and Measham, F. (2022) Building a Sustainable Queer Nightlife in London: Queer Creatives, COVID-19 and Community in the Capital, London: Arts Council England, Available from: publications. aston.ac.uk/id/eprint/45892/1/LondonQueerNightlife_v7_High_res.pdf [Accessed 18 June 2024].

McCormack, M. and Measham, F. (2024) 'Contemporary Drag in the Shadow of RuPaul's Drag Race: Adaption, elevation and contestation', in M. Edward and S. Farrier (eds) Drag Vistas & Visions: Drag in a Changing Scene, Volume 3, London: Bloomsbury.

McCormack, M. and Wignall, L. (2022) 'Drag Performers' Perspectives on the Mainstreaming of British Drag: Towards a sociology of contemporary drag', Sociology, 56(1): 3–20.

Mercer, J. and Sarson, C. (2020) 'Fifteen Seconds of Fame: RuPaul's Drag Race, camp and "memeability"', Celebrity Studies, 11(4): 479–492.

Mercer, J., Sarson, C. and Hakim, J. (2020) 'Introduction: Charisma, Uniqueness, Nerve and Talent: RuPaul's Drag Race and the cultural politics of fame', Celebrity Studies, 11(4): 383–385.

Newton, E. (1979) Mother Camp: Female Impersonators in America, Chicago: University of Chicago Press.

Rojek, C. (2001) Celebrity, London: Reaktion Books.

Rubin, G. (1993) 'Misguided, Dangerous, and Wrong: An analysis of antipornography politics', in A. Assiter and A. Carol (eds) Bad Girls and Dirty Pictures: The Challenge to Reclaim Feminism, London: Pluto Press, pp 18–40.

Rupp, L.J. and Taylor, V. (2003) Drag Queens at the 801 Cabaret, Chicago: University of Chicago Press.

Siddons, E. (2019) 'The Extraordinary Rise of Drag Bunch: A dining delight or a betrayal of queer history?', The Guardian [online] 17 March, Available from: theguardian.com/culture/2019/mar/17/the-extraordinary-rise-of-drag-brunch-a-dining-delight-or-a-betrayal-of-queer-history [Accessed 29 March 2024].

Vesey, A. (2017). '"A Way to Sell Your Records": Pop Stardom and the Politics of Drag Professionalization on RuPaul's Drag Race', Television & New Media, 18(7): 589–604.

Index

References to endnotes show both the page number and the note number (38n15).